DUNKIRK
TO
D-DAY

As Bill Williams did in his victory message on 8 May 1945,
I dedicate this book to the non-regular officers and men, the women of
the ATS and civilians, and the regular officers and men of the
RAOC with whom they worked so hard and well, together with the
Ordnance Corps of the British Empire: India, Canada, Australia,
New Zealand and South Africa. Their achievement was monumental.

Front cover image: Lanchester scout car and DUKW.

Back cover image: DUKW and from COO meeting photograph, June 1942: Back row standing: Col. Davis[1], Col. Hunt (WO). 2nd row: Mr McOnie, Col. Warwick[2], Gen. Geake (WO). 3rd row: Brig. de Wolff (Donnington), Col. Hildreth (WO). 4th row: Mr Boddy, DCS Planning Officer, Brig. R.F. Johnson. On right: Gen. Williams (WO), Col. Bell (Weedon), Brig. Crosland (Branston), Col. Lewis, Miss Perks.

1. Fernyhough lists Colonel T.W. Davis as succeeding Colonel Robinson at Feltham, but this photograph pre-dates this.
2. Fernyhough lists Colonel H.B. Warwick as a member of the working party that selected Chilwell as the Motor Transport Centre.

DUNKIRK
TO
D-DAY

THE MEN AND WOMEN OF THE RAOC
AND RE-ARMING THE BRITISH ARMY

PHILIP HAMLYN WILLIAMS

PEN & SWORD
HISTORY
AN IMPRINT OF PEN & SWORD BOOKS LTD
YORKSHIRE – PHILADELPHIA

First published in Great Britain in 2021 by
PEN AND SWORD HISTORY
An imprint of
Pen & Sword Books Ltd
Yorkshire – Philadelphia

ISBN 978 1 52679 430 7

A CIP catalogue record for this book is available from the British Library.

Typeset in Times New Roman 11.5/14 by
SJmagic DESIGN SERVICES, India.
Printed and bound by CPI Group (UK) Ltd, Croydon CR0 4YY

Pen & Sword Books Limited incorporates the imprints of Atlas, Archaeology,
Aviation, Discovery, Family History, Fiction, History, Maritime, Military, Military
Classics, Politics, Select, Transport, True Crime, Air World, Frontline Publishing,
Leo Cooper, Remember When, Seaforth Publishing, The Praetorian Press,
Wharncliffe Local History, Wharncliffe Transport, Wharncliffe True Crime and
White Owl.

For a complete list of Pen & Sword titles please contact
PEN & SWORD BOOKS LIMITED
47 Church Street, Barnsley, South Yorkshire, S70 2AS, England
E-mail: enquiries@pen-and-sword.co.uk
Website: www.pen-and-sword.co.uk

Or
PEN AND SWORD BOOKS
1950 Lawrence Rd, Havertown, PA 19083, USA
E-mail: Uspen-and-sword@casematepublishers.com
Website: www.penandswordbooks.com

Contents

Foreword

As the President of the Royal Army Ordnance Corps (RAOC) Council, it might be expected that a book dedicated to the personnel of the RAOC is going to get my vote, and it most definitely does. However, there is a bit more to this tale than merely recording the good works of our RAOC predecessors and one does not need to have an RAOC connection to relish its contents.

The author is certainly not the first son to be intrigued as to what his father did 'in the war'. However, few then discover that their father was actively engaged in *two* world wars and their mother in one. Even fewer then uncover a veritable treasure trove of memorabilia with both photographic and written documents contained in diaries and albums that have been meticulously recorded and preserved for posterity to enrich the story and demonstrate the scale of the contribution to answer that 'What did you do in the war, Daddy?' question, so richly and proudly told here and with no need for false modesty or indeed exaggeration because the evidence is clear for all to behold. (Incidentally, if, as we are told, this manuscript was proofread by my old friend and former comrade, Clive Elderton, then we can have absolutely no doubt as to its historical accuracy and all-round provenance as he is supremely well informed on matters of military history in general and those pertaining to the RAOC in particular.)

Awareness that the father in question, Leslie 'Bill' Williams, held senior rank at the time of the Second World War, would lead to an assumption that he had considerable responsibilities and a key role, but the letters R, A, O and C, or even the words the initials stand for do not offer an immediate explanation. Therefore, I can only applaud and admire the forensic way in which Phil set out to discover what the RAOC was actually responsible for, and what it was not, and how the entire support organization of the British Army functioned and developed from the time of the First World War and beyond the Second World War. He sets this out, to those who will be fascinated by both the social history and the military history of this period, with absolute clarity. Moreover, he recognizes and articulates the significance of the introduction of motor transport and armoured vehicles, the mechanization of the armies of the world, which is perhaps the most profound change militarily in the period under review, and paints the verbal picture for us of just what this meant to those charged with supporting the people and the equipment that eventually made up a massive organization operating all around the world.

Commanders of land campaigns throughout history have been required to acknowledge the importance of supply and medical support. Some – Marlborough, Wellington and Montgomery, for example – have grasped the need to plan ahead thoroughly to avoid being overly constrained by the limits of support available, whilst others have chosen to take chances with support systems, sometimes gambling successfully and enjoying dramatic victories, but on other occasions being defeated by failing to comprehend what was practically feasible: Napoleon, Rommel, Patton perhaps, who once famously said, 'My men can eat their belts, but my tanks have got to have gas.' However, as this book makes so crystal clear, the introduction of vehicles in the twentieth century did not actually make supporting an army on the move easier. If anything, the reverse applies. Yes, greater distances might be covered over a period of time, but the complexity of the organization to be supported is changed dramatically. The 'friction' – the term used by Martin van Creveld, the military theorist and historian, in his book *Supplying War* – within such a mechanized army increases hugely and the demands over distance for ammunition, food, clothing, fuel, spare parts, military kit, the difficulties of communicating, plus the challenge of maintaining its equipment and vehicles, all also actually increase substantially, literally because of the sheer number of 'moving parts'. Yet, this is exactly the sort of army that Bill Williams and his kind were being required to sustain from Dunkirk to D-Day.

We are allowed to enjoy and share Phil's discovery that alongside his father, there was a group of people, many from the Class of '22 as Phil calls them, most of whom, having served as young officers in the First World War went on to have significant roles in supporting the mechanized army of the Second World War. As he puts it, 'In my research the same names kept reappearing.' What intrigues us as we read is that this group is a bridge in time from one world war to the next. We feel we get to know them as people: loyal, committed, open to change, driven by a sense of duty and nicely old fashioned. We follow Betty too, from PA to wife and finally as our author's mother, for it is she who has recorded the key events of the story in the diaries and albums, whilst adding some delightful personal vignettes. By following this whole group, we learn the scale of the challenge of supporting the army of the First World War and how it adjusted to the demands of equipping and sustaining the extended army of the Second World War. We also learn of the essential need for the individuals in the group, progressing as they do through various roles, to embrace developments in the commercial world, especially in the motor industry, in order to judge what needs to be adopted by the army in order to transform its supply services. Some of the group become 'captains of industry' in their own right, some move seamlessly from the military to the commercial sphere and then bring new knowledge and understanding back to the military under the mobilization of the nation's finest talents in the Second World War, some make big contributions to industry after the war. (Any reader interested in modern-day links between industry, academia and the military might care to look at the work of the RLC Foundation via their website rlcfoundation.com.) Above all though, whilst we are reading about the provision of things – ammunition, armaments, spare parts, vehicles, items of clothing, bits of equipment and so on – we are reminded that it is people that matter most of all in designing and implementing the systems and processes that make these things available to an army. There is plenty of leadership and management in this story.

Today, all this military support would be called logistics. The British Army still has a Corps of Royal Electrical and Mechanical Engineers (REME) to maintain its equipment, whose formation we read about here, but alongside, it has a Royal Logistic Corps (RLC) formed in 1993 from the RAOC, the Royal Corps of Transport (which itself had emerged from the RASC whose roles are described herein, in 1965), the Royal Pioneer Corps (a massive organization in its own right in the Second World War), the Army Catering Corps and the Postal and Courier Services of the Royal Engineers. Everything that the RAOC used to do is done within the RLC and much more besides, as the supply function is now delivered by the same organization that is responsible for movements and distribution, catering and food services, remnants of the pioneer function and postal and courier services. The fact that we still have an RAOC Council for me to preside over and a thriving RAOC Association, with a mix of geographical and trade branches across the UK, is down to the support given by the RLC to all its Forming Corps and to the fact that there are still plenty of former soldiers who proudly served within the RAOC and who enjoy the fellowship and community support afforded by belonging to a body that allows them to still engage with their former comrades. We shall continue for as long as there is a demand and a need, acknowledging our advancing years.

Bill Williams would recognize much that the RLC does today. I suspect he would have some perceptive questions about what has changed from 'his day', some of it for the good and some that would give him legitimate cause for concern about dissipated expertise. His story, and that of his wife, friends and colleagues, so brilliantly set out for us by Phil in *Dunkirk to D-Day* is history, but I commend it as much for its relevance to us all, military or civilian alike. Bill's portrait hangs in the RLC headquarters' officers' mess. I have walked past it countless times since I was commissioned into the RAOC in 1973. I wish I had known then what I know now, about Bill and his family, his work and his colleagues, but above all of their accomplishments. I would have been better prepared for my chosen profession if I had.

Malcolm Wood
Major General (Retired) Malcolm Wood CBE
President of the RAOC Council

Author's Note

At Dunkirk, the British Army had lost most of its equipment, yet of D-Day, only four years later, Max Hastings would write:

> To almost every man of the Allied Armies, the predominant
> memory of the campaign, beyond the horror of battle, was
> the astounding efficiency of the supply services.[1]

None of this happened by accident. It was by dint of hard work, a willingness to learn from mistakes, and an openness to new ideas. I believe it was also the product of the previous experience of those who led the Royal Army Ordnance Corps.

I have spent the last five years researching and writing about how the British Army was supplied in the two world wars. In my research the same names kept reappearing. I needed to find out who these people were: what had prepared them for the task they undertook, what they did afterwards and what impact the huge burden they carried had on their lives. I had focused on the supply of vehicles and armaments and, in particular, on the role played by the men and women of the RAOC and the very many civilians who worked with them. For them, it was a monumental task.

All biographers are debtors. I owe my biggest debt to my mother, Betty, who as a young woman diligently and, I think, lovingly recorded the deeds of her boss, Bill Williams, who, much later, would be her husband and my father. In recording his deeds, she wrote a good deal about those around him. Bill was Controller of Ordnance Services in the Second World War. Fortuitously for us, she also wrote vivid, and in places, charmingly naïve diaries of the overseas trips they made. This whole archive I have now passed to the care of the Royal Logistic Corps Museum.

I am also in debt to a number who were, I am sure, my father's friends. Jack Omond, son of an historian, who wrote a remarkably frank account of his service in the Great War and later at Gallipoli. Charles de Wolff, a larger-than-life character, whose unpublished memoir is in the archive of the Royal Logistic Corps, the successor to the RAOC. That archive also holds notes of lectures given by Tom Leahy, who was the mentor of many young officers in the First World War, and copies of the *RAOC Gazette* in which so many obituaries were published. The Imperial War Museum holds the papers of Dicky Richards, another larger-than-life character, who was Bill's friend and rival over many years. The National Archives holds war diaries of many of those in the book. I researched census returns and other public records in order to piece together family trees. I am indebted to those who wrote the histories of the companies for whom a number worked: Pilkington, Vickers, Dunlop and Rootes. I am grateful to Juliet Campbell and Lizzie Campbell (no relation), the daughters of two of the men in the story, who contacted me and provided much-needed flesh with which to cover the bare bones.

My hope is that I have managed to tell the stories faithfully, for they will never be repeated. They take us from the world of the pony and trap, via pre-First World War East Africa and Malaya, through the mud of Flanders and thence to the farthest reaches of the British Empire and the exciting developments of the 1930s, before the gruelling conflict of the Second World War. Thereafter, for some it was an early death, for others it was British industry of the 1950s, a country that had never had it so good.

I thank Brigadier Clive Elderton, Trustee of the Royal Logistic Corps Archive, and also my sister, Marian Bond, for reading my manuscript. I thank my wife, Maggie, for reading my draft, but more so for her support in this five-year quest. Claire Hopkins of Pen and Sword thought this book should be published and I thank her for her confidence. Major General Malcolm Wood has written the foreword to this book. He also kindly invited me, representing my father, to the one hundredth anniversary of the RAOC Officers' Club. I felt then, and feel now, that the massive contribution of those about whom I have written is being properly acknowledged.

Cast of Characters

Body, Major General K.M. (Joe) CMG, CB, OBE – DOS

Campbell, Major General Levin H – Director US Army Ordnance

Cansdale, Major General Cyril, CBE – Class of '22, DOS BOAR

Chalmers, Bob – Managing Director Tecalemit

Clark, Brigadier C.C. (Nobby) Order of Merit – DOS Detroit

Clarke, Brigadier Terry, CBE – DOS Second Army, later Conservative MP

Cox, Brigadier Basil, CBE – Middle East, Didcot, Tel-el-Kebir

Coxhead, Ernest – Worshipful Company of Carmen

Cutforth, Major General Sir Lancelot (Cutters) KBE, CB – DDOS 21st Army Group, DOS

de Wolff, Brigadier Charles (Wolffy) CB, CBE – Class of '22, COO Donnington

Denniston, Major General JG (Jim) CBE – DOS 21st Army Group

Geake, Major General Clifford (Geako) CB, CBE – DCS, DOS CMF

Goldstein, Brigadier Alfred CBE – Class of '22, COO Greenford

Haigh, Brigadier Cecil – Class of '22, DDOS, DOS Eleventh Army

Hardy, Brigadier Gordon CBE, Order of Merit – Class of '22 Washington, COO Donnington

Hiam, Brigadier RM (Bob) OBE – COO Old Dalby, Caen and Antwerp, Sales Director of Dunlop

Hildreth, Major General Sir John KBE – DOS, Bill's No. 2

Hill, Major General Sir Basil KBE, CB, DSO – Controller of Ordnance Services 1938–41

Hoare, Major General Lionel – COO Woolwich

Horne, Major General Gerald, CB, CBE – DDOS, DOS

Hunt, Colonel A.J.M. (Dick) OBE – Bill's eyes and ears

Johnson, Brigadier R.F. – barrister, journalist, great friend

Johnson-Davies, Colonel Kenneth, Barrister, Secretary of the Motor Trade Association, COO COD Greenford

Kenward, Sir Harold – Director Dunlop

Lea-Cox Brigadier M CB, CBE – DDOS War Office

Leahy, Brigadier Tom, CMG, DSO – Divisional Ordnance Officer, 3rd Cavalry Division, 1914, Military Mission in Washington First World War, COO Gibraltar 1925

Lillico, Bob – Lucas Industries

Omond, Brigadier Jack, MBE, MC – Class of '22, writer of his experiences in the First World War, Head of RAOC Training

Palmer, Major General Geoffrey CBE – Class of '22, COO Bicester, COO Chilwell

Parsons, Major General Sir Harold KBE – Director of Ordnance Service, France, 1914–18

Perks, Betty – my mother and Bill's wartime PA

Perks, Frank – builder, Betty's father

Pickthall, Brigadier Wallace CBE – Class of '22, DOS Allied HQ Mediterranean

Preston, Colonel Stan CBE – COO 206 BOD India, President of the 'Canbedoneans'

Readman, Major General Edgar (Reddy) CBE – COO Chilwell, Director of English Steel Corporation

Reynolds, Brigadier C.G. (Digger), Chilwell, Washington

Richards, Gordon – Chairman Solex Carburettors, Bill's best man

Richards, Major General WW (Dicky) CB, CBE, MC – Class of '22, DCS, DOS, DQMG (ME)

Riddell-Webster, General Sir Thomas, GCB DSO – QMG Middle East, then QMG in succession to Venning

Robinson, Brigadier DS (Robby), OBE – COO Derby, Inspector of Ordnance Overseas, Dunlop

Rootes, Sir William – co-founder Rootes Motor Group

Sewell, Brigadier Arthur – COO Feltham, Tecalemit

Stower, Colonel Tiny MC – Bill's friend from the First World War

Swiney, Major General Sir Neville KBE, MC – Class of '22, DOS, DOS ME

Tankard, Brigadier Ernest, OBE, MC – Chilwell, Middle East, COO Bicester

Valon, Major General A.R., CB, OBE, MC – Director of REME

Venning, General Sir Walter, GCB CMG CBE MC – QMG, then Director-General Ministry of Supply Mission in Washington

Warren, Colonel Dan, OBE – Chilwell, Middle East, Jaguar Cars
Weeks, General Sir Ronald, KCB, CBE, DSO, MC, TD – DCIGS,
	Director of Army Equipment, Chairman of Vickers and of Pilkington
Whitaker, Brigadier Harry CBE – Chilwell, Tel-el-Kebir, COO Feltham
Williams, Major General Sir Leslie (Bill) KBE, CB, MC – Class of '22,
	COS, DOS, Export Director of Rootes Motor Group

Glossary

ADOS	Assistant Director of Ordnance Services
AOD	Advanced Ordnance Depot
ATS	Auxiliary Territorial Service
BAD	Base Ammunition Depot
BAS	British Army Staff
BEF	British Expeditionary Force
BOD	Base Ordnance Depot
CAD	Central Ammunition Depot
CB	Commander of The Most Honourable Order of the Bath
CBE	Commander of the Most Excellent Order the British Empire
CO	Commanding Officer
COD	Central Ordnance Depot
COO	Chief Ordnance Officer
COS	Controller of Ordnance Services
DADOS	Deputy Assistant Director of Ordnance Services
DCS	Director of Clothing and Stores
DDOS	Deputy Director of Ordnance Services
DOS	Director of Ordnance Services
DQMG	Deputy Quartermaster General
GHQ	General Headquarters
IAOC	Indian Army Ordnance Corps
IWM	Imperial War Museum
KBE	Knight of the Most Excellent Order the British Empire
LHW	Leslie Hamlyn Williams (Bill Williams)
MBE	Member of the Most Excellent Order the British Empire
NMP	Nancy Mary Perks (Betty pre-1948)
NMW	Nancy Mary Williams (Betty post-1948)
MC	Military Cross
MT	Motor Transport

NCO	Non-Commissioned Officer
OBD	Ordnance Beach Detachment
OBE	Officer of the Most Excellent Order the British Empire
OFP	Ordnance Field Park
PoW	Prisoner of War
QMG	Quartermaster General
RAF	Royal Air Force
RAOC	Royal Army Ordnance Corps
RASC	Royal Army Service Corps
REME	Royal Electrical and Mechanical Engineers
RLC	Royal Logistic Corps
SMMT	Society of Motor Manufacturers and Traders

Chapter 1

The Photograph

In the spring of 1965, a woman, no longer young, sat at the bedside of her husband of sixteen years. He was an old soldier, dying, not of physical wounds, but of the exhaustion of service in two world wars. She had, on her knee, her notebook with page after page covered with her version of Pitman shorthand, as she wrote down his memories of a world long gone: childhood in Victorian south London, work as an office boy in the City of London, life as a young man trading in East Africa and rubber planting in Malaya.

A quarter of a century earlier, she had begun to compile a record of his deeds. Over the years of the Second World War, as thick album succeeded thick album, that record became more personal, but, equally, about more than simply him: some twelve 4-inch-thick albums spanning twenty years from 1938, just before the outbreak of the Second World War. She married him, in 1948, at the halfway-mark in the albums. He had married first in 1915.

The focus of the albums was the man she loved, and those who worked with him on one of the most monumental tasks ever undertaken by British soldiers: that of supplying a newly mechanized army with all the equipment it needed to do its job.

With the albums, she left diaries, written by her as a wide-eyed girl of 24 who had never been further from her Midlands home than Skegness. The diaries were of trips made during the Second World War to the USA, the Middle East and Africa: worlds of wonder.

The woman was Betty Perks, the daughter of a Midlands builder, Frank Perks, who had carried out building work for the Royal Army Ordnance Corps (RAOC) in the 1930s. Frank became friends with the officer with whom he mostly dealt, Colonel Bill Williams, or that mad b***er Bill Williams, as Frank would refer to him. When Betty left school, she had been determined to work, and so went to secretarial college. On gaining her certificates, her father spoke to Bill, and a job was found for her at the Army Centre for Mechanization at Chilwell, run by the RAOC and which Bill had created. In due course, she became Bill's secretary. When war broke out, Bill was posted to the War Office as Director of Warlike Stores, but Betty remained at Chilwell. In September 1941, she too was posted to the War Office as Bill's PA, from which time she began to compile her record.

The albums could have been a dry record of work done. For those eager for this, they would be a disappointment. For they contain press cuttings and copies of speeches, but also dinner menus, invitations, Christmas cards – there is even a pressed flower, the provenance of which is revealed in one of the diaries. After the war years, the task described in the albums became the challenges faced by the British motor industry of the 1950s, supplying a wider world still hungry for British manufacturing. There is all manner of memorabilia: souvenir brochures of short sea voyages on ships, including the *Queen Elizabeth* and *Queen Mary*, and invitations to all kinds of events: City Livery Company dinners, boxing and football matches. There are many photographs, including of Bill marching in the funeral procession of King George VI, but also snaps from overseas trips and studio images of Middle Eastern customers viewing the Queen's Coronation parade.

I wonder, sometimes, how often Bill and Betty would have opened up the albums to remember.

*

On the wall of Bill's room hung a photograph of a group of soldiers, some old and distinguished, but most, young and eager. He probably looked at it every day of his life. In 1957, thirty-five years after the photograph was taken, the *RAOC Gazette* published an article about the soldiers in it. Bill was there, much younger, slim and handsome; so were others Betty had known, in the Second World War, as equally driven but middle-aged men. In the front row was their Colonel-in-Chief, the Duke of York (later King George VI). The photograph was taken on the occasion of the Duke's inspection of the RAOC at its Hilsea headquarters. This had coincided with the final day of the first ordnance officer's course after the end of the Great War, and the younger faces were those of officers who had attended the course: the Class of '22.

It was the sort of course where friends for life were made, not unlike university these days. Bill would have remembered Dicky, his friend and rival over so many years. They had met in France in 1916, at St Venant, when Dicky commanded an ammunition train and when Bill was Ordnance Officer to the 19th Division, Les Papillons, under his hero, General Tom Bridges. Bill remembered Dicky as the life and soul of the course. He would also have remembered Charles de Wolff, 'Wolffy', for they and their young wives had shared digs in Blackheath from where they travelled daily to Woolwich. Bill definitely would have remembered his bicycle, and how Wolffy had played a practical joke by placing a drawing pin, sharp side up, on the bicycle seat, and how he, Bill, did not flinch.

There were others. Jack Omond, standing next to Bill, who had written a very honest account of the lot of ordnance officers in the First World War (I draw on this in Chapter 4). According to Brigadier C.H.E. Lowther, who wrote his obituary, he was one of the 'lost generation'. In a sense, most of those mentioned in this book are of that 'lost generation' who came to adulthood just before or during the Great War.

Geoffrey Palmer joined as a private in the Honourable Artillery Company (HAC), and was always very proud of his service in the ranks. Wallace 'Picky' Pickthall was commissioned in the West Yorkshire Regiment in January 1913 and crossed to France in November 1914. Cyril Cansdale had served in the London Regiment as a territorial for two years before the outbreak of war. He was commissioned and joined the Army Ordnance Department, as it was then known, in December 1914. The Territorial Army had been formed in 1908, drawing together the former rifle volunteers and Yeomanry. The London Regiment had within it battalions focused on Greater London areas, but also trades and countries of origin. For example, the London Scottish was the 14th Battalion. The HAC was a battalion, but declined to be given a number.

Then there were others on the course who were in the Royal Artillery, and, so, not in the photograph. Gordon Hardy had served in the Royal Garrison Artillery attached to the RAOC. Neville Swiney was army through and through. On graduation, he was Senior-Under-Officer at the Royal Military Academy in 1916 before crossing to France.

They each had had hands-on experience of supplying an army in the field. However, their formal education in the complexities of ordnance had been lacking, and a course had been brought together to fill that knowledge gap. It extended over some two years, so we might, as I say, liken it to a degree course at university, although, in this case, it was only for men, and they worked at close quarters and without the benefit of any long vacations. They would have got to know each other well. There would have been friendships and rivalries. They were seen by their seniors

3

as the group of young officers who would rebuild the newly named Royal Army Ordnance Corps after the horrors of the Great War. The course also had on it an officer from each of the Canadian and Indian Army Ordnance Corps, and these relationships would prove important. There were thirty-two young officers in all, seven of whom had been awarded the Military Cross, three an OBE and one a CBE for service during the war.

A word about the CBE. It had been awarded to Wolffy for rescuing a Russian princess. At the end of the First World War, Wolffy had been posted to support the White Russian Army. The story of the rescue is contained in an autobiography he wrote, which is in the Imperial War Museum archive and, very sadly, is marked strictly not for publication. It is well worth reading, and I also draw on it in Chapter 4. In it, he also tells of a dinner he and his wife attended in 1920 with his then CO, Basil Hill (who would lead the RAOC in the years before the Second World War). It seems that Hill's wife noticed Wolffy's CBE, and asked her husband, who then had a more junior decoration, when he was going to get one: embarrassment mingled with amusement. The Order of the British Empire had only just been introduced by King George V.

Alfred Goldstein was also not in the photograph, since he was in the Royal Garrison Artillery and, so, not then in the RAOC. He did, however, come top of the course. In researching his background, I came across him referred to as both Goldstein and Goldstone. His obituary in the *RAOC Gazette* is headed Goldstone, but the author, Major General Sir John Hildreth, writes of him with great affection as Alfred Goldstein, adding that he married in the 300-year-old synagogue in Portsmouth in 1936. I fear that his name and ancestry would prove a glass ceiling in the years to come.

In 1962 there was an exchange of letters published in the *RAOC Gazette* about the course, and one of these came from Goldstein. It begins with a discussion about the actual dates of the course, and continues:

> It will be a matter of interest to those now in the Corps, that not only were eleven future RAOC Brigadiers on this Course, but also five future Major Generals, RAOC, i.e., Major Generals Sir Leslie Williams, Sir Neville Swiney, W. W. ('Dicky') Richards, Geoffrey W. Palmer and Cyril Cansdale. This remarkable instance of an Ordnance Officers Course producing no less than five Major Generals and eleven Brigadiers, is likely to be an all-time record in the RAOC.[1]

It seems that memory has endless capacity to play tricks, for, in a later issue, Charles de Wolff offered a couple of humorous recollections (including that of the drawing pin), but also that he thought the course lasted fifteen months at the most. Be that as it may, the course was undoubtedly demanding. It covered a large range of subjects, as is clear from the exam papers filed in the archives: carriages, mathematics, range finding, electrical engineering, small arms and machine guns, physics, ammunition and chemistry, equipment other than guns, ordnance organization, motor vehicles and machinery. In the archive there are also the workbooks belonging to Dicky Richards on chemistry, which clearly included metallurgy.

Alfred Goldstein had passed out top of the course, but with Bill Williams second. Bill would recall many years later, how, initially, the course had him completely flummoxed. It was the maths (he had no idea what trigonometry was), and the others took great delight in teasing him. He had, after all, left school at the age of fifteen. Now, he was 29 as were a number of the others; one or two were younger and a half dozen a bit older.

Others in the photograph would have been fountains of knowledge for the Class of '22. Seated to the right of the Duke was Lieutenant General Sir Travers Clarke who had been Quartermaster General in France for most of the war, and who wrote this about ordnance men: 'Ordnance was the ever-present help of the British soldier in an ordeal of unexampled severity.' Next to Clarke was Sir Harold Parsons who had been Director of Ordnance Services in France for nearly the whole of the war, a massive task. To the left of the Duke was Sir John Stevens who had come out of retirement in 1914 to be Director of Ordnance and Equipment at the War Office. Distinguished men, but perhaps of an earlier world.

Lieutenant Colonel Jasper Baker, at the right end of the front row, was a little younger than the generals. He had come to the then Army Ordnance Department from the Royal Marines and wrote a vivid account of the first stages of the First World War, which Major General Forbes drew on in his history of the Army Ordnance Services. Baker would also to rise to the rank of major general and become a colonel commandant of the RAOC. Next to Baker is H.S. Bush, who was Ordnance Officer Commanding Hilsea. Captain C.W. Bacon, at the left end of the front row, was the adjutant at Hilsea and next to him, H.L. Wethered was the chief instructor on the course. Captain Arthur Valon (back row, second along), who was a mechanical engineer and whom de Wolff remembered lecturing on the course during the Duke's visit, also became a major general as Director of the Royal Electrical and Mechanical Engineers (REME) and later Colonel Commandant of REME. W.M. Stokes had served on the committee which had developed the course. He was later one of the pioneers at the Corsham underground ammunition depot near Bath.

*

In June 1940, some say by a miracle, an army returned to England from Dunkirk. In the next few weeks, more men would return, as would a small amount of their equipment; the vast majority had been left behind. Also lost were experienced men who had fought the rear-guard action; many had died and many more were taken prisoner. Amongst these were experienced men of the Royal Army Ordnance Corps who had been supplying and maintaining the anti-aircraft batteries protecting the retreat.

Back in the War Office, temporary Major General Bill Williams was three months into a six-month 'probationary period' as Director of Warlike Stores; only, there were now precious few such stores to direct, and an army needing to be rearmed quickly, to stave off the expected invasion.

Other RAOC officers had returned from France. Charles de Wolff had come back in the previous November. Before mobilization, he had been building a massive armament depot at Donnington in deepest Shropshire; the idea had been his: to create a replacement for the Woolwich Arsenal far away from the risk of enemy air attack. Wisely, the then Director of Ordnance Services, Major General Basil Hill, had given de Wolff the job to do. He had, though, been mobilized and sent to France along with everyone else, until the War Office saw the error of their ways and sent him back to his vital job in hand. Dicky Richards, who had set up a massive general stores depot in Le Havre, returned after Dunkirk, albeit briefly, before being sent out to join General Wavell in Egypt. Geoffrey Palmer, who had commanded the Warlike Stores Depot at Nantes, came home; I do not know whether he was a survivor of the SS *Lancastria*, which sunk off Nantes with the loss of 3,000 lives. There is evidence that he had suffered trauma. Cyril Cansdale, who was ordnance officer to the Lines of Communication, returned, as did Clifford Geake who had been with Palmer in Nantes.

June 1940 must have been truly a terrifying time. Some years later, on 31 March 1946, Major General C.H. 'Geako' Geake wrote to Bill, apologizing for being unable to attend Bill's leaving party, and in the letter, he reminisces:

> I suppose you do know without my telling you – though I'm sure you won't admit it – that you personally saved the Corps from a horrid crash in 1939–42? Anyhow, be that as it may, I know that I owe everything to meeting you in a passage in W.O. on about 25th June 1940.

'Geako' (Clifford Geake) was not a name I found in the records of the ordnance officers' course, but he plays an important role in this story so I dug a little. He was not on that first course because he was serving as Ordnance Officer in Bermuda. After Bermuda, he served at Hereford, Stirling and the War Office before being posted to Hong Kong.

These men were surely suffering from shock, but they had to pick themselves up and get to the mammoth task that lay ahead. They shared an unparalleled advantage: some twenty years earlier they had been knitted together as a team on, or soon after, that first ordnance officers' course following the end of the Great War.

*

In the early spring of 1944, Major General Bill Williams, known to the quarter of a million men and women of the RAOC by his nickname 'Willie', was working every hour that God sent, with those of the Class of '22 and many more besides, to achieve the impossible. They had to supply the hundreds of thousands of troops undertaking the most daring seaborne invasion ever attempted: D-Day. Failure of supply would mean total failure, as had so often been the case in the past. The pressure was enormous, the memories of Dunkirk haunting.

On 23 May 1944, some fifty officers of the RAOC and the Canadian Ordnance Corps had gathered in the Debating Hall of the Royal Empire Society in London to listen to Bill; rather like the scene in the film *A Bridge Too Far* where General Horrocks addresses his officers.

Bill spoke first. He was by then Controller of Ordnance Services as well as Director of Warlike Stores, which meant that he was responsible for the supply of all vehicles, guns, radio and ammunition; the buck stopped with him.

Dicky spoke next. Major General W.W. 'Dicky' Richards was Director of Clothing and Stores and supplied everything from socks to stretchers. Before joining the army in 1914, Dicky had worked in one of the massive textile warehouses close to London Docks.

Then came Jim Denniston, a former Seaforth Highlander, who was Director of Ordnance Services for the 21st Army Group. Denniston, who had attended the 1928 ordnance officers' course, said this:

> We in the Expeditionary Force are the 'happy few'. Let us remember that there may be, in our bases behind, many who are thinking of our good fortune; let us remember that they, too, would very willingly take our places in the front. To those who are behind, I would say, do not forget there are officers who will be landing a few hours after the first British troops set foot in the war theatre and the conditions under which they will work, for days and weeks, will be beyond description. General Williams has stressed a point which I had very much in mind – speed. Speed and efficiency, not only at the beginning but right through. I seem to remember a slogan in the Middle East regarding tanks – 'anything connected with tanks will be done at the double!' That is what we all need now.[2]

The fourth speaker was the Quartermaster General who expressed his confidence in the ability of the RAOC to 'deliver the goods'. The Colonel Commandant, Major General Jasper Baker, sent a message of encouragement.

In the audience were a number of others who had been in the photograph. Charles de Wolff, Geoffrey Palmer (who had built the all-purpose depot at Bicester specifically for D-Day), Alfred Goldstein (in command of the depot at Greenford which was to be first port of call for the invasion force) and Cyril Cansdale, who was Deputy Director of Ordnance Services and in charge of field operations. There were also temporary officers from industry, who had brought with them their experience and knowledge of modern methods. Former steel industry director, Brigadier Edgar (Reddie) Readman, who was running the massive Motor Transport depot at Chilwell. Former Dunlop manager, Colonel Bob Hiam, who had commanded the armaments depot at Old Dalby, which supplied power tools and, famously, Bailey bridges. Hiam would command the second depot to be set up in France following the invasion and go on to command the depot at Antwerp supplying the final push into Germany. A fellow Dunlop man, Colonel Robbie Robinson, was not present since he had been given the role of Inspecting Officer Overseas, and he was already at work planning supply for the invasion of Burma. Former manager at Tecalemit (the garage machinery manufacturer), Colonel Arthur Sewell, was in command of the depot at Feltham, which was at the forefront in developing effective packaging that would become increasingly important in South East Asia.

From later ordnance officers' courses were Lancelot Cutforth, who had been commissioned into the Gunners in 1918, seeing service in the final two months of the First World War, and who was Jim Denniston's number two, and Terry Clarke, Director of Ordnance Services for the Second Army, who would later become a Conservative Member of Parliament. Cutforth would always be known by the single word, 'Cutters'. Another significant name was that of John Hildreth, who was Bill's right-hand man. Not present was Bill's eyes and ears, Dick Hunt. Others, from the course of '22 and later courses, were in the Middle East, supplying the Eighth Army as it fought its way up through Italy, and included Neville Swiney, Geako and Harry Whitaker.

As Bill said in his speech, this meeting marked the culmination of years of hard work and cruel learning through experience.

Only a few weeks earlier Bill and Betty had returned from their second trip to the USA where Bill had gone armed with a letter from General Montgomery:

> I am seriously perturbed to find that there is a grave shortage of certain essential fast moving spare parts and equipment for Tanks and Vehicles. The supply of spares for power units for Tanks is of the utmost importance, and unless adequate supplies are received in good time, it will seriously affect forthcoming operations.
>
> Major General Williams is representing my interest in this most important and vital problem and I should be most grateful if you would give him every possible assistance.[3]

The British Army was hugely dependent upon supplies of guns and vehicles from the USA as well as from British companies, especially motor companies. The problem was that politicians prefer numbers that make good headlines: the total number of tanks supplied; far less interesting, but no less vital, were spare parts. For example, a Churchill tank engine has 4,000 parts. To maintain a squadron of one hundred Churchills, landing reserves of 190 tons of spare parts are needed to cover fourteen days.[4]

Betty had written diaries of these trips, as well as carefully pasting photographs, newspaper cuttings, dinner menus and travel tickets in her albums. The second American trip had followed one a year earlier where, as a wide-eyed girl of 24, she had made a vivid record of all she had seen. In between the trips to America, there had been a six-week tour of inspection of the Middle East and Africa, which itself had followed an earlier trip Bill had made to North Africa to hear his men's experiences in the field. This first-hand information had been vital and had enabled Bill to understand the challenges that a massive seaborne invasion would face.

Of course, it wasn't all overseas trips, however vital they were. Most of the time, for Bill, it was dogged hard work in the War Office and around the UK. For Dicky and a number of others of the Class of '22, though, it had been in North Africa and the Middle East where the main land war was waged.

Another name comes to be mentioned, that of Ronald Weeks. In the early years of the war the army was grappling with the profusion of equipment, its selection, supply, storage and maintenance. As I tell later, the maintenance question was addressed by the formation of the Royal Electrical and Mechanical Engineers. All this came under the Quartermaster General and, as I read it, the span of responsibility became so great that it was necessary to create the appointment of a Director of Army Equipment to ease the load and better support Bill as Director of Warlike Stores. The man appointed had considerable experience in industry and the army. His name was Ronald Weeks.

Each of these men had been moulded by their experience in the Great War and the jobs they had done in the interwar years. These I explore, but first I needed to trace whence came those members of the Class of '22 and others, to see what, in their upbringing, might have equipped them for the job that lay ahead.

Chapter 2

Family and Childhood in Victorian London

Leslie Williams would, for most of his life, be known as Bill; it was the army way. But on 13 June 1891, when he was born and, I suspect, for the next ten or so years, the army would not even have entered his head. The family home, a little terraced house in the poorer part of Dulwich in south London, had within it just about the only family heirloom, a kneehole chest with the date 1772 written on the back of a drawer. Leslie, as a young boy, would sit at the desk and pretend to be a businessman in the City of London; that was when he was not playing with electricity – rigging up bells and electric shocks to surprise his parents.

His father, Alfred, had, in the 1850s, worked in the City, with premises at 46 Cornhill when he started out in partnership with a Mr Watson, as stationers and dispatch box manufacturers. The partnership was dissolved on 2 December 1857, and Alfred went on his own. He took premises at 135 Fenchurch Street which, for some years, he may well have owned. In 1863, he became a Freeman of the City of London. His business expanded and, in 1865, he described himself as 'travelling bag, trunk, dressing & writing case maker and cutler' and then, ten years later, as 'a master cutler employing one man and two boys'. His great-nephew, Peter Wilson, later wrote,

> I believe he had a severe financial reverse at some time and probably that valuable property [135 Fenchurch Street] had to go. He was inter-alia an inventor, and once buttonholed a Minister while the Sudan Campaign was on, and his device for shallow craft, and canalizing for that purpose, was adopted – but too late for use in the relief of Gordon.[1]

11

As an inventor, Alfred held several patents. He was awarded prizes for his patent raft seat: a medal from the Royal Cornwall Polytechnic Society and a medal from the International Exhibition of Navigation, Travelling Commerce and Manufacturers, Liverpool, in 1886. There is a picture of him with his 'Topsy-Turvy', a miniature playground big wheel.

By the time Leslie was born, Alfred, at age 60 had seen the best days of his career; he now described himself as an engineer, and sold gas equipment. He had invented a patent gas turner-regulator. The family lived modestly, although Alfred found time and money for the occasional trip to Monte Carlo, with his friend Allerton, to try their luck in the casinos. I sometimes wonder whether Alfred ever met Charles deville Wells, famed for having broken the bank at Monte Carlo; Wells was a distant cousin.[2]

I shall tell more of Leslie since, inevitably, I know more about him, but, first, a word on some of his future brothers-in-arms.

Jack Omond was older than the others, born in Edinburgh on 19 April 1884. His father, George, was born in Perthshire, and the *Oxford Dictionary of National Biography* describes him as a Scottish advocate and a prolific author of history. Jack's mother was an Edinburgh girl, Margaret, and he had two older and one younger sisters.

Ronald Weeks was born in 1890 in County Durham where his father, Richard, was a mining engineer. It was a Durham family, that had been farming for generations. The engineering profession was clearly remunerative, for their house was described in the 1891 census as having fourteen rooms, with three servants and a governess. Ronald also came from a big family, having one younger brother and three younger sisters. His mother, Susan McIntyre, had Scots parents, but had been born in Jarrow.

1891 was a significant year, for, as well as Leslie, in January, Geoffrey Woodroffe Palmer was born in Paddington. His father was William, a stock exchange clerk, and his mother Maud; he had five sisters and three brothers. His grandfather and great-grandfather had both been schoolmasters.

Another 1891 birth was Wallace Pickthall, who was born on 9 November in Otley in Devon. By the time of the 1901 census, the family had moved to Bedford. His father, Walter, was shown as being of 'independent means' and his mother was from Germany. He had a younger brother and younger sister. His younger brother, Henry, died in Central Macedonia, Greece, on 8 December 1918 whilst serving with the Royal Field Artillery.

In 1892, Dicky Richards was born in St Helier on Jersey in the Channel Islands. He was baptized William Watson, but, in the army, soon became Dicky. His father, Thomas, had been a draper's assistant. In the next-door house there lived three women, also named Richards: one aged 68; another, Elizabeth, then aged 35, also a draper's assistant; and Jessie, aged 33, a dressmaker. It might not have been totally by chance that Dicky would, in the Second World War, become RAOC Director of Clothing and Stores. His mother, Mary, came from a line of Jersey fishermen.

Cyril Cansdale was born in Gibraltar in 1892, where his father, Arthur, was a British soldier. Arthur was the son of an agricultural labourer in Suffolk. By the time of the 1901 census, the family had returned to England to Prittlewell in Essex, where Arthur managed a wine and spirits store. Cyril had one older and two younger brothers, one of whom died at the outbreak of the First World War and another in France on 29 September 1918. His mother, Jane, had been born in Ireland and died in 1917 in an Essex lunatic asylum: we might, perhaps, assume through mental illness prompted by grief. Harry Whitaker was born on 30 September 1892, the son of a Tooting umbrella and walking stick maker

Charles Esmond de Wolff was born in 1893 in Camberwell. I read first that his grandfather was a Polish émigré. Further research revealed rather more.[3] The family was part of the Polish aristocracy, and both grandfather and great-grandfather had served as cavalry officers in the French army. The defeat of the French, in 1870, had prompted the move to England. In 1901, the family was then living in Wimbledon, and Charles's father, also Charles, was working as an examiner in the Exchequer and Audit Department. His mother, Hetty, died just after the end of the First World War.

Edgar 'Reddy' Readman was born in 1893 in Sheffield, the son of Ernest Readman, a local education committee assistant supervisor, and Mary Platt. He had one younger sister. His grandfather, William, had been an engine driver.

Gordon Hardy was born in Kensington in 1894. His father was an illustrator for the *Strand Magazine* and illustrated a number of books including Arthur Conan Doyle's novel *Beyond the City*. The family moved to Chobham in Surrey by the time of the 1901 census. Both his father and his mother, Ida, came from Gloucestershire. Clifford 'Geako' Geake was born in Plymouth in 1894, the son of Thomas, a solicitor. His mother, Jane, like his father, was Cornish. Clifford had two older, and one younger, sisters. They lost their father in 1907, and their mother ten years later.

Jim Denniston was born in 1895 in Epsom in Surrey, the son of Thomas, a Scot who had moved south to work as an insurance broker. His mother, Beatrice, was Thomas's second wife. She had been born in Dublin in 1869.

Alfred Goldstein was born in 1896 in Hampstead to Nathan Goldstein, a financial agent originally from Dover, and Kate, a Londoner. He had one older and three younger brothers. A.J.M. 'Dick' Hunt was born in the shadow of Woolwich Arsenal in 1897. His father, John, worked at the Arsenal. His mother, Edith, looked after Dick and his brother and sister. Dick would become a boy soldier in the Army Ordnance Corps.

Neville Swiney, an only child, was born in India in 1897, son of Royal Engineer, later, Brigadier General Alexander Swiney. His mother, Marguerite, was Welsh. His grandfather had also been born in India and, with his wife Mary, had had five children, Alexander being the youngest. He had been in government service. In 1901, Neville was living in Wales with his maternal grandfather, a solicitor. Lancelot Cutforth was born in 1899 in York, the son of George Cutforth, a leather producer for boots and shoes, and Elizabeth Hardy who was shown in the census as assisting her husband in the business. They lived at 56 Micklegate, York. George's father, Joseph, was also a leather producer and came from Lincoln.

Arthur Sewell was born in Leicester in 1901, son of Arthur, an electrical engineer, and Matilda who came from neighbouring Warwickshire. He had one older and one younger brother. Bob Hiam was born in 1905 in Somerset, son of Robert, a French-born draughtsman who worked for the railways. His mother, Mary, died also in 1905, we might presume in childbirth. He had two sisters, Eva, who later married in Kuala Lumpur, and Mary born 1904. In 1911, the three children were recorded as living with a housekeeper in Pangbourne, Berkshire. Their father died in 1962. John Hildreth was born in India in 1908. His father, Harold, and mother, Edith, had also been born in India. By the time of the 1911 census the family was living in Dublin and John had a younger brother, Henry. Harold was then a captain in the Royal Army Medical Corps.

D.S. 'Robbie' Robinson remains a mystery. As will become clear, he wrote the obituaries of a number of the others and had much to say that adds flesh to the story, but no one seems to have written following his death. He was a contemporary of Bob Hiam. I could find a D.S. Robinson born in 1908 and who died after 1985. The last record I could find of the D.S. Robinson, who served in the RAOC, was a small advertisement in the *RAOC Gazette* for someone to help him and his then disabled wife in their home, but that was all. For this reason alone, this book could never be just a biography of my father; it is about a remarkable group of people which had as its leader, Bill Williams.

But, now, back to Leslie. The family home, at 32, Trossachs Road, had two downstairs rooms separated by sliding doors, and a small front garden. It housed Leslie and Alfred, and Alfred's much younger wife, Mildred Mercy. It would, within the space of four years, also house Leslie's brother, Cecil. Of the two boys and their father, I quote, again, words of Peter Wilson, 'As a small boy I remember "Uncle" [had] rather a bristly moustache, [and] at Christmas times, a little brusque – more than justified with small noisy and over excited boys.'

Mildred's pride and joy was a little conservatory adjoining the house, I assume, to the rear. Leslie later recalled an old woman who would come in once a week to do the washing and being rewarded by a mug of ale in addition to her wages. The sight of this old woman up to her ears in soap suds and steam and then cooling off after her efforts by drinking her ale, must have been 'a wondrous sight to a little boy who in so many ways must have been protected from the world by his mother'. The quotation is from my own mother who clearly loved both mother and son.

Alfred and Mildred had married in 1889, some seven years after the death of Eliza, Alfred's first wife of twenty-four years. Alfred and Eliza had married on 31 January 1858 and they had had one daughter, Kate Mary. They had lived first at 46 Cornhill, and Kate Mary had been baptized at St Michael Cornhill on 23 November 1858. During the 1860s, Alfred's private address was given as 8 Montagu Villas, West Green Road, Tottenham. By 1881, the family had moved to Rosedale, St Mary's Road, Peckham. Sadly, Eliza would only live for one more year.

Alfred was then taken under the wing of Eliza's sister, Emily Crawcour, who ran Parsonage House School at Balfour Road, Ilford described as a 'collegiate school for girls preparing Oxford and Cambridge Examinations and junior classes on the kindergarten system'. Emily's daughter, Lizzie, worked there as a teacher, as did her good friend, Mildred Mercy. The family are said to have expressed surprise when Alfred and Mildred announced they were to be married.

In 1878 Kate Mary, then aged 19, married Harvey Barton, an assessor and collector of Inland Revenue, with whom Alfred didn't get on. Leslie adored Kate Mary's daughter, Ruby, and viewed as her 'ideal' woman, tall and fair and gentle. It had been Mildred who had stilled the troubled waters between Alfred and Harvey. The Bartons lived in a big house on Champion Hill not far from Dulwich. Leslie remembered most particularly the garden which had a mulberry tree, and that he was allowed to collect leaves for his silkworms. It was always a great joy for him to visit his 'nieces', Ruby and her sister Norah.

Alfred's mother, Mary, had died in 1864 and his father, Richard, in 1879. Richard had been born in 1799 and had spent his childhood above his father's (also Richard) wax and tallow chandler's premises at 408 The Strand, just by the Nell Gwynne Tavern. It would have been a noisy and smelly childhood. The Strand was not far from the Thames, which was rapidly becoming an open sewer, not to mention the horse droppings that littered London streets. It was also a busy and bustling area. Almost directly opposite was a shop window which enchanted Alfred's father. It was the premises of John Weiss, surgical instrument maker. I can imagine the young Richard staring at the shop window, wondering at the gleaming instruments. By 1851, he would be recorded on the census of that year as head of the household at 62 The Strand where he then managed the Weiss business.

Alfred's father and his brother, William Smith Williams, who would later be known as the reader at publishers Smith, Elder & Co. who first recognized the genius of Charlotte Brontë, had both become orphans in 1813. Their mother had died two years earlier. They then disappeared from the public record until William re-emerged in 1817 apprenticed to publishers Taylor & Hessey; Richard was recorded present at the baptism of his daughter, Mary, on 1 October 1820, when he was described as a surgeon's instrument maker. I suspect that he may well have been apprenticed to Weiss on his father's death.

Alfred was born in August 1830, two years before the Great Reform Act which began to extend the suffrage to more men, but, at that date, no women. He was baptized Alfred Hamlyn at St Mary Magdalene, Bermondsey, on 31 October 1830 with his brother William Fleetwood, who had been born in 1826. We have a family photograph of a small boy whom we always assumed had died in childhood; perhaps he was William Fleetwood.

A brief word about these second names. A Thomas Fleetwood was recorded as attending Richard's brother's wedding in 1826. It may be that the lack of any reference to Richard at the wedding could be the result of the birth of his son? I infer that Fleetwood was a friend of the brothers. The name Hamlyn is important, but I don't know why! Leslie made an almost dying wish that my sister and I should change our surname to Hamlyn Williams. The 'adored' Ruby recalled a conversation with Mildred, during which Mildred had asked whether Ruby had given the name Hamlyn to any of her children, adding that she should have done for it was a 'very important' name. My mother searched long and hard to find its origin. There was a Hamlyn-Williams family at Clovelly in Devon. Could Richard have known them?

In 1841, Alfred was living with his father, mother and sister in Allen Street, Lambeth. He once told Leslie that he had been at school at East Horsley in Surrey. This may well have been one of the occasions when Alfred would take his sons by train to East Horsley to go fishing and enjoy the country lanes by pony and trap.

Alfred was recorded on the 1851 census as living at 62 The Strand with his father, mother and sister. This was a year I am quite sure Alfred would not quickly forget. It was, of course, the year of the Great Exhibition at the Crystal Palace, celebrating industrial advances. In the early part of 1851, Richard Williams was acting as secretary to the group of surgical instrument makers preparing their displays for the Great Exhibition. For the exhibition, Weiss had produced a most marvellous instrument comprising 1,851 knives. This was clearly a bit of showing off. However, it must have inspired Alfred in the inventions he would patent over the course of his career. Alfred's younger son, Cecil, would go on to be an engineer. Leslie, as we shall see, was certainly no stranger to engineering.

By 1861, Richard was shown as living at 62 The Strand employing thirty men, three boys and 'a female'. His business had prospered. John Weiss & Son are mentioned in the Sherlock Holmes story, *Silver Blaze*, as manufacturers of a cornea knife. Jack the Ripper is said by some to have used a Weiss scalpel. Leslie, of course, never knew his grandfather, but invention and engineering were clearly stamped on his DNA.

Leslie's childhood, if not idyllic, certainly offered a solid foundation to later life, and there were happy memories. One was being taken on Sunday mornings by his father, along with his brother, to The Crown in Dulwich village to drink ginger beer, often with ice-cream floating in it. Another was of his parents wearing evening dress to go to see Gilbert and Sullivan. A further memory was of Uncle Rowland's wedding to Auntie

Emily, the daughter of a Suffolk farmer. Rowland was Mildred's brother. Suffolk was always a favourite holiday destination, particularly Lowestoft, perhaps because Alfred's mother had come from Bawdsley in Suffolk. The Wilcockson wedding in 1902 was clearly one to remember: playing in the haystacks, collecting eggs and, of course, the wedding treats. Another, less happy, memory was of his father 'teaching him to swim' by throwing him in a pool. To my knowledge, Leslie never learned to swim.

Unusually, at the end of the nineteenth century, Leslie went to a dame school where the three Rs were taught. Such schools were run by women from their own homes and had been popular. In the mid-part of the century, they had been called into question in terms of the quality of education they were actually providing. A great many closed, and children instead attended the growing number of charity and church schools. From his dame school, Leslie went the short distance from Trossachs Road to Alleyn's School.

The name Alleyn is synonymous with Dulwich, for it was the Jacobean actor Edward Alleyn who, in 1605, bought the Manor of Dulwich and, in 1610, set up the foundation of Alleyn's College of God's Gift. The original college was built between 1613 and 1616 at the southern end of the main street in the hamlet of Dulwich. Alleyn's School came into existence, in its own right, in 1882. Alleyn's took boys from the age of 8 until 16, and its focus was on English, maths, elementary sciences and French, intended to equip pupils for a career in trade or commerce. Scholarships were then available to transfer to Dulwich College for a further two years for university entrance or the professions. New school buildings were erected in 1887, and Latin and German were added to the curriculum. Dr Smith had been master of the Lower School from 1875, and took the headship of Alleyn's from 1882 until his retirement in 1902, by which time the school had nearly 700 pupils.

Significantly for Leslie, Smith was succeeded by H.B. Baker, a scientist who split the school into modern and science sides, the former concentrating on French and German with the addition of bookkeeping and shorthand, whilst the latter focused on subjects which would equip boys for careers as 'electrical engineers, manufacturing chemists or possibly inventors'. Baker taught the ideals of honesty, manners and work. Games had their part to play, but, when they were finished, pupils should devote themselves to their work. Baker took up an appointment at Oxford before completing a year, but his changes were continued by F. Collins who held the post of headmaster until 1920. A feature throughout was the presence of drill in the daily curriculum. Collins had a gymnasium erected and efforts were made to instruct all boys in the use of a rifle.[4]

Leslie talked of his schooldays, and my mother inferred, from what he told her, that he was something of a loner at Alleyn's. His great love was the natural world, and he could be found at the bottom of the playing fields in search of chrysalises of hawk and other moths and indeed the moths themselves. Right from the beginning of Dr Smith's tenure, Alleyn's had had a strong reputation for excellence in natural sciences. The playing fields held no spell for Leslie, since he was hindered in ball games by short sight. Not so, drill; he remembered with pride the day when the drill sergeant called him forward to lead the file of marchers, because his bearing was so soldierly. This may have sown a seed.

In the classroom, he loved science, particularly electricity. He enjoyed the experiments, and, at home, would surprise his parents with bells and electric shocks in his sanctum, his room with the kneehole chest. He was less keen on languages, and negotiated a deal with his German teacher under which he would clean the master's bicycle in preference to attending class. I remain unclear as to how strictly the school was in practice divided between modern and science.

In 1906 Alfred became ill and died. Leslie, who had been longing to leave school, grasped the opportunity to help his mother, then in a straightened financial situation, by leaving and taking a job. Mildred sold the house and took a position as housekeeper at the Conservative Club in St James's Street. Cecil moved to the City of London School and Leslie moved into digs. Leslie and Cecil would meet at Leslie's digs for Sunday breakfast of smoked haddock, a tradition which Leslie honoured throughout his life.

Leslie's childhood and education were thus cut short, but what of the others in this story? The 1901 census shows Ronald Weeks as attending the Mount School in Northallerton as a boarder. It places Geoffrey Palmer at boarding school in Eastbourne. I tried to trace which, but it seems that Eastbourne at the time had attracted a good number of boys' boarding schools. I could find that Charles de Wolff went to the Strand School between 1909 and 1910, before which he had attended Portsmouth Grammar School. Lancelot Cutforth became head boy of his prep school in York. Of the others, I could find little of their primary education.

Chapter 3

The World of Work in Edwardian London, East Africa and Malaya

The job Leslie found was as office boy to papermakers, James Spicer & Sons, in the City. I wondered whether the job with James Spicer had come about through a family contact. Leslie's father's first wife had been the daughter of a printer; could there have been a connection? I obtained one of Alfred's patent applications, and it was printed by Spottiswood, the same company which printed much of Smith, Elder & Co.'s output; perhaps that was a connection? Spicer Brothers featured in the catalogue of the Great Exhibition as contracted wholesale stationers to the exhibition. Perhaps Richard and Alfred got to known them? It could be the Alleyn's had contact with potential employers for their pupils. We don't know. The job was rewarded by the princely sum of seven shillings and sixpence a week. I reflected on this, and, of course, an apprenticeship or an articled clerkship was out of the question, since a premium would have been required and Mildred had no money. Leslie recalled making many mistakes, including spilling ink. Nevertheless, the clerk, for whom he worked, rewarded him with the gift of a Bible when he moved on to his next job.

It is not clear how long Leslie worked for Spicer, but at some point, he moved jobs to join Robert Gardner Mountains and here I can use Leslie's own words, as, in his last months, he recalled his second job:

> I worked as a clerk for Gardner Mountain the insurance brokers. I had to work very hard indeed and had the magnificent wage of 10 shillings a week. Many evenings we had to stay on to deal with invoices brought in by the directors, who spent the afternoon at Lloyds placing insurances. Mr Howes, the chief clerk, would give us sixpence and send us across the road to buy sandwiches

and then we would work sometimes till nine at night to get the invoices cleared.

At the time I was working for Gardner Mountain, I used to walk along Leadenhall Street looking with longing eyes at the advertisements of the various shipping companies, scenes of lovely ships sailing down palm lined coasts, and I used to feel a great restlessness and a tremendous urge to travel.

My good fairy must've heard my thoughts, because one day an old friend of my father, a Mr Baines, asked if I would join him in a company he was forming to go to Portuguese East Africa to trade with the natives. I, of course, jumped at the chance and, after a few months – the time it took Baines to get enough money put up by friends to finance the company – I was able to tender my resignation from Gardner Mountain.

When I told the chaps in the office that I was going to Africa, they just didn't believe me. Throughout my time with them, they had not been very pleasant to me; possibly I had been to a better school than they and perhaps spoke with a better accent, and they would just be unpleasantly jealous. So, I was able to leave the office with a great feeling of relief.

The company Baines had formed gave me an outfit allowance of £120, and so I immediately began to collect together my kit: pith helmet, various suits of white duck and of course camping equipment.[2]

During the last two years in which he had worked for Gardner Mountain, he had joined the 14th (County of London) Battalion The London Regiment (London Scottish) as a territorial with the rank of private. This he loved. It had been the London Scottish, because his maternal grandmother was a Nisbet, a family of the clan Campbell. They would meet at Buckingham Gate for regular sessions of drill under the eye of Sergeant Duncan Tovey, whom Leslie would come to admire greatly and would mention every time he passed Tovey's home in Worplesden in Surrey. In order to leave for Africa, Leslie had to buy himself out of the regiment. His discharge certificate records that he enlisted on 8 February 1909 and was discharged on 9 October 1911.

The mention of 1911 brings in the census for that year which helps in locating some of the others in the story. Jim Denniston was at

Haileybury School, probably best known for preparing young men for service in India and elsewhere in the Empire. Alfred Goldstein was also listed as being at school, but in London, living with his parents, siblings and two servants. Neville Swiney is shown as a boarder at a school for boys in Cheltenham. Cheltenham seems to have been the English home of the Swiney family, a number having chosen to be buried there. The census shows Wallace Pickthall as a gentleman cadet at the Royal Military College Camberley, which merged with the Royal Military Academy Woolwich in 1947 to create the RMA Sandhurst. Lancelot Cutforth became head boy of St Peter's York and his daughter, Lizzie Campbell, who kindly provided detail of her father's upbringing, added that Lancelot had been awarded a scholarship to Cambridge, but was unable to take it up having been called up on leaving school.

Ronald Weeks, alone among those mentioned in this book, was, by 1909, studying at university, at Gonville and Caius College, Cambridge. His secondary education had been at Charterhouse School in Surrey. I found his name in the *Book of Matriculations and Degrees* with the award of a degree of Batchelor of Arts in 1912. His obituary in *The Times* adds that he captained the Cambridge Association Football XI. T.C. Barker in his book, *The Glassmakers*, adds further that he

> came to Pilkington with the strongest recommendations from the Cambridge University Appointments Board which had started to provide promising graduates to various business concerns, notably Brunner, Mond in Cheshire.[1]

Brunner, Mond would later become part of ICI.

Edgar Readman was living at home with his parents in Sheffield and working as a junior clerk in the steelworks. By 1911, the Cansdales were still in Prittlewell, but Cyril's father was then an insurance collector and Cyril was working as a civil servant. The Palmer family had moved to Green Hurst Park, Hurst Green, Oxted in Surrey, and Geoffrey was listed as a stock exchange clerk.

Dicky Richards' obituary records that he came to London to work in one of the City's largest textile warehouses. He joined F Company of the London Scottish in around 1911. He then went overseas. Also overseas, I think, was Gordon Hardy, since I couldn't find his name on the 1911 census, but his name did appear on a passenger list returning from the USA in 1914.

Charles de Wolff's memoirs show that he attended Birkbeck College in the University of London, where he was awarded a degree of Bachelor of Laws. In the 1911 census, he was shown as living with his parents in Wimbledon, and, at age 17, working as a solicitor's clerk; the Birkbeck degree course was part-time.

Leslie was rather more adventurous, for he set sail for East Africa in the autumn of 1911. Once more I am fortunate to have his own words to tell the story:

> I sailed to Africa on the German East Africa liner, Admiral. Our first port of call was Lisbon, and then Marseille where Baines came on board. From there we went to Naples, and he and I visited Pompeii.
>
> Together this voyage was, of course, a wonderful experience for me; in fact, it was all my dreams coming true.
>
> On board one day, a very handsome tall young man approached me and said we had met before. He was mistaken, and I told him so. He thought we had been to the same school together. He realized his mistake and introduced himself as Stafford, the Marquis of Stafford, heir to the Duke of Sutherland. He was extremely kind to me and befriended me for the rest of the voyage. There is a picture of him on the station in Mombasa in the albums, and I took another picture at that same spot of Betty and she took one of me when we visited Mombasa again many years later.

The name the Duke of Sutherland rang a bell, and so I looked him up. This young man, played by Peter Egan, appears in the film *Chariots of Fire* as the one member of the British Olympic Committee who understood the principled stand being made by Eric Liddell, the Scots Christian who wouldn't run on Sunday. The Duke went on to have a distinguished political career.

To continue with Leslie's account:

> From Naples we sailed to Port Said where the ship was to be coaled – for all ships were fuelled by coal in those days, there was no oil. I have never seen anything quite so fantastic as the coaling process. I saw hordes of men (coolie types) each

carrying a basket on his head, going like a line of ants up one gangway, heaving the coal into the bunkers, and coming off the ship by another gangway. Just an endless line of men gradually filling up the bunkers for the rest of our journey.

All the passengers were advised to leave the ship for this coaling, as the coal dust went everywhere. When we returned there was literally a quarter of an inch of dust wherever you looked.

Port Said was a fascination to me, I suppose my first glimpse of the East. We passengers were besieged by men selling all kinds of things and I eventually found my way to Simon Artz, the great shop where all kinds of eastern wares can be bought. It was like an Aladdin's Cave to me.

The voyage down the Red Sea was terrible, the heat was terrific and there was no air conditioning in those days.[3]

Leslie crossed the equator and was dubbed Porpoise by King Neptune. His certificate of baptism is in Betty's album. Sadly, he does not describe the actual scene but I do remember him telling of a ceremony.

He arrived at Lourenço Marques, the capital of Mozambique, and would have been struck by the well-preserved Portuguese colonial architecture amid the bustle of a port on the Indian Ocean. It seems he went from there first to Mozambique Island on an Arab dhow, a journey of three days truly from hell. The seas were mountainous, and he was tied to the mast to prevent him being washed overboard. All the food on board became soaked with seawater. Returning from the island, he landed at Beira and he continues the account:

> I went on foot from Beira to the Portuguese border near Blantyre, seeking out trade and trading with the natives groundnuts and mealies [maize cobs]. We had brought out with us bales and bales of 'Manchester goods', cheap coloured cottons, brass wire and beads. These were our barter goods.
>
> Wherever we stopped to make camp, native boys would come to the camp to find out who we were and I instructed my head-boy to let me know whenever they came in wanting to sell things to me. By this means I bought a lovely collection

of spears, chiefs' sticks, tom toms and other curios. I have most of them still [sadly sold after Leslie died], and each one brings back to my mind the days I spent in Portuguese East Africa.[4]

The journey on foot was of some 500 miles. I suspect that the route would be quite close to that now followed by the Trans-Zambezia Railway built in the 1920s when Beira became a major port. I think that a sense of what the journey may have been like may be gained from an article written by a man who had gone to Mozambique to mine minerals at about the same time. He describes the coastal regions as relatively flat and covered in thornbushes. He suggests that the 'natives' were not keen on their Portuguese 'masters' and had created 'no go' areas, leaving relatively narrow strips of land safe for white men. He does add that, when natives found they were dealing with the British, their attitude became more friendly.

Blantyre, in what is now Malawi, had only been in existence for thirty years at the time of Leslie's arrival. It had become the capital of the British protectorate of Nyasaland in 1889. There is a lovely book, *Blantyre: Glimpses of the Early Days*, which gives a sense of what it was like. It was named after the birthplace of David Livingstone, the famous explorer. Looking through the book, the impression is of a European town in Africa, but not one where native Africans were kept down; prosperity spread to a degree throughout. There are pictures of ox carts, but also Model-T Fords. It boasted a railway station; the line to Lake Nyasa opened in 1908.[5]

Three further anecdotes of East Africa give some more flavour. The first was a visit to a Portuguese Army post where Leslie met the officer commanding, 'a very large, rather oily, rumbustious fellow dressed in a bedraggled so-called white uniform' who offered all the lavish hospitality he could – including 'any girl you like to choose'.

Leslie's second encounter was a good deal more terrifying. He was camping, and was wakened by the feeling of something passing over his bed. To his horror he saw this 'horrible puff adder' slithering off his legs. He immediately grabbed his shot gun and killed it. My mother adds 'that was certainly a near thing, as a bite from one of these snakes is fatal'.

The third was his memory of the Africa Hotel in Zanzibar, which was where all the 'great white hunters' stayed. It had clearly impressed him, for, when he went back to Zanzibar during the Second World War, he asked the Resident's ADC to book him a room there. The young man was horrified, and explained that the hotel had become a 'low seaman's dive'. Leslie did visit it, and saw the courtyard he remembered with a pool and a turtle swimming at the bottom.

Baines's company did not flourish; my mother suggests this was because Baines drank the profits. Either way, Leslie, stuck in East Africa, had to find another job. This was a time when the gold mines in South Africa were desperately short of labour and had set up an organization, The Witwatersrand Native Labour Association, to recruit labour from neighbouring countries. This organization itself needed staff, and Leslie was recruited.

Witwatersrand or WINLA, as it was known, was a substantial organization recruiting many thousands of natives from Mozambique and other African countries. The recruits would be sent to the mining areas for relatively short periods, but without their families and with pay that was only slightly better than their daily living would gain for them back home. Whilst there are no specific reports of ill-treatment, the reputation of the Englishman did suffer, and I would take this as evidence of the unpopularity of the system.[6] I suspect that, for Leslie and many others, it was a way to earn a living, and, in Leslie's circumstances, one with little alternative.

Leslie's time in East Africa was brought to an abrupt end when he contracted blackwater fever and had to return to England. It is difficult to put a date on his return, but he took a job back in insurance, this time with the Liverpool, London & Globe Insurance Company at their offices at 1 Cornhill in the City of London. He worked in the basement offices, but, in his lunch-break, would make a point of venturing out to see how 'city gents' dressed and behaved. He spent the substantial sum of £5 on a good suit.

During his time in Cornhill, he was given a ticket by his uncle to a reception at the Mansion House, who also lent him white tie and tails. Leslie recalled two memories of the evening: looking down from the gallery on the assembled glittering throng, and then meeting a friendly and cheerful man whom he later discovered was Winston Churchill.

None of this was enough to keep him in England, and he was soon making plans to venture overseas once more, this time to Malaya, as an assistant on a rubber estate.

I looked through the newspapers of the time to see what was being said about rubber planting, and found a full-page spread in the *Illustrated London News* of April 1912, which laid down the challenge to young men. The article begins by recalling from the days of 'our great grandfathers' the tradition of the grand tour for adventurous young men, but then reminds the reader that 'Improved methods of locomotion have annihilated space', so that the modern youth is as likely to visit Calcutta or Peking, as Venice or Rome. It then sets out enticing images of the East before talking of Malaya, and the opportunities for young men in going out to be an assistant on a rubber plantation. There had been earlier pieces in the press on rubber planting, including the report of a major exhibition held in London in 1907 where the opportunities of rubber planting had been shown to a British public hungry for adventure and opportunity.

I also found a book which offered advice to those considering rubber planting:

> The first essentials for a successful planter's life are a sound physique, an aptitude for controlling native labour and a readiness to dispense with the superfluities of life. The life is, of course, an out-door one, and a certain amount of sport is usually to be had, but the Federated Malay States is not pre-eminently a sporting country. As a rule, however, nowadays some opportunity for playing games can be found and, of course, a planter has plenty of exercise in the course of his work. The backbone of an estate labour force is generally South Indian, and, to deal with his coolies satisfactorily, the young planter must as soon as possible acquire some knowledge of the Tamil language. He must also acquire sufficient Malay to get on with the Malays, Chinese and other Asiatics.[7]

The decades either side of the turn of the century had witnessed a new transport phenomenon, the internal combustion engine but also, and then to a much greater degree, the bicycle. They both need tyres, and tyres needed rubber. Until the end of the nineteenth century, rubber had only grown wild in South America and parts of Africa. In the late 1880s, some rubber plants were brought out to Singapore from Kew Gardens, and the planters found the conditions to be perfect. Rain came evenly throughout the year, and there was little variation in temperature; it was never cold. The soil was ideally suited to the growing of rubber. With the formation of the Federation of Malay States as a British protectorate, opportunities were created for young entrepreneurs to buy land on the Malay peninsula. The jungle would be cleared and rubber planted. It was a five-year project before rubber could be taken from the plant in any quantities, and so required capital. In time, bigger business became involved, not least the East Indian trader, Guthries.

Leslie, clearly, had made up his mind that rubber planting was to be his next career move. Elsewhere, the advice on offer suggested that it would be a five-year commitment, and that, certainly to begin with, wages would be meagre and not enough to 'support a wife'. Leslie was single at that point, and so need not have been deterred. He pressed ahead with job applications, and later recalled an interview with a 'very distinguished looking man with a white beard' who turned out to be a cousin of his father. This was most likely Thornton Arthur Williams who was a partner in Alston Hamilton & Co., London and Ceylon Merchants. In the event Leslie took a job as assistant at the Elphil Rubber Estate, Sungel Siput, Ipoh, Perak.

My mother did some research into the Elphil estate, and discovered that its name came from the two children, Elfrida and Phillip, of Alfred Duarte Machado. Machado had managed the neighbouring Kamwning Rubber Estate for several years and had persuaded Guthries to buy the land on the opposite side of Sungei Siput, a town in Perak some 600 kilometres from Singapore. Machado had died in 1910, and had left the running of the estate in the hands of assistants.[8]

I have found a record of an L.H. Williams sailing for Sydney via Singapore on 18 April 1913 on the P&O steam ship, *Marmora*. It may, of course, be a different L.H. Williams, but the date would seem to fit quite well. Leslie would therefore have arrived in Singapore before travelling up the Malay peninsula past Kuala Lumpur to Sungei Siput, where he was housed in a bungalow with the other assistants. By 1913, Singapore was firmly established as part of the British Empire. It was a stopping-off point, as well as a prosperous state in its own right. It had been founded by Raffles in 1819, and, by 1913, boasted the famous Raffles Hotel. There is no record of whether Leslie stayed at Raffles, but he certainly told my mother more than once how taken he had been by Singapore and by the East generally.

The next part I remember, since it was one of the Sunday morning stories he would tell to my sister and me. It was his daily life on the Elphil Estate. He would get up early and parade his coolies and give them their dose of quinine to combat malaria. They would then set out on the daily work of hacking their way through the jungle before rubber could be planted.

Another story from Malaya was the explanation of his love of Lea & Perrins sauce and of curry. In both cases, they were employed in Malaya to disguise the taste of the meat which, by the time it had come up from Singapore, was pretty smelly. For the third story, I let my mother's words speak for themselves: 'He recounted with some shame and a lot of humour the occasion in Malaya when he got too tight at a party and had to be wheeled home in a barrow.'

It was neither meat nor alcohol which brought the Malayan adventure to a close, but the recurrence of the blackwater fever. I couldn't find his name on passenger lists for the voyage home, and, so, have no real idea when it was, save that it had to be long enough before the outbreak of the First World War for him to have two further short-lived jobs in London.

The first was for a girl who ran a typewriting service in an office on the corner of Bedford Street, and was really a straightforward selling of the service. This led him to the second job via 'a very interesting man' who worked for the *Overseas Daily Mirror*. This newspaper was no more than the *Daily Mirror* itself inserted in a cover filled solely with advertising. Leslie's job was to sell the advertising space; he was taken on to continue his success in selling.

We can assume that Leslie was back living in digs and enjoying his work. He would, though, have been all too aware of the news being reported by his colleagues on the *Daily Mirror* news desk. Oddly, certainly to me, the war that was being discussed in June and July 1914 concerned Ireland, and the political talk centred around Prime Minister Asquith and the burden he was carrying. We know now that the assassination of Archduke Ferdinand on 28 June would be seen as possibly the defining moment of the twentieth century. It was reported in the *Mirror*, and, on 1 July, there was a short report of the speech Asquith made in Parliament sending the nation's sympathy, but adding his description of the event as 'one of those inscrutable crimes which almost makes us despair of the progress of mankind'. On 27 July, the headline of the paper, which boasted a circulation of one million copies a day, was a question,

'Will the Archduke's murder be avenged in Europe's Blood?' The front-page pictures, though, were of Ireland and the report that British troops had opened fire on Irish 'gunrunners'. Only a week later, the front page of the *Mirror* reported that King George had signed mobilization orders.

I have already mentioned the account Jack Omond wrote of his experience in the First World War.[9] He begins it with his reflection of Great Britain in that summer of 1914, pointing out, as I have, that it 'was immersed in an acute domestic political controversy when the news of the assassination of Archduke Franz Ferdinand of Austria with his consort the Duchess of Hohenburg at Sarajavo caused a ten-day newspaper sensation in most English homes'. He continues:

> The immediate feeling was one of horror against the perpetrators of this political murder, and many bitter comments were made in the country against the peoples of South-Eastern Europe; for this fresh crime reminded people that a comparably short time had elapsed since the murder of the King of Serbia in Belgrade in 1903.
>
> After the funeral of the Archduke and Duchess, domestic politics surged to the front in Great Britain once more amidst much confused talk about Ireland, and hurried conferences in London and Dublin. The international situation, full of danger and difficulty was forgotten, and gun-running in different parts of Ireland became one of the chief topics of conversation and debate in all the drawing-rooms and clubs of London. Civil war within the confines of the British Isles was discussed with scarcely bated breath, and long friendships were shattered as they had been once before with the Irish question.
>
> Meanwhile the enemy without the gate was fast preparing the final blow which was to destroy the peace of the world, and to inflict the horrors of a modern war on all who dared stand in the destroyers' path. The ultimatum addressed to Serbia by the Austrian government came as a rude reminder that the hour had come when domestic quarrels must be laid to one side and the nation prepare itself for what perhaps would be the greatest struggle it had ever fought. Hope that the conflict which now threatened might be avoided

lived on from hour to hour until the announcement was made in the Houses of Parliament that Great Britain would consider herself in a state of war with the German Empire from midnight of August 4th unless the Imperial German Government recalled the troops which had actually violated the neutrality of Belgium.

It is worth recalling that Omond's father was a prolific historian. Omond himself would go on to publish at least one acclaimed history in his *Parliament and the Army 1642–1904*, published by Cambridge University Press in 1935. How he came to write this particular book is interesting. He was attending the army class at the London School of Economics in 1927/8, when Professor Graham Wallas was lecturing on army control and observed that no one had written a study of it and suggested that someone in his audience now might.

On the subject of England on the point of war, Omond continues:

When the morning papers brought the news to the country districts of England where evening papers do not penetrate, a state of war had already existed for a few hours. Nobody was surprised. The feeling indeed was one of thankfulness that the Government of the day had determined to stand by our treaty obligations to Belgium and by our neighbours and friends the French people. The cost was not counted by any but a few who would have sacrificed the nation's honour with as much levity of spirit as the German Chancellor exhibited when he talked about a solemn international treaty as a 'scrap of paper'.

The feeling of unpreparedness for war, which might have struck an unmilitary nation when confronted with the perfect mechanism of the mighty German hosts, did not strike this nation as a whole until many months had passed. Confidence in the Navy and Old Army was supreme. The Territorials had volunteered to go wherever they were wanted, and recruits were pouring in of their own sweet will at such a rate that the standard of physical fitness had to be raised instead of lowered, which is the general practice in war time. 'Business as usual' was the cry.

However, all business could not be as usual. With lengthy lists of casualties, and an idea that everyone would be wanted, the great question was what to join, when most branches of the army rejected any but those who were physically fit in every respect. As was said at the time of the Wars of the French Revolution, 'The threat of invasion fixed every loyal pair of shoulders for a Red Coat,' so it was in the British Empire of 1914.'

Omond continues by explaining that the Army Ordnance Department announced that it had need of a number of officers. He tells how 'it was easy in those days to get a commission, unlike later on'; he suggests that it was essentially a form-filling exercise and a medical examination. He, or indeed many of those following this route, had little idea of what the AOD was, but it demanded the wearing of khaki and afforded a commission, as well as a generous kit allowance. On this basis, Jack Omond reported to Woolwich for initial training on a Tuesday in October 1914.

Chapter 4

The Great War

Leslie's path to Flanders was rather different. On the declaration of war, despite protestation from the *Daily Mirror*, Leslie volunteered and was sent to a cadet unit. I took this from his obituary as it appeared many years later in the *London Scottish Magazine*. My further researches suggest that these units did not come in until 1916, and so his training may more probably have been at the Royal Military College at Camberley. His brother, Cecil, had joined the Royal Naval Volunteer Reserve, and he told me many years later of the euphoria that gripped the young men of the nation at the prospect of being able to serve King and Country. It is hard to imagine what their mother thought. We do know Geako's mother's views. Clifford Geake told in an interview what he remembered of 4 August 1914. He had joined the army as a cadet at the Royal Military College at Woolwich in February 1914 and was back in Plymouth on leave. On hearing the declaration of war, he recalled 'bouncing into his mother and saying, "Hooray the war has begun."' He remembered, too, her reply: 'You'll be sorry before it's over.' Geake records 'how right she was'.[1]

Leslie found his path to the front tortuous. He spent four months in initial training before being gazetted 2nd Lieutenant Infantry on 11 December 1914. He was posted to the 8th Battalion of the Suffolk Regiment on 22 December. The choice of the Suffolks, I would have thought, came from the family connection with the county and childhood memories. The first months of 1915 were spent at Crowborough on a junior officers' course. He was then posted to Colchester and was appointed machine-gun officer. This was the only officer in the battalion with a motorbike and, my mother notes, he 'had tremendous fun haring about the countryside, yet his life was not full enough'.

This lack of fulfilment found a response in a chance meeting. He was travelling by train, and entered into conversation with a fellow officer who told him that he was in the Army Ordnance Department. He began to tell Bill what the department did. What he might have said was articulated a few years later by an AOD officer who would, I think, have a profound influence on Bill's career. You may notice that I am now using the name 'Bill', since, I suspect, that Leslie disappeared with the entry into the army.

This AOD officer was Tom Leahy of whom I will have more to say later. For now, this is some of what he said about his work. 'The Army Ordnance Department is, as regards supply of ammunition, guns, equipment, clothing and stores of all kinds, the William Whiteley of the Army.' Whiteley's was a well-known department store of the time and Leahy sums up the AOD role rather neatly:

> In addition, therefore, to being the Universal Source of Supply, it is also the Universal Repairing Agency and Universal Salvage Department for the Army, as regards the whole of its fighting stores.[2]

For, as we will see, it was also responsible for salvage and repair of what was serviceable.

My suspicion is that it was the technicalities of the work that Bill found attractive: the science, but possibly also the organizational challenges. Whatever it was, it persuaded him to seek an interview, following which he was accepted and was sent on the staff officers' course at Camberley, from which he was posted to Advance Ordnance Depot (AOD) Colchester and, he recalled, Bomb Disposal. His commanding officer was Colonel Trimnell, a man near retirement insistent that his young officers, although not at the front, should none the less 'rough it'. Bill was required to sleep in the office. Quite how this fitted with his family life is not clear, for, on 2 May 1915, he married his childhood friend, Mabel Eleanor Lovett, at St Barnabas Dulwich. We may assume that marriage did not interfere unduly with his work, for, on 1 July, he was promoted to lieutenant AOD.

The aspect of 'roughing it' is echoed by Jack Omond who tells how, at Woolwich, the recruits were provided with

> trestle beds of three boards with a couple of hard mattresses known in the army as 'biscuits', a somewhat sudden change

from the comfortable beds in which we were accustomed to sleep, but in those early days we rather gloried in such things.

Like many young men around him, Bill was keen to get to France to do his bit. He may have seen in his former newspaper a report of an appeal by Lord Kitchener for the whole nation to become engaged in the production of war material to relieve the shortage being faced by troops. He would have been by then fully aware of the key role of the AOD in getting the guns and ammunition to the troops and then of maintaining them. Leahy though offers a reminder of the difficulties that a raw ordnance officer would face when he describes the peacetime process of training which was, to all intents and purposes, really an apprenticeship for officers who had already served elsewhere in the army. It was started with an entrance exam in mathematics and mechanics. Those who passed, restricted to some sixteen such officers each year, would

> undertake a ten month course at Ordnance College covering subjects including instruction in gunnery material, store accounting, machinery, chemistry, electricity, optics, gun construction, ballistics and general instructions as to the maintenance of guns, all kinds of ammunition and majority of equipment and stores.

Those who successfully completed the first course would go on to a second, after which they would have seven years in which to master their job. This would include a thorough knowledge of the 'vocabulary', a list in two thick volumes of the many pieces of equipment the army used. They would also need to master the 'scale of issues', which is the entitlement of soldiers to different pieces of equipment. In this the ordnance officer was acting on behalf of the taxpayer 'to ensure that waste was kept to a minimum and there was no profligacy. They would also and importantly be skilled in gun and ammunition inspection'.[2]

Bill, and many like him, including Jack Omond, would need to master all of this in a matter of months, but always in the knowledge that in the field there would be experienced men like Leahy at the end of a phone line to advise and counsel. Although at Woolwich and so in the thick of armament production, Omond tells how it took a good while for the recruits to gain an understanding of ordnance work. The focus was on the 'vademecum of all Ordnance personnel – the Prized Vocabulary of Stores'. He explains that it was a

> two volume book – parts I and II subdivided into all sorts of Sections such as Camp Equipment, Harness and Saddlery, Barrack and Hospital Equipment, Guns, Howitzers, Machine Guns and their component parts – paints, oils – in fact it is a general price list of all stores in use in the army.[3]

Following his time at Woolwich, Omond was posted to an ordnance depot in an unnamed town with a port, a castle and a large variety of military activity:

> Naval vessels of various sorts predominated in the harbour, and there were constant comings and goings among them. Destroyers, old torpedo boats, private steam yachts engaged on patrol work, and a certain cross channel steamer well-known to travellers to Ireland via Holyhead, but now armed and under orders of the Admiralty, had this harbour as their main base. There were constant stories of enemy submarines sheltering in bays in the near-neighbourhood, and these tales grew in number, and in intensity after the sinking of the 'Lusitania'. If all the sinkings recounted were true, the German Fleet must have had serious food for reflection.[4]

Jack had fallen on his feet for, as he puts it, everyone from the chief ordnance officer to the messenger took pains to ensure he learned his trade, which was essentially to equip units leaving for France. He writes of the difficulties this posed, with shortages of just about everything, in spite of pleas by Kitchener for donations of blankets and such like. He writes of the news coming back from the front of dreadful casualties:

> The winter was wearing on with the papers filled with stories of the terrible conditions under which our men were fighting near Ypres, in Ploegsteert Wood and east of Bethune. Drafts were constantly leaving for the front from the troops

based at the Depot. One particular unit had suffered heavy casualties among the officers it had sent out, and gained the ill-omened title of the 'Suicide Club'.

In the autumn of 1915, Omond's Chief Ordnance Officer (COO) was asked to recommend officers to take up duties with divisions heading for France, and he put Omond's name forward. This was welcome news, and Jack headed for Aldershot where he was seriously impressed by the high level of activity and, in particular, from nearby Farnborough, the amount of aircraft action. His first task as Deputy Assistant Director of Ordnance Services (DADOS) was to ensure that his division was fully and properly equipped before they left for France. He adds that the division had been one of Kitchener's first, but its departure had been delayed since its officers and men were being continually taken to replace losses in other divisions. It was in December that his division crossed to France, and Omond was part of the advance party leaving on 14 December.

Bill crossed to France, just ten days later, on Christmas Eve 1915 and served first in the Calais Ordnance Depot for just under two months. Incidentally, my researches revealed that Colonel Trimnell was mentioned as Chief Ordnance Officer at Calais. It may be that he transferred at the same time as Bill, or, more probably, my father's memory was failing him as morphine took hold. I can imagine Bill utterly captivated by what he found in Calais. Tom Leahy describes the make-up of the Calais workshops, covering 22,000 square yards and which worked alongside the ordnance depot. It was a hive of activity and surely a source of endless fascination to a young man like Bill. There were armourers, artificers, fitters, pattern makers, moulders, cycle fitters, blacksmiths and hammer men, carpenters, painters, saddlers, tentmakers, tinsmiths, wheelers, boot-makers and storemen; probably over 1,000 men and 600 women supervised by 'the Chief Inspector of Ordnance Machinery and, under him, three assistant Inspectors, an Assistant Inspector of Armourers and a Boot Inspector'.

It was in Calais that, by chance, Bill met his brother Cecil, who had transferred to the army and was serving as a lieutenant in the Pembroke Yeomanry. It was also at Calais, or perhaps the railhead at nearby St Venant, where he met Dicky Richards who, at least at one period, had commanded an ammunition train. There is an intriguing piece of evidence suggesting that Dicky had travelled much further afield, for he was awarded a Japanese medal. Japan had joined with the Entente in 1914, and soon took possession of the then former German colonies in the eastern seas. Dicky was also awarded an MC.

I made brief mention of some of the others in previous chapters and, here, add a little more. Geoffrey Palmer served in the HAC in France until the Armistice, being promoted to captain in 1918. After three years in the Army Cyclists Corps, of which he was adjutant, Wallace 'Picky' Pickthall was in 1917 attached to the Army Ordnance Department. Cyril Cansdale was commissioned and joined the AOD in December 1914. He went to France in 1915 and served throughout. Gordon Hardy served in the Royal Garrison Artillery attached to the AOD. Neville Swiney served in the Royal Field Artillery, being awarded the MC whilst serving in his battery.

Charles de Wolff's experience of the war was a little different.[6] He was commissioned into the Sussex Regiment, but then was posted to Gallipoli. He had passed a musketry course with distinction and was made musket officer. He kept a love of shooting throughout his life, as indeed did my uncle Cecil who was a frequent competitor at Bisley. In 1915, Wolffy left for Egypt and thence to the Dardanelles. He tells how he left Alexandria on a troopship as the only infantry officer on board, the remainder being a Yeomanry brigade under Lord Lovat who had come out as cavalry expecting to patrol the Suez Canal. During the voyage, they were redirected as infantry, and Wolffy took on the task of showing them how to wear the infantry webbing they were given. He adds that, tragically, a great many were killed very soon after landing, their training having been about riding horses and not how to fight from trenches. He recalled the blizzard of November 1915 which blew for three days. Soldiers from both sides moved to their parapets to escape the trenches full of icy water.

Equipment was in short supply, and boots were repaired on the spot by teams of repairers from that home of shoe manufacture, Northampton, but never with great success given the absence of proper blocking equipment to keep the boots in shape. De Wolff was deputed to show the system of boot repairs to the visiting QMG who afterwards asked, 'Tell me de Wolff, what exactly do you know about boot repairs?' 'Nothing,' he replied. 'I thought not, but you tell a damned good story!'

De Wolff would become known for his storytelling. One such was about beer. Rations were bleak in the extreme, and it was decided to provide beer for the troops. When it arrived, those charged with unloading it sampled it instead. A guard was ordered to stop the sampling but instead they followed suit, as did the next guard, all blind drunk. The culprits were court-martialled but, because only a few could be found who had not drunk of the beer, they were let off with only a reprimand.

At the end of 1915, de Wolff volunteered for Salonika where he served until he left for Russia in February 1919. There was little military action, the mere presence of the British being enough. In early 1916 de Wolff directed his energies to a revue entitled *Hello Salonika*, which played to full houses wherever it went over a period of three and a half months. This was followed by *Bonjour Salonique*, which was even more successful and was reported in the *Daily Mail* of 27 November 1916. The *Porstmouth Evening News* of 19 December 1916 also carried a report:

> AUTHOR AT SALONIKA—Captain C. Esmond de Wolff, formerly a pupil of the Portsmouth Grammar School, whose revue Hello Salonika had a most successful run of four months, is now managing another one, Bonjour Salonique, which is even more successful and is playing to crowded houses. Captain de Wolff had a narrow escape in Salonika last July, being very badly burned in an explosion, and was for three months in hospital. He is now, however, quite fit again.

The period of illness was spent in Malta where it was discovered that he had lost his hearing. He did not though lose his sense of humour. He recounts the nursing sister asking him a question which he couldn't hear and he asked her to write it down. This she did: 'How are your bowels?'

Geako was commissioned in the Royal Garrison Artillery on 3 November 1914 and posted to 48 Heavy Battery RGA (60-pounders drawn by eight shire horses – a wonderful sight, he recalled). He crossed to France in February 1915 with one other equally green second lieutenant who was killed the next day. Of the fifteen in his class at Woolwich, only three survived the war. The job of the 60-pounders was to target opposing batteries. The lighter 18-pounders were used by the Royal Field Artillery, for example, in the barrages that preceded infantry advances. Geako and his colleagues would have seen at first hand the scandalous shortage of ammunition and heavy weapons in the first year of the war. They would then have witnessed the improvements resulting from the appointment of Lloyd George as Minister of Supply and the way he drew in the whole industrial muscle of the country in the war effort, led by his 'men of push and go'.[8]

The larger guns worked in close liaison with the Royal Flying Corps who would identify targets and provide feedback on range finding. One RFC 'boy', as he put it, would be on the ground with the artillery men. Armed with a radio, he could receive a Morse code message from the pilot looking down at the action.

On one occasion the boy mistakenly picked up the messages coming from a German aircraft. Geake remembered a German shell falling short of their battery, and then hearing the Morse message from the German pilot. The next shell still fell short, but not by as much. The whole battery heard the confirmatory Morse message and braced themselves, for the next shell could well be on target. In the event it fell on a hedge a short but safe distance away. The Morse message reported 'OK'; the German pilot clearly thought the battery was in the hedge. Relief all round.

As a battery, both officers and other ranks were billeted in local farms and so were spared the horrors of the trenches and lived in comparative comfort. Leave home, other than when wounded, only really came in the last two years of the war. On one such wounded leave, Geake married the woman who would be his wife for the next sixty-seven years. He served with his battery at Ypres and the Somme until the Armistice.[7]

James Guy (Jim) Denniston served first as private in the London Scottish, and was then commissioned on 13 August 1915 in the Seaforth Highlanders. He served in France and then in Egypt.

Ronald Weeks was commissioned in the Prince of Wales's Volunteers and later gained a regular commission in the Rifle Brigade where he gained a reputation for leadership and initiative in battle. He was awarded an MC in January 1917, a DSO in January 1918, a Bar to the MC in July 1918 and the Croix de Guerre, as well as being mentioned in dispatches. He ended the war as a major in the Rifle Brigade.[9]

Alfred Goldstein was commissioned from the Royal Military Academy at Woolwich, 'The Shop', to the Gunners; he served from 1916 until the end of the war in France with the 154 Siege Battery RA, and there he rose to the rank of major, in command of the battery, at the age of twenty-two. He was twice wounded whilst in action with the battery and he carried a number of pieces of shrapnel in his arm for the rest of his life.[10]

Harry Whitaker was commissioned into the AOD in 1915 from the Honourable Artillery Company and served as DADOS to the 12th Division. On 2 March 1916, following two weeks with the 35th Division, Bill too was appointed DADOS, in his case, to the 19th Division with the temporary rank of captain. Jack Omond was also a DADOS, and in his remarkably frank account of his experience of war, described the duties of a DADOS. The day-to-day role was to ensure that his division was supplied with all it needed from boots and uniforms to guns and camp equipment. These duties demanded of him a high degree of accuracy to ensure that precisely what was needed was received. Here he describes a typical day:

> Railhead being within easy distance, DADOS walks down to the station about 7.45 am and sees how the unloading of trucks is getting on. [Stores and equipment were despatched daily from Base, such as the Calais Depot, by train to the many railheads supplying the fronts] He also has a look at the stores collected at Railhead for return to Base, in case there is anything he can use for issue, or in his Armourer's shop. If there is, he instructs the AOC Sergeant who is supervising the unloading of stores from the train, to collect it. DADOS then goes off to breakfast with an appetite sharpened by his morning walk. He does full justice to his porridge, bacon and eggs, coffee, toast, butter and marmalade. He exchanges morning greetings with his mess mates, reads letters and papers and smokes in the ante-room. He discusses whether it is possible to combine forces with any of them in car-outings he or they may be going on. [The DADOS is part of Divisional HQ and will mess with officers with other duties in support of the division such as Army Service Corps and Army Veterinary Corps.] He goes off to have a look at his store or dump where issues, of stores received at the railhead that morning, are already in progress. He visits his Armourer's shop and inquires how the repair and overhaul of machine guns stand, and inspects the record of work done to see if it is keeping up to the monthly average. He ascertains the position of repairs of a number of Very pistols, and how soon the manufacture of tin rocket covers will be completed for the GOC is pressing for an early delivery to the Infantry Brigades in the line.

He next takes a turn round the boot-makers shop. He then proceeds to his office. There he finds a pile of papers on his table. Their importance varies very considerably but something has to be done about them all. DADOS issues his instructions to his Chief Clerk as to their disposal, probably keeping a number to handle by himself later on. It is now time to visit Divisional Headquarters. This visit is paid at least once a day, for it is the best method of keeping au fait with what is moving in the mind of Q [Q or Quartermaster] staff and thence by the process of deduction DADOS knows what his GOC is thinking. The morning is now well on its way, and lunch time will soon arrive. DADOS fills up the time by paying a visit to the Quartermaster's Store to see that they are not accumulating clothing etc. in undue quantities, and by signing a number of indents and letters in his office.

After lunch he sets out by car to local purchase stores for units or to visit different COS to talk over difficulties that may have arisen. The Divisional Salvage Dump, baths and laundries, Workshops and Gun Park must all be visited. Whether he gets back until after tea or not depends on the distance he has to travel. But, in any case on his return, he must go back to his office once again, go over various papers, write his War Diary, and arrange his programme of work for the following day. He eventually goes off to his billet about 11 o'clock glad enough to get there, as he has been on the go since seven o'clock in the morning.[11]

On a research visit to the National Archives, I looked up the *War Diary* written by my father as DADOS of the 19th Division: pithy, brief – and certainly not a mine of information. Omond provides another view of a couple of aspects of his daily round. First, transport which was the bailiwick of the Army Service Corps. He writes first:

It was interesting to visit the wagon-lines where the stables were, and to note the arrangements made for the comfort of the animals. Stables were improvised wherever possible. For instance, a long wall bounding a cemetery had a lean-to stable built against it with a roof of tarred felt and floor of hard beaten slag. Each horse had its allocated stall, its own nose bag and hay-net. The whole place was kept swept and garnished, better in fact that many stables in this country. Watering troughs were placed in the vicinity, and careful grooming insisted upon. In winter every horse or mule was provided with a horse rug, and many dandy-brushes were issued by DADOS. Harness was clean and the metal work brightly polished. Collar chains were kept highly burnished by shaking in sandbags.

It wasn't only animal-powered transport that was lovingly cared for:

> Lorries were all kept most beautifully clean, and the engines most highly polished. Woe betide the unlucky man in charge of a lorry if his vehicle was dirty through any avoidable cause. At times it looked, and smelt, as if some lorries were cleansed with petrol but, anyhow, the smartness and efficiency of the M.T. vehicle provision was something of which the RASC had every reason to be proud.

These were the early days of motor vehicles and so breakdowns were frequent, but equally frequently and effectively addressed:

> Another admirable part of the MT organization were the travelling workshops where all sorts of repairs were done to all classes of MT vehicles. These workshops were carried round in two or three lorries and given a supply of spare parts, there seemed to be little repair work that could not be carried out.

One aspect of repair work would come to a head in the war of a quarter of a century later, since the AOC also had a workshop infrastructure from the small mobile workshop to much larger units at army level.

> Of great interests were the Light Workshops belonging to Ordnance and run by an Inspector of Ordnance Machinery [IOM]. Here were field guns – 18 pdrs and

4.5" Howitzers – damaged in all sorts of ways. I remember one 4.5" Howitzer in particular. It was almost broken in two, just beyond the shield, by premature explosion of the shell in the bore.

I was intrigued by the division of responsibility between the RASC and RAOC and am grateful to Juliet Campbell, whose book, *One Small Island and Two World Wars,* on her father's RASC career sheds helpful light. Wilfred Collings, an officer in the Army Service Corps, had served in the 13th Division at Gallipoli and, following the withdrawal from the ill-fated campaign, was posted to Mesopotamia, again with the 13th. It was during this campaign that motorized transport began to take the place of wagons drawn by mules, and it was natural that the new motorized transport should be operated by the RASC and, in the absence of any alternative, be maintained by them also. It is important to remember that we are talking about the relatively early days of motoring, and of vehicles, that would require frequent maintenance, which the driver himself would often carry out.

In 1917 Wilfred was posted from the 13th Division as transport officer to the Indian Cavalry Division. It was during that year that the potential of vehicle companies in desert conditions was plainly seen, and soon the original Ford Van companies, equipped with 5cwt Ford vans, multiplied until there were twenty-five and a new ASC branch of QMG staff under a brigadier general was formed in Baghdad. It also didn't take long for this brigadier general to see that Collings's talents were being wasted, and that he should return to the Corps and qualify as a mechanical transport officer.

The course took place in Basra, and Collings describes his experience:

> The course presented no difficulties. There were vehicles of every type available to practise on, and I had a go on everything from motorcycles to heavy lorries – I even tried a Caterpillar tractor.
>
> Basra itself had been completely transformed since we landed there two years before. A vast camp covered several square miles of what had been desert, some areas tented, but much, including the Base M.T. Depot, housed in wooden huts with an electric light and fans.

One of the things the Base M.T. Depot was doing was forming up new Ford Van Companies and sending them off up river. The vans were arriving by the hundreds from America in packing cases partly broken down, and had to be assembled.

The Officer Commanding the Base M.T. Depot was one Col Archibald. He was a delicate looking man with a sallow complexion and light ginger hair. He was one of the small band of ASC officers who had specialized in M.T. in the pre-war days and had qualified on courses with civilian manufacturers of motor vehicles. The depot which he now commanded had grown into a large complex consisting of a workshop company, a stores department holding stocks of spare parts, a vehicle park which received all-new vehicles arriving and issued them as required, and a reinforcement and training section.[12]

I believe that this account makes it clear that, certainly during the First World War, vehicles were very much the bailiwick of the ASC. The growth in the number of armoured fighting vehicles, which, with their armaments, were maintained by the AOD would, in the Second World War, create a dilemma for the General Staff. This was an issue that would land on the desk of Ronald Weeks in the spring of 1941 and would result in the formation of REME eighteen months later.

Among the divisions that were part of Kitchener's Second Army was the 19th, formed on 11 September 1914. By March 1915 the division had been clothed in khaki, rifles and machine guns had been issued to infantry, transport was formed and the division left for France between 16 and 18 July 1915. Major General Tom Bridges had taken over command on 13 December 1915. It was Bridges who introduced the 'Butterfly' as the division emblem; they soon became known as 'La Division Papillon'. On 7 March 1916 Bill Williams took up the appointment as DADOS.

On 1 July 2016, I went to Lincoln Castle at 7 am where, perhaps, a hundred people had gathered to remember those whose lives were lost on the first morning of the Battle of the Somme. At that point I had only a half-memory that my father, Bill Williams, had fought on the Somme, but I didn't know when or where. So, straight after the commemoration, I returned home and got out Bill's service records and found that he had indeed served with the 19th Division. The official history of the 19th confirmed that, on the evening of 1 July 1916, Major General Bridges was called upon to take the village of La Boiselle, without which progress on the flank was impossible. Such was the confusion following the unprecedented carnage of the morning that no straightforward plan was possible. As Everard Wyrall puts it in his *History of the 19th Division 1914–1918*, 'an extraordinarily difficult task now faced the 19th Division'.[13]

The progress of battle is described in the official history; here I just want to record some of the key pronouncements. The following order of the day was issued on 4 August 1916 on behalf of General Bridges and I try to imagine my father reading it. Although not in the trenches, ordnance officers were near enough to see and hear all that was going on. They would be at risk of shelling when bringing equipment and ammunition up to the fighting troops:

> The Divisional Commander wishes to thank all ranks of the Division for the way in which, during the last 10 days, they have upheld the best traditions of discipline and hard fighting. The Division leaves a name behind it in the Fourth Army which will never be forgotten.
>
> The battle of the Somme is still unfinished, and every effort is being made to wrest the full fruits of victory from the enemy and to gain such positions as will seriously dislocate his defensive system.
>
> To this end fresh troops are required and the 19th Division will take its place at once in the defensive line in order to release another division for the attack.
>
> When this is understood by the troops, the Divisional Commander is confident that they will play their part ungrudgingly and that every individual will continue to put forth his best efforts in this critical period.[14]

Jack Omond's division was moved to the Somme, just one month later, in August 1916:

> Life was to be under canvas at Forked Tree Camp which was pitched on the side of a hill, looking down into Bray-sur-Somme where the French and British armies joined hands. The camp was beside a cross-country road from Albert to Bray.

The water supply was insufficient, and it all had to be carried for some considerable distance. The countryside itself was fine, open, rolling country, where crops must have abounded in more peaceful times. Now it was thick with troops returning from or going forward to the seething cauldron of the battle which ceased neither day nor night. Railheads and roads had been constructed in every direction. Tents and horse lines were to be seen on every side. Disused gun pits and trenches were much in evidence. Empty ammunition boxes and cartridge cases were collected in gigantic heaps at intervals along the roads. Screens, which had been erected to hide the traffic on certain roads before the 1st of July, were still fluttering in the wind, and heaps of broken rifles, discarded equipment – salvage in fact – clearly illustrated the waste of war.

The nearer the front, the more congested did everything seem to be, and the greater the number of people and things, useful and useless, on the ground. Close to [the tented] Divisional Headquarters was a valley, known as Happy Valley, where there were many units of all sorts, British infantry, Artillery, French gunners, horse lines, all pell-mell to the eye of the casual observer. Yet, it was always possible to find a unit, and even an individual, if the search was prosecuted with intelligence. Shanties, camping arrangements of all sorts, from bivouacs under wagons to tents, circular, single, linen, were dotted about. When the sun shone, the scene was bright enough, but when it rained – ugh! The mud, the discomfort, the misery, and the chilled look of man and beast.

There was another camp of similar character, which rejoiced in the name of the Citadel. If anything, it was a more depressing place on a wet day, and it was even more congested. It was much noisier for the noise of the heavy guns seemed to echo through the valley where it stood with greater violence than at Happy Valley. As a matter of fact, I believe it was nearer to the front. Curiously enough, these places were but seldom shelled by the Germans. They must have known, whether their airmen told them or not, that British troops were using those valleys. Why they left them alone, it will be always difficult to understand.[15]

In September 1916 Jack recorded seeing the then top-secret tanks 'waddling about on a firm piece of grassy land near a railway, in the presence of HRH Prince of Wales'. Tanks first saw action on 15 September 1916 on the Somme and are destined to feature frequently in this story. Their first major successful battle was at Cambrai in November 1917.[16] Edgar Readman had served first as a lieutenant in the South Staffordshire Regiment, and then in the Tank Battalion, being promoted to captain on 30 November 1917. This first-hand knowledge of tanks would prove of great value in the task he undertook a quarter of a century later.

Jack Omond served with his division until January 1917, when he was ordered to take up the role of DADOS to the British Mission to the Portuguese Division, a post which he held until March 1918 when he was posted to headquarters at Ranchicourt. This posting was not to last long, for he was invalided back to England for the remainder of the war. His time with the Portuguese Division presented him with a whole new range of challenges. The Portuguese soldiers had arrived hopelessly unprepared for what awaited them. The cold of that winter proved almost unbearable for men used to a more benign climate. The food offered by the British was so alien as to be inedible. With no common language, any communication was slow and prone to inaccuracy.

In his account, Omond spends a little time reflecting on the lot of civilians caught up in the war zone. In common, probably with all combatant nations, the young men had gone to war leaving old men and women to tend the farms. They also acted as hosts in the many billets which had spare rooms formerly occupied by sons and husbands. Some civilians had moved away altogether to safer homes with friends and relations. Omond's experience of billets was, with only two exceptions, very positive: landladies were welcoming; many had lost sons and so took to British soldiers in a motherly way. Old men wanted to talk of their own exploits in earlier conflicts and a sympathetic ear earned both respect and friendship.

The 19th Division was redeployed ready for the Ypres offensive. This demanded of the DADOS long hours of work organizing dumps and ensuring that the division was fully prepared for the fight ahead. Bill Williams was mentioned in dispatches on 9 April 1917 for gallantry and devotion to duty. He served with the division until November 1917. The division went on through to the end. Following the battle of Ypres in 1917, Major General Bridges was severely injured. Nevertheless, he wrote again to praise the efforts of his men, not least those in the supply line such as ordnance. Wyrall adds:

> It should, however, be remembered always that in winning great success for their divisions, the infantry in the front line could not have done so had it not been for the splendid cooperation of all arms of the Division: the RA, T.M. Batteries. pioneers and RE, Signallers, and medical units, were constantly in the shell-swept area. The services of DADOS and his personnel in replacing and repairing destroyed and damaged weapons and equipment during the operations were simply immense. The Army Service Corps and Veterinary Corps were invaluable.[17]

There is, in Bill's archive, a handwritten letter to him from General Bridges from hospital thanking him for

> the great services you rendered the Division here since you joined. I am by no means insensible to all the hard work you have put in and am grateful to you for it. I hope the New Year's honours will give you some recognition.[18]

Bill was awarded the MC in the *London Gazette* of 1 January 1918 for devotion to duty. The pencil-written letter is in a folder marked 'keep'. Bridges was one of Bill's heroes and his name features significantly in the context of the involvement of the USA in the First World War.

American businesses had been significant suppliers to the Entente forces from the start, but in April 1917 the USA entered the war on the side of the Entente. One of the first acts by the British was to send missions to the USA to explore just what their involvement would mean. General Tom Bridges led the army mission as part of the mission led by Foreign Secretary Balfour.[19] Later Tom Leahy would be posted to Washington as part of the British Army presence there.

A chance meeting with his friend Tiny Stower, a former London Scottish private as Bill had been, facilitated Bill's move to Italy, which entailed him taking over the post held by Stower and Stower taking over as DADOS of the 19th. Italy had entered the war on the side of the

Allies in May 1915 with the objective of seizing territory from their old rivals, the Austrians. For two years they captured important mountain positions, and, by 1917, were in a position to try to capture the prize of Trieste. The Italians, however, were becoming more and more war-weary, and, on 20 October, the Germans reinforced the Austrians and broke through the Italian line, throwing it back on the River Piave. The British responded with the redeployment of two corps from the Second Army on the Western Front. Bill Williams was appointed DADOS to Italian GHQ at Padua and promoted major on 27 November 1917.[20] This, though, would not last for long.

The revolution in Russia had resulted in it leaving the war. Its consequent removal of the German Eastern Front, allowed a German redeployment to the west which, in turn, triggered the return to France of the Corps deployed in Italy. Bill was posted to the Home Establishment as DADOS of Western Command at Chester. It was here that he saw out the remainder of the war.

The mention of Russia once again brings Charles de Wolff into the story. I have already told that his CBE was awarded for his saving of a Russian princess. He had come to serve at Novorassick in Russia after the revolution in support of the White Russian Army. He recounts how a Royal Navy destroyer docked and he was invited on board where he met a Colonel Edwards. After some conversation the Colonel handed de Wolff a Bible and asked him to swear not to repeat what he was about to be told, a request Wolffy found surprising to say the least; nevertheless he obliged. The colonel then told him that Grand Duchess Olga Alexandrovna, her husband and baby had escaped when the Tsar was murdered, and were living under an assumed name in poverty some 150 miles into Red Russian territory. Would de Wolff and his Russian fellow officer, who knew the Duchess, be prepared to attempt to rescue her? De Wolff, of course, said yes, provided his commanding officer agreed. The commanding officer was even more put off by the need to swear on the Bible as de Wolff had been, but he assented, provided de Wolff returned safely.

Wolffy and his Russian companion set off first by train and then crossed into Red Russian territory. They were convinced they were being followed, but, nonetheless, pressed on and eventually arrived at the town where the duchess was hiding. They came to the house and Wolffy's companion was welcomed with much hugging and kissing.

Wolffy explained that they had been sent by King George V, the cousin of the duchess, to ensure her safe passage to England. She refused their help, explaining that she was not going to desert her homeland. Shortly afterwards, a message reached the house that the two men who had been following de Wolff had let their whereabouts be known and they could expect to be arrested the next day with the likelihood of later being shot.

In the light of this, the duchess changed her mind and journeyed first with de Wolff into White Russian territory and then, on the subsequent retreat of the White Russians, she and her family evacuated to England where they stayed first with the king, then with the Princess Alexandra. They finally departed for Denmark where they joined other exiled members of the family. De Wolff was rewarded with a CBE and, following a gap of a few years, the Duchess remained in touch with him for the rest of her life. De Wolff concluded his posting to Russia with an evacuation when the Red Army finally gained full control. Much equipment was left behind.[21]

The reinforced Western Front, resulting from the removal of Russia, gave the Germans the manpower to mount a decisive assault which they did in March 1918 causing the Entente forces to retreat.[22] The advance over battle-scarred ground eventually stuttered to a halt and the Entente, crucially now with significant American reinforcements, began their advance which eventually led on 11 November 1918 to the Armistice. The men who would make up the Class of '22 had been through hell, albeit with lighter moments; but, unlike so many of their countrymen, they had survived.

Chapter 5

Interwar Years and Mobilization

The ending of the Great War was followed all too quickly by the epidemic of Spanish flu which claimed the lives of 228,000 people in the UK.[1] This was the equivalent of a quarter of those British soldiers who had died in the conflict. Of those who had survived, many were wounded and many more returned to an industrial landscape that had been transformed by war but which, in the absence of war production, needed many fewer workers. The many women who had taken men's jobs were sent home, preference being given to the returning soldiers. The 1920s would see a continuing decline of traditional heavy manufacturing, despite Lloyd George's promise of a land fit for heroes. However, the interwar years would represent a shift rather than an overall decline, with the growth of new industries, particularly motor vehicles.

What happened to Bill following demobilization wasn't entirely clear. My mother wrote this:

> Leslie, [my mother always called him by his Christian name] on returning to London, went to the Daily Mirror office to arrange to take up his civilian job again. There, to his dismay, he found that men had stayed behind and had advanced in their jobs and it was proposed that Leslie should re-join the paper at the level of seniority he held when he volunteered for the army in 1914, thus allowing his actual juniors at the time to become his bosses on his return. I'm afraid Leslie did not like that idea at all, as he had already heard that certain of the temporary Ordnance Officers were to be selected and, if they wished, they could obtain a regular commission. He really let rip [at] the Mirror office and told them exactly where they could go.

The records show that he was gazetted captain and ordnance officer 4th class (acting major and ordnance officer 3rd class) on 1 January 1919 and returned to Chester. It was here that he began a hobby that I remember vividly from my childhood: collecting Chinese porcelain, which was broken and which he would painstakingly repair. My mother notes that it was at Chester that he bought a large Imari plate for the then enormous sum of £3. Another hobby was buying and bringing back into working order of bracket clocks, one of which I still have.

Among the many thousands who were demobilized along with Bill were Reddy Readman, Harry Whitaker, Arthur Sewell and Ronald Weeks. Whitaker's experience was not unlike Bill's and he rejoined the RAOC.

Edgar Readman was demobilized in 1919 and returned to the steel industry in what, in 1928, would become the English Steel Corporation formed from the steel activities of Vickers, Armstrong and Cammell Laird.[2] In the recession following the end of the war, the steel industry was rationalized and the new English Steel Corporation brought together the River Don works of Vickers and the Cyclops and Grimesthorpe works of Cammell Laird.[3] Readman rose to hold a managing director post; he remained in the Territorial Army for the whole interwar period.

Arthur Sewell, who latterly had served in the RAF, left in 1920 and spent nine years (1920–29) in the USA marketing lubrication and car valeting equipment for the Alemite Corporation. He returned to the UK in 1929 and joined Tecalemit, the garage equipment manufacturer.[4]

Ronald Weeks returned to Pilkington, despite overtures from the Rifle Brigade for him to stay in the army. Pilkington Brothers traced its history back to 1906 and was very much a family concern. However, by the 1920s it was feeling the strain of being run as a small partnership when, in reality, it had grown into a major company employing thousands of workers in and around its home of St Helens in Lancashire. Ronald Weeks had been taken on as a trainee from university and surely had returned from four years in the army a good deal older and wiser. This was recognized by the company, which appointed him, at the age of 30, as works manager at their Cowley Hill plant which manufactured plate glass. Major Weeks, as he was always known, acted as 'lieutenant' to family member and main board director, Lord Cozens-Hardy.[5] Weeks threw himself into the detail of plant management and the technicalities of plate-glass manufacture. In 1928, he was appointed a main board director alongside younger members of the family. Weeks himself had, in effect, joined the family in 1922 when he married Evelyn Elsie Haynes, a granddaughter of William (Roby) Pilkington.

The 1930s brought in major management changes. Pilkington was suffering from stiff competition from Belgian glassmakers, and this was not helped by the high sterling exchange rate with its link to the gold standard. Financial results were poor and action was needed. An executive committee was formed from main board directors, but with each given a clear line of responsibility. Ronald Weeks retained his responsibilities for Cowley Hill, but added Doncaster Plate Glass Works and also Technical Services. Of perhaps greater significance to our story was Weeks's involvement with Management Research Group No. 1, which was a grouping of major companies including ICI, Lever Brothers, Standard Telephones and Rowntrees, to explore modern management issues. The group had been founded by Seebohm Rowntree in 1926. The immediate focus for Pilkington was methods of recruiting and training future senior managers.[6]

Weeks wrote a paper for his executive committee colleagues in which he reflected on the way industry had organized itself into large and complex units, and had thereby created the need for a new type of skilled administrator. The problem was that no organization was then training young men and women to fulfil this role. Weeks identified three functions within Pilkington where such people needed to be recruited: secretarial/legal/accountancy, manufacturing and commercial, and he concluded that a university education was preferable in all but in selling, where he thought that a suitable school leaver could be taught 'on the job'. In 1933, Pilkington recruited its first cohort of trainees and all appeared to be well until it became clear that career progression was being hindered by those existing managers long in their posts, not least family members. This would continue to present problems for some years.

The executive committee addressed other issues. It introduced budgetary control and a finance committee, again drawing on experience from others in the Management Research Group No. 1. It introduced a personnel function and, in due course, a research department, drawing together expertise from throughout the group.

Ronald Weeks was successfully furthering both his career and the fortunes of his company, but he was also garnering the skills he would later bring to bear in wartime.

The 1920s was a time of rebuilding for British industry more generally. The demands, particularly of trench warfare in the First World War, had led to the creation of an astonishing network of companies and works devoted principally to the production of ammunition and all that went with it. There were thus projectile factories, explosives factories, fuse factories and shell-filling factories. Some were privately owned, some in various kinds of partnership with the Ministry of Munitions, and some owned and run by the Ministry. At the heart of it all was the Royal Arsenal at Woolwich. The coming of peace meant that the demands on these establishments ceased, and, by 1921, only a handful were still active: the Woolwich Arsenal, the Royal Small Arms Factory at Enfield, and the Explosives Factory at Waltham Abbey. Some small factories also remained: Hereford, cartridge cases at Birtley and explosives at Irvine. The total number employed at 9,000 was a fraction of what it had been. Ian Hay, writing the *Short History of the Royal Ordnance Factories*, expresses shock at the rashness of the closures.[7] When I read it, I found myself nodding, but then it became clear: of course most would be closed, the need had gone, and there would never be another war demanding weaponry on that scale. The factories that remained open ticked over supplying the services with what they needed. This is an important point, for, certainly in terms of ammunition, it was all three services which were supplied.

Looking more widely at the economy, I have already referred to the decline of the heavy industries, companies which contributed so much to the war effort, like Vickers, Armstrong Whitworth and Beardmore, and the steel industry more generally, which felt the chill of declining orders for battleships and guns. There was a north–south divide with the Midlands and the South benefiting increasingly from 'new industries'. Coventry, Birmingham, Luton and Dagenham were set to benefit from the astonishing growth in the demand for motor vehicles. In the mid-1920s the national grid began to make electricity more freely available. Chemical industries grew, as did plastics with the development of Bakelite.

The funding for the army had been drastically cut under the ten-year rule, the assumption that no major conflict was foreseeable in the next ten years. The army thus shrunk in size, as had ordnance. There were depots at Woolwich, Didcot and Weedon and then depots attached to each home command HQ. Overseas, there was the Empire that needed protection, there was Ireland and the protectorates in the Middle East where a British presence was required to keep the former Ottoman Empire at bay. Ordnance had a role in each of these. RAOC officers and senior NCOs were frequently seconded to the Indian Army Ordnance Corps; indeed, until the 1930s, the officers and senior NCOs in the IAOC were exclusively British.

Those officers of the Class of '22 would, over the ensuing years, find themselves posted either to the War Office, to depots, to home commands and overseas. Cyril Cansdale was posted to Northern Ireland, Singapore, Scottish Command and the War Office. Wallace Pickthall served in Malta, Tidworth, Hilsea and Aldershot.

Jack Omond, together with Cecil Haigh and P.W. Kidd, was assigned to a force returning to Gallipoli to keep the peace following the end of the Greek-Turkish war. Jack Omond kept a diary, from reading which it seems to have been a time of little activity but much discomfort and many ghosts.[8] They arrived in October 1922, and Omond describes the voyage, mentioning those places engraved on many a soldier's memories from the disastrous campaign of only six years before: Mitylene, Lemnos and Lancashire Landing. He later visited the beach carrying the name of the Lancashires and observed:

> How troops ever landed on those beaches in the face of rifle and machine gun fire, with barbed wire entanglements on the sand cliffs to climb, and carrying 200 rounds of ammunition, water-bottle, rifle etc., it is impossible to imagine. How the positions gained were held is also marvellous, when the lie of the land is considered. The running of an Ordnance depot on the Beach which was under observation from Kum Kale Fort on the Asiatic side is another marvel, as the Navy never succeeded in silencing that fort at all.

Of the remainder of the account, the weather was as experienced by de Wolff and others in 1915, compounded by having to spend winter under canvas; huts only arrived in time for the spring of 1923. Omond notes the passing of his ninth wedding anniversary, adding that, like most in their short married life, it was spent apart. There is much anxiety about promotions, with Omond firm in his assertion that he was senior to both Haigh and Kidd by virtue of the date he joined the AOD. Seniority mattered if an officer had ambitions for a military career, since the number of posts was limited by an establishment; again, as observed later by de Wolff. I know my own father kept a list of officers in order of seniority, from which he could plot his own chances of promotion; the paper is in his archive. Omond refers to a letter received from Cyril Cansdale in January 1923 saying that a new establishment of posts had been approved. Relief all round.

Charles de Wolff was posted first to London District where, following two months of court martial duty, he served under Basil Hill. Hill had amongst, much else, commanded one of the depot ships at Gallipoli. He had been commissioned in the Royal Marine Artillery in 1897 and in 1903, 'while still a subaltern was appointed an assistant professor at the Royal Naval College. Greenwich, in 1903'. He transferred to the Army Ordnance Department in 1908. In 1914 he was serving in China and was present at the Siege of Tsingtau. After Gallipoli, he served in the Egyptian Expeditionary Force as ADOS Alexandria. He was awarded the DSO in 1917 and mentioned three times in dispatches. For a young man like de Wolff, it must have been enormously valuable to serve under a man of such ability and with such experience.

There was yet another side to Hill: his sporting prowess. In the RAOC, as with the rest of the army and indeed the armed forces generally, sport played an important part. In nearly every obituary in the *RAOC Gazette*, there are recorded the sporting achievements of the deceased. With Hill, these achievements were indeed great. He played rugby for England nine times between 1903 and 1907, including as captain against both Wales and France in that latter year. He looks the part, tall and distinguished.[9]

From this viewpoint in London District, de Wolff saw the process of disposal of surplus equipment and what can only be called the frauds that took place. Following the Armistice, the RAOC had had the massive task of the clean-up, but, by 1922, this had largely been done and the world was facing a 'new normal'.

Cutters' first service was in the clean-up operation in France and Belgium which followed the end of the war. Almost immediately after his marriage in 1925, he and his new wife Vera were sent to the Indian North West Frontier at Risalpur and Kohat. There he was seconded to the RAF, whilst remaining a gunner, and was awarded his wings. His daughter, Lizzie Campbell, told me that he served with V Squadron flying with Bilney, later air-vice marshal, and Sanderson, later air marshal. She added that this flying was to supplement his army pay: 'he flew a Bristol fighter and loved it.' Lizzie's sister was born in 1930, and the small family was sent out to Shanghai and Tientsin. On their return, he transferred to Ordnance in 1931, 'as I believe a number of his contemporaries felt they could have more challenging openings'. He straight away attended the ordnance officers' course where he was described by the course commander as 'quiet, reliable and efficient'.

Bill was posted to Gibraltar, and I suspect that this was a much-sought-·after posting. I imagine Mabel delighted at the prospect of colonial life in such a benign climate. Mabel was petite and pretty, sociable and an accomplished musician and bridge player; so, just about the ideal army wife. Shortly after the end of the First World War, Bill had met another second cousin, Richard Smith Williams, who had married Marian McKenzie, also an accomplished musician and music teacher. I understand that Marian had taught Mabel at some point.

In Gibraltar, Bill was Ordnance Officer for the Army, but also Inspecting Ordnance Officer for the Navy, which required him to spend time on board ships. In the course of this, he met American naval officers. I can imagine the conversations, one of which led to one American officer arranging the shipment of a Model-T Ford for Bill for the princely sum of £55. It must have been quite an occasion when the car was brought ashore on the Admiral's Barge. It was the first civilian vehicle on the Rock. He cared for, improved and tuned the car until eventually it was christened the Rolls-Ford. It took Bill and Mabel on holidays right through Spain and along into France. He had always been captivated by motor vehicles; this was the first of many he would own. It was also the car through which he learned about how the internal combustion engine worked, and how cars were built and maintained. A high point in Bill's posting was a visit on holiday by his mother. He recalled carrying her in his arms off the ship and then taking her everywhere in the Rolls-Ford.

As Ordnance Officer for the Army, Bill was responsible for maintaining the massive guns which defended the Straits of Gibraltar. It was his habit to walk up the Rock early in the morning to avoid the heat of the day. I remember, as a child, visiting the Rock on holiday, and being taken into the caverns within the Rock, and seeing the guns and the shells lined up ready. In the RLC archive I found the letter of thanks Bill had written to Major Gray, the then Ordnance Officer, who had taken so much trouble in showing me and my sister around. Not that it is relevant to this book, we were shown round HMS *Ark Royal* – quite an experience.

A possibly longer-lasting experience for Bill was being commanded by Tom Leahy. I have already quoted Leahy in the chapter on the Great War. He had been Ordnance Officer to the Third Cavalry Division in Belgium in September 1914 and then held significant posts in the lines of communication and at corps and army level. I doubt whether there was much about ordnance that he didn't know. This was evident from the text held in the RAOC archive of lectures he gave to trainee officers, from which I quoted. My mother recalled my father remembering Leahy teaching him to salute with a sword. I am sure that this was but a small part. Bill delivered the eulogy at Leahy's funeral.

The posting was unquestionably a wonderful experience. Life on the Rock suited them well, with weekend parties in the Spanish countryside or on the beach. During their time there, there were visits from the Prince of Wales, amongst others. I have a silver cigarette box which had been presented to Bill to mark the production of *Aladdin* for which he had done the lighting. Clearly, he must have involved himself in the life of the garrison. They lived in a small house away from the crowded town, en route to the Moorish castle, where Bill had load after load of soil trucked in to create a garden which became his pride and joy, until the arrival of the Rolls-Ford.

The after-effects of the Great War lingered with a great many of those who had survived physically. I know that Bill had nightmares until his death, some forty-five years after its end. I suspect that the mental injury, caused by the war, damaged relationships as much as it had people and I understand that Bill's and Mabel's marriage came under strain from which it would not recover. The army though was an unforgiving institution, and so divorce was unthinkable. They soldiered on, with Bill finding solace in his work, and Mabel in her music and socializing. The National Archives does though hold record of a divorce involving Bill's friend, Dicky Richards. It cites Richards as the appellant and his wife as respondent, with a named co-respondent. Richards married again and his second wife, Alice Marie, survived him. However, with Richards also a Roman Catholic, divorce was, I suspect, rather more than frowned upon and may well have held back his army career.

Bill and Mabel did agree that, after four and a half years in a wonderful climate, a home posting in the south would have been welcomed.

They returned to England in early December 1926 to Hilsea, the new headquarters of the RAOC, and so, at least initially, all would have been well. Bill would have renewed his friendship with Neville Swiney who was then adjutant at Hilsea. Sadly, January 1927 had something a good deal colder in store, as Bill was posted to Stirling. As young children, my sister and I accompanied our parents for a short holiday in the Trossachs near Stirling, which had been a favourite haunt during the posting. He spoke warmly of his Scots ancestry; he was a Nisbet of the clan Campbell, through his maternal grandmother.

In February 1925, a remarkable event had taken place which had severely shaken the Corps. Major General Sir Harold Parsons, after only four months as Colonel Commandant RAOC, died at the age of sixty-one. His death was not reported in the *RAOC Gazette* as an obituary; instead, a whole supplement was devoted to him. As has already been stated, he served for nearly the whole of the First World War as Director of Ordnance Services in France and so oversaw and directed the incredible progress the Corps made in the war years. He is credited with the birth of the RAOC as it would be for most of the twentieth century.

In the late 1920s, cuts in defence spending meant that the number of available posts was further restricted. Bill had been lucky. Charles de Wolff, whose hearing was getting worse, could see pretty dim prospects ahead and so he looked around at opportunities in civilian life. He tells how, just as he was about to leave, two officers died in post, thus freeing them for others. De Wolff was first promised an overseas posting, but, when this didn't materialize, he was appointed Inspector of Ordnance for four years which he found fascinating, taking him to many areas of ordnance work.

For Bill, the Stirling posting came to an end in June 1928 when, with a promotion to major, he was posted to the British Army of the Rhine in Weisbaden to join Leahy once more to complete the massive job of repatriating British war equipment. This took just over a year and, in October 1929, Bill was posted to Didcot for four months. Didcot had been the major new depot of the First World War, and so had employed the most up-to-date thinking, something that would surface with a vengeance later. In 1934 Didcot also pioneered NCR mechanical accounting under Alfred Goldstein.[10]

On 3 March 1930, Bill took up what turned out to be a highly significant posting at Catterick in Northern Command. Alfred Goldstein had been posted there in 1926 and so their paths may have crossed; more particularly Goldstein may have employed his exceptional intelligence and organizing ability, which had been evident on the course and would also surface later. During Goldstein's tenure at Catterick, this command depot was completely re-planned in order to replace the Curragh (now in the Republic of Ireland) and, more significantly, to become a centre for mechanized units.[11] Steer, in his book *To the Warrior his Arms*, describes it as 'the jewel in the crown', with new workshops to maintain tracked fighting vehicles.[12] It received the mechanized units from the British Army of the Rhine which then formed the 5th Division.

In 1927, an experimental mechanized force had been set up under Colonel Fuller based on two battalions of the Royal Tank Corps, but this was disbanded in 1928. Thought, though, was being given to mechanization and, in particular, how vehicles in a mobile force could be maintained. This would, in 1941, become a live issue for Dicky Richards in North Africa. Back in 1930, Dicky had been posted to nearby York, and this provided an opportunity for the friendship between Bill and Dicky to grow, and, surely, a sharing of ideas around the whole area of mechanization. Dicky had previously been posted to Tidworth in Wiltshire, a command depot largely for artillery. Prior to that he had been attached to the RAF in Iraq. His final between-the-wars posting was as Chief Technical Adviser to the British Military Mission in Egypt.[13] All this would prove a vital learning ground for what lay ahead.

Steer refers to a number of articles which appeared in the *RAOC Gazette* on the issue of mechanization. One five-page article in October 1929 explored the particular significance for ordnance of mechanization.[14] The workshop, particularly mobile workshop, activity of the RAOC began to increase rapidly. Arguments raged over which corps should take responsibility for the repair and maintenance of vehicles: the Royal Army Service Corps, which had the largest fleet of soft-skinned wheeled vehicles ('B Vehicles'), or the RAOC which had taken on the maintenance of armoured vehicles ('A Vehicles'). The decision, taken in the late 1920s, was for the RASC to keep the maintenance of its own fleet, but for responsibility of the whole of the remainder to pass to the RAOC. The plan was for 'B' vehicles to go to a new depot being set up at Farnborough, and for 'A' vehicles to go to Woolwich, where the last remaining tanks from the Great War had gone. Command depots would hold and maintain the vehicles in use by their battalions.

Bill worked at Catterick on the day-to-day running of the mechanized vehicle depot; he also took a great interest in the morale of his RAOC men. He encouraged a garden competition. Many years later, a then much older NCO wrote a confession to a dreadful misdeed:

> The Colonel was a great gardening enthusiast, and in two or three short years his inspiration turned the wilderness of our 9 Section Lines into a blaze of colour and beauty, and won for us all the gardening trophies of Catterick Camp and, indeed, at every horticultural show in North Yorkshire for miles around.
>
> One of the most spectacular exhibits was a glorious display of carefully attended lupins blooming outside the entrance to the Colonel's office. I was duty NCO one day and my girlfriend – now Mrs Hodgson – came along to see me in the evening. We were talking together to the night watchman at the entrance to the Depot gates, when my wife, spying the lupins, casually asked the night watchman if she could have a few. Supposing that such a question could never be meant seriously, he airily agreed and we carried on talking. A few minutes later, to our utmost astonishment and terror, my wife reappeared with an armful of the precious lupins. The watchman and I looked towards the Colonel's office, now dreadfully naked. We dared not wonder what the following morning would bring.[15]

Bill had also arranged for the construction of a recreation institute, which was subsequently named the Williams Institute. It was a busy time, and his tenure at Catterick was extended past the conventional three years. At least part of the building work on the Catterick site was undertaken by Long Eaton builder, F. Perks & Son, and Bill began a friendship with Frank Perks which would last the latter's lifetime. Frank's daughter, Betty, remembered being driven to Catterick at the age of 11 and seeing, from the back seat of the car, this rather dashing soldier. On other occasions in the Perks household, Frank would speak of that 'mad b****r Bill Williams'. Bill was a very determined man.

The Perks family had moved from Kent via the West Midlands to Long Eaton in the late nineteenth century. By the time Betty was entering her teens, the building company was busy building houses. It is not possible to miss the astonishing number of 1920s and 1930s semi-detached houses that surround our towns and cities. The major growth was around London, but certainly in the Midlands and elsewhere in the south a very great number of such houses were built. These in turn created demand for furniture, and Long Eaton would benefit from this as its traditional craft of lace-making declined. The textile skills, though, were re-employed in making new artificial fabrics by companies such as Courtaulds and British Celanese, for which the parent of one of Betty's friends worked.

The opportunities for leisure multiplied. There were three cinemas in Long Eaton: The Scala, The Palace and The Empire. Films were Betty's passion, and she would go each Saturday, sometimes twice. Later the Empire added a ballroom, built by Perks, as the fashion for dancing took hold. Betty and her friends were members of the local tennis club and the whole family would go the short distance to watch Derby County play football and Derbyshire play cricket. Whilst it may have had three modern cinemas, the high street was still dominated by a great many small shops, most of which had delivery boys. Elsewhere, Sainsbury's, Marks & Spencer and Woolworths were slowly changing the face of retail.

The international situation was also changing, with the rise of Hitler in Germany. The ten-year rule was placed on hold and a certain level of expenditure on rearmament undertaken. This focused on Woolwich, but plans were also made for new armaments factories to supply the guns and ammunition that would be needed for a second war on a global scale. Plans were put in place for the creation of forty-five royal ordnance factories. A number would be engineering, tasked with the manufacture of artillery and small arms. There would then be the manufacture of explosives and the filling of shells. All horribly familiar. Particularly the latter were to be located away from areas of population and the risk of aerial attack. Priority was given to the navy and air force and so, for the army, progress was slow. By 1939 twenty-three factories had been planned, but, by the time war broke out, only seven were in production. Four engineering factories at Nottingham, Birtley in County Durham, Blackburn and Dalmuir on Clydeside; an explosives factory at Irvine in Ayrshire; a shell-filling factory at Hereford, with another at Chorley which began production in 1940.[16]

In addition, and importantly, the British motor industry began to flex its muscles in the cause of rearmament, but again the primary focus was on aircraft. There were still a great many motor companies all feeling the pressure of mass production methods used more widely in the USA. Lord Nuffield, as he later became, had under his wing Morris and Wolseley. There was then Austin and, as I will mention more later, the Rootes Group. From the USA there was Ford in Dagenham and Vauxhall in Luton. There were also the smaller manufacturers of heavy vehicles: Dennis, Leyland and AEC, to name but a few. Jaguar would be important in aircraft engine production.[17]

Guns and ammunition would need secure storage, and Charles de Wolff wrote in the early 1930s, 'a brilliant appreciation of the likely effect of aerial warfare on the important equipment stored at Woolwich.' This was written in a letter to the *RAOC Gazette* following de Wolff's death. The writer, Lieutenant Colonel D.R. Pudney, continues,

> bearing in mind how ill-prepared Britain was at the beginning of the Second World War, this concept of second-guessing aerial bombardment of London and recommending relocation of its vital stores to a safe area of Shropshire was a piece of incredible foresight.[18]

That safe part of Shropshire was Donnington, of which more later.

Bill had been promoted to brevet lieutenant colonel on 1 July 1933. In November 1934, he was instructed to visit the site of the derelict former National Shell Filling Factory at Chilwell near Nottingham. Frank Perks had worked as a supervisor in 1917 and 1918 following service as an officer in the Pioneer Corps where his experience of managing building had been put to full advantage. On 2 July 1918 he led his men and women to continue production, despite the shock and devastation caused by a massive explosion the previous day which had cost 134 lives.[19] The factory actually increased production until the end of the war. It was then used as a depot for bulk storage, until 1926 when it was abandoned to weeds and brambles.

Following the November visit, Bill wrote a report which included the following key section:

> The problem [of setting up an Army Centre for Mechanization at Chilwell] appears to divide itself into three main areas:
>
> 1. Lay-out of the new depot, storage methods, and types of racks, etc. to be used.

2. The best methods of meeting demands and continuing services to Command Depots during the move [from Farnborough]
3. Systems of accounting and provision, and assimilation of the latest methods from large business firms, where they can be applied

Of the above, the most urgent question is No. 1, and I should like to deal with it on the following lines:

1. Visit Farnborough for one week, concentrating on storage and racking problems only
2. Visit certain representative civilian firms to inspect their racking and storage methods:
   a. Morris
   b. Austin
   c. Wolseley
   d. Hillman-Humber Commer combine
   e. BSA Combine
   f. Sunbeam Talbot Darracq Combine
   g. Dunlop
   h. Brown Bros, London (motor component and accessary factors)
   i. C.T. Riches & Co. London
3. Visit RASC Depot at Feltham
4. Inspect all plans, drawings, etc. of the proposed layout and at Chilwell
5. Visit Chilwell for a couple of days

In Bill's archive are further detailed reports and plans, which include arrangements for bringing both 'A' and 'B' vehicles to Chilwell.[20] Another significant business name which emerges is Tecalemit, which was and still is a major supplier of garage equipment of which Chilwell needed a great deal. The importance of the motor industry in this story cannot be overstated.

Bill returned to Catterick, and reported that the site was suitable for an army centre of mechanization. He was posted to Farnborough in April 1935, promoted to colonel and began to build his team.

I pause at this point, because I am certain that it was team-building, more than almost anything, that enabled the RAOC to become the organization of which Max Hastings wrote his words of praise on D-Day. I am equally sure that it wasn't just Bill's team-building. It is possible to see in the Middle East, the thumbprint also of Dicky Richards on the team he had out there. And it wasn't just those who became generals; Charles de Wolff was a remarkable leader.

At Chilwell a number of names emerge of men who would have significant roles in the coming conflict: Digger Reynolds, then of the Australian Staff Corps, and who was on the seventh ordnance officers' course along with Jim Denniston and would go out to Singapore to enlarge the Alexandra Depot and then undertake a number of roles including a major one on D-Day; Victor Lonsdale would become Deputy Director of Warlike Stores for Ammunition; and George Crawford, Director of Ordnance Services at the end of the 1950s. Reynolds led the team at Chilwell which masterminded the army vehicles parts list, no simple task given the large number of makes and models, and the imperative of supplying the right part for the vehicle in question anywhere in the world.

A.J.M. 'Dick' Hunt was another Chilwell pioneer, and would later become Bill's 'eyes and ears' when Bill moved to the War Office. Bill, writing on Hunt's death in July 1961, recalled him at Chilwell as 'one of the best members of the team who were responsible for the creation, not only of the Motor Transport organization, but for the foundation of the systems and methods which are now used throughout the Corps'. Another was Vic Ebbage who would be posted to Hong Kong where he was taken prisoner by the Japanese. Harry Sims was a civilian stores superintendent and he went on to be part of the team setting up COD Derby in 1939 and COD Feltham in 1943. There were, of course, others in those early days. Ernest Tankard was on the ordnance officers' course in 1923/4 and had won an MC whilst serving in the Royal Field Artillery in the First World War and, with Basil Cox and Harry Whitaker, would play a major role in the Middle East.

Another significant name was Dan Warren who then worked at SS Cars (Jaguar) and who arranged for spare parts for Bill's adored silver-grey Jaguar. Bill had previously driven an Austin and then a Sunbeam; his interest in vehicles was a good deal more than professional! Alongside Dan Warren was Sergeant Spalding, an excellent mechanic, who followed Bill from Catterick and would keep the precious Jaguar in perfect working order. I found in the biography of Jaguar's founder, Sir William Lyons, a reference to an Eric Warren who had, in 1935, followed William Lyons from Brown & Mallalieu in Blackpool to SS Cars as sales manager.[21] I don't know whether Eric and Dan are one and the same man, or possibly related.

Perhaps at the other end of the spectrum were two of Bill's bosses: Major General Lionel Hoare who was Chief Ordnance Officer at Woolwich and Basil Hill who was by then Director of Ordnance Services. Major General Sir Basil Hill, as he later became, was undoubtedly the talisman of the RAOC in the interwar years, of whom Jack Omond wrote this:

> Building on the final and, in some respects, the grudging respect which the Corps had earned during the 1914–18 War, he strove his hardest to ensure that Commands and units knew what the Corps could and did do continuously to help in the vast field of military administration.[22]

Hill had been appointed Director of Ordnance Services and Colonel Commandant RAOC in 1936. In July 1939 he was appointed Controller of Ordnance Services. His name is linked to that of Lionel Hoare, just below him in that all-important list of seniority. Hoare was born to the great banking family at Staplehurst, Kent, in 1881, just one year after Hill. Hoare went to Eton and served as a gunner subaltern in the Boer War. He was awarded a DSO for his service in the First World War. Writing on Hill's death, he told how

> I took over from him three times – as Adjutant at the Red Barracks; at the School of Instruction, Hilsea; and as ADOS, MG0.7, War Office, and, in the two former cases, his house and garden as well. In every case it was in apple-pie order. At the School of Instruction, he had revolutionized the Provision system, which was a major reform.
>
> I must add a personal note, probably unknown to anyone. When he was made DOS, he was just senior to me (and incidentally far abler!), but with characteristic generosity he told me that if I had been selected over his head he would have willingly and loyally served under me.[23]

Hoare was a great support to Bill in the monumental task of building Chilwell at a time when defence spending was being directed to aircraft production.

At Farnborough, Bill had lived in the Officers' Club. At Chilwell, he moved with Mabel to Woodside House, a fine 1920s building with wonderful views of Nottinghamshire.

Also at Woodside House came George Cook as butler. George had been a coalminer in the nearby Nottingham coalfield, and joined the Grenadier Guards as an officer's servant, a role he filled in an exemplary manner. The officer, whom he was serving, married, but his new wife took a dislike to George who was dismissed with a bad reference. In spite of this, he applied for the job of butler at Woodside House and Bill interviewed him and liked him straight away. George would remain with Bill for the remainder of Bill's life and died within six months of Bill's death. When my sister and I were little, George was cook, decorator and gardener and devoted friend of Fluffy our cat. Truly a lovely man.

In 1935 the view from Woodside House would have been marred by the sight of the derelict shell-filling factory. Work began immediately with Royal Engineers working alongside men from F. Perks & Sons who were already on site with a care and maintenance brief. I know Bill was only too delighted at the prospect of working again with his friend from Catterick.

Another Perks entered the story on 11 May 1936 when, on leaving secretarial college, Betty took a job as a temporary civil servant typist. She was assistant to Bill's personal assistant, Miss Drew. When Miss Drew left the following year in order to marry, Betty moved into her seat and from this point on, I have her wonderful personal record.

Key to the Chilwell project were systems. The army had never before set up an organization capable of supplying and maintaining a large number of quite different vehicles. At its peak in 1944, Chilwell would handle some 800,000 different parts. Bill, in conjunction with Lionel Hoare and Basil Hill, realized that they needed help, and so Bill wrote a great many letters to leaders of the motor industry, component manufacturers and distributors of all kinds. From these letters came the help requested, but also friendships developed, many of which would last a good number of years. Betty described what she witnessed:

> Leslie made a particular point of getting to know the leading members of Industry and he paid visits to motor

manufacturers and makers of components (e.g. Lucas and Dunlop) and he learnt as much as he could of their methods of supply and distribution. He used to say he 'picked their brains'. It was one thing to see what other people did and the methods they used, but it was another to be able to discriminate and use the most efficient and most appropriate methods for the use of the Army. Leslie was a most humble man in this respect; he always insisted in giving credit where credit was due.

Betty noted that, in response to Bill's approaches, he welcomed these visitors from the businesses: Sir Peter Bennett of Lucas, Harold Kenward of Dunlop, Bob Lillico of Lucas, Lord Nuffield, Sir William and Sir Reginald Rootes, Sir Patrick Ashley Cooper of the Hudsons Bay Company, Sir Patrick Hennesey, Sir Roland Smith and Stanford Cooper of Fords.

I suspect top of the list came the Rootes brothers, William and Reggie who, from their Kent-based garage business had, through acquisition, created perhaps the foremost British motor group of the 1930s; I say this on the basis that Morris and Austin were then separate companies. William Rootes, in particular, would be of enormous help to Bill but also to the war effort generally.

One man at Dunlop, who made a massive contribution, was Harold Kenward. In Bill's archive there is an appreciation of him written for his remembrance service on his untimely death in 1947. It is not clear whether Bill wrote it or merely obtained a copy of it. It tells how Kenward was a Sussex man born in 1894. He was the son of a bootmaker and joined Dunlop as an accounts clerk in 1911. The author of the appreciation, who recalls knowing him from those 'early days at Aston Cross', also tells how Kenward worked with Lord Austin on recruiting men from the motor industry for the RAOC.[24] Kenward had volunteered in 1914 and served in the Royal Field Artillery with a horse-drawn 18-pounder. He had been wounded in the Battle of the Somme, but had gone back until demobilization in 1919 when he rejoined Dunlop. He held a number of posts in the commercial department and became London manager in 1924. He, like Hiam and Robinson, would have witnessed the tremendous developments in the motor industry, not least in the way it was managed.

The bigger challenge, for Bill, was as much to convince the army bureaucracy, as to develop the strong systems which would stand the strain of war. Betty watched from her then junior position:

> He spent days in London at the War Office badgering the finance section for more money so that he could improve the services and organization of Chilwell. He had many battles with the Civil Service to get his schemes approved. He developed a very canny technique. He would not approach the head of the branch concerned, but always made a point of finding out which more junior member of staff actually dealt with the matter in hand and then would contact that particular person. The very fact that the senior army officer had approached the junior civil servant did the trick, as they invariably fell for the flattery and Leslie got his way.

It was not only Chilwell where developments were taking place. Major Harris, who co-authored with Alan Fernyhough *The History of the RAOC 1920–1945*, wrote an article in the *RAOC Gazette* in 1959 looking back twenty years. In it he notes the then leadership of the Corps: 'At the War Office the post of Controller of Ordnance Services was created and occupied by Major General Basil Hill, with Major General K.M. Body succeeding him as DOS. Brigadier Valon was promoted to major general in the post of Principal Ordnance Mechanical Engineer. Harris then provides a snapshot of the progress then made with mechanization:

> The Mobile Division had been formed, and it and the 1st Tank Brigade re-equipped with the Light Tank, the Infantry Tank and the Morris Armoured Reconnaissance Car; more than 500 carriers had been issued to the infantry. All but two of the horsed cavalry regiments were to be mechanized during the year, and the artillery regiments (lately brigades) re-equipped with the 25 / 18 pounder gun on pneumatic tyred wheels by mid-1939.[25]

Harris records the efforts being made at Chilwell, but also the essential painstaking work being carried out by Lieutenant Colonel Swiney, of the

Class of '22, in completely rewriting the tables of war equipment for an army with mechanical vehicles instead of horses.

In terms of engagements, Harris lists the theatres of potential conflict as Palestine and Egypt. In 1936, Palestine had been the posting for Geoffrey Palmer, and Egypt for Dicky Richards. De Wolff had been posted to Malta, sailing out on a troopship on 16 January 1933. He succeeded Harry Whitaker, who returned first to Aldershot and then Hilsea before joining Bill at Chilwell.

It is hard to know how typical de Wolff's experience was of an overseas peacetime posting, but I suspect it offers an albeit well-spiced flavour. His wife and their English cook plus pets followed him to Malta by P&O liner. Life was agreeable. They had three horses and both rode regularly. In terms of work, he had come out as a major but, with the return of his chief of service to England, was promoted to lieutenant colonel. He tells how he and his fellow chiefs of service would each sit in their offices communicating by memo. Wolffy suggested to the commanding officer that a daily meeting over a drink might be more efficient. This was sharply rejected, because it turned out that the CO was teetotal. A compromise with a meeting with soft drinks proved very effective.[26]

De Wolff clearly made an impression in Malta, for he received a very positive reference from the Governor General and had been remembered by the Secretary for War, Leslie Hore-Belisha. Notwithstanding this, de Wolff considered that he had reached as high as he could with his deafness, and so submitted his retirement papers. These were rejected and he was asked to set up the new Woolwich at Donnington in Shropshire which he had advocated, a task he set to with relish.

Returning to Bill, it is here that Betty's record really comes into play. The first part seems almost a retrospective, for, at the start of the first volume, there is a full-page photograph of Bill followed by images from the evacuation of the Rhine in 1929. There are then photographs from Catterick with a sequence of images of the Williams Institute. There is the group photograph of the senior officers' course which Bill attended from May to July 1933. His posting to Chilwell is recorded in a press cutting. There are then extensive press cuttings from the visit of journalists to the then reopened Chilwell depot in April 1938. There is a separate album of photographs of the new depot taken on the same occasion. Betty's volume has photographs of the people involved and press cuttings telling of the progress made, life on the base and the men and women who worked there. There must have been a huge sense of achievement for all involved, not least Bill.

The Munich crisis of 1938 raised the tempo of preparations, and Bill joined a team of officers that crossed to France to reconnoitre the most suitable places to form the bases in the event of war breaking out. Betty recalls some of what Bill told her. 'All the officers travelled in civilian clothes and as civilians; one man was particularly security conscious – hiding behind closed curtains and watching if they were being followed.'

Barely a year later, on 10 May 1939, disaster struck as major fire took hold of the Chilwell tyre store. The arsonist was found, prosecuted and sent to Lincoln gaol. The more positive outcome was that a new bespoke tyre store could be built. Also, in May 1939, there was a major exhibition of army equipment in nearby Nottingham. Betty then records what she terms as 'those days of peace', with a programme for Derby Day at Epsom Races and the programme for the Livery Dinner at the Worshipful Company of Coach Makers and Coach Harness Makers in the City of London, an echo from earlier times.

It is clear, from other documents in Bill's archive, that contact with industry continued, this time not so much to tap their brains, as to encourage suitably skilled men to join the RAOC Reserve and so be ready for call-up should war be declared. John Hildreth wrote about this in his note to Robbie Robinson's obituary of Bob Hiam:

> Before the war that longsighted man the then Colonel Leslie Williams – at Chilwell – had personally recruited a number of the ablest young executives into the Army Officers Emergency Reserve RAOC so that, immediately war came, a group of very useful officers was available to the Corps. We, the regulars, laughingly referred to them as the Dunlop Light Infantry, though not all were from Dunlop. Those like Bob Hiam, D.S. Robinson, Dennis Hayes, Gilbert Way and Eric Baker – all were close friends and colleagues and all did a great deal to raise the standard and enhance the reputation of the Corps. Do not let us forget them.[27]

The political developments of the summer of 1939 are well known. For Bill they would mean promotion on 29 August 1939 to brigadier with the job of Deputy Director of Ordnance Services (Motor Transport) based at the War Office. Lord Nuffield, whose many businesses were playing important roles, visited and had clearly been impressed by what Bill had achieved at Chilwell, for, at a meeting with Secretary of State for War, Leslie Hore-Belisha, when the job of DDOS (Motor Transport) came up, Hore-Belishsa is reported to have said, 'why not Williams at Chilwell?'

Whilst no one could have known more about the job than he, it must have been daunting to enter the corridors of the War Office, no longer as a visitor, but as part of the senior establishment. His domestic accommodation, and so both his wife and butler, remained at the Woodside House to which he would return on frequent visits. In London he had rooms at the Junior Army & Navy Club in Whitehall Court close to QMG House where his office was.

On Sunday 3 September 1939, on the declaration of war, he was indeed at Chilwell, and chaired a remarkable meeting where permanent ordnance officers sat side by side with those who had come from the territorials or volunteer reserves, including TA Colonel Edgar Platt, 'Reddy' Readman, Bob Hiam and Robbie Robinson from Dunlop, Arthur Sewell from Tecalemit and Dan Warren from SS Cars. Kenneth Johnson-Davies was also probably present, but came from a different background. He was a barrister, a former scholar at St Catherine's College, Cambridge, and had served in the RASC in the First World War. On demobilization, he remained in the Territorial Army. In the 1930s he was Secretary of the Motor Traders' Association and joined the RAOC with a number of others from the motor trade. He would undertake the task of setting up the Greenford depot in West London. After the war he would write a number of books on law and the motor trade. Of the others joining from the motor trade, Colonel Browne, who went out to India to set up 206 IBOD (see Chapter 11), was from Morris Motors. Colonel McCausland, who was an ever-present source of inspiration at Chilwell, came from Provincial and Suburban Garages Ltd. J.W. Mackillop from Jackson Garages, Aberdeen, later commanded the Tanks and Vehicles Organization.

With Bill's appointment to the War Office, Brigadier Harry Whitaker was appointed COO of Chilwell. That September, of course, much else was taking place.

For Ordnance, Geoffrey Palmer returned from three years in Palestine to become COO of 1 BOD at Nantes; Dicky Richards returned from Egypt to become COO of 2 BOD at Le Havre; 'Geako' Geake returned from Hong Kong to join Dicky at Le Havre; Cyril Cansdale became DDOS Lines of Communication.

Charles de Wolff had received an order to return from three years in Malta to begin to set up his brainchild, the new depot in Shropshire. That was in March 1939 and he had spent the summer planning what might be. In September, on the declaration of war, he too was posted to France. In his not-to-be-published memoir, he records that his serial number was 0003 as Q Staff; that Lord Gort's, as Commanding Officer, was 0001, and that 0002 was given to 'G' Staff. He thus crossed to France as the senior lieutenant colonel to join the Staff at GHQ. I suspect that much discussion subsequently took place concerning this appointment, for the depot at Donnington was under construction and was seen as most urgent. De Wolff returned from France in November 1939 to continue oversight of the project which would bear fruit after Dunkirk and for the duration of the war.

Ronald Weeks had remained in the Territorial Army whilst working for Pilkington, and, from 1934 to 1939, 'was a most successful commanding officer of the 5th Battalion of the South Lancashire Regiment TA'.[28] At the outbreak of war he was made G.S.O.1 of the 66th Division and crossed to France with the BEF.

What did all this mean in reality?

'The British Army which crossed to France in 1939 differed from other armies at that time in being fully mechanized.' So wrote the author of the official report on the British Expeditionary Force. He continued, 'The Army was however better equipped on paper than in practice.'[29] It is appropriate at this point to take a step back to see the reality behind this boast. Whilst there were indeed vehicles, there were inadequate spare parts; there were tanks, but nothing like the type and number needed. There were ordnance men, but not enough, insufficiently trained and not using common systems and procedures. In 1938 Colonel R.F. Johnson had been given the task writing a new edition of *The Ordnance Manual (War)*, effectively the ordnance 'bible'. The new edition was demanded by the study and experimentation of new methods, including the work done at Chilwell on procedures for Base Ordnance Depots and Ordnance Field Parks. On 2 January 1943, Johnson wrote to Bill with congratulations on his being awarded a CB and added this:

> Most people know what you have done to modernize the Ordnance. Some of us – I, for one – realize that the

modernization of the Army itself depended, in no small measure, on the pioneer work you did in pre-war days, in the teeth of difficulties which had defeated so many of your predecessors.

R.F., as he was known, had been on the second ordnance officers' course with Harry Whitaker. In the mid-1930s he served in Hong Kong and earned the nickname 'Rim-fire', for 'not being the easiest man to work with, but one had to admire his qualities of perception, originality and drive'. He had qualified as a barrister before the First World War, and had worked as a journalist before becoming a regular soldier in 1917. The writer of his obituary suggests that Sir John Reith had once offered him a job as Director of Programmes, but R.F. had preferred to remain in the RAOC. After he retired, he went back to journalism at the Colonial Office News Branch, before dedicating himself to writing.[30] Tragically for the BEF, Johnson's changes had not been fully implemented and training in them had barely begun.

Whilst procedures may have been lacking, talented people most certainly were not. The name Dicky Richards will appear at key points in this story for his energy was prodigious. Dicky was COO at Le Havre and had secured premises at Quai Transatlantique. The story goes that he was becoming increasing frustrated at the non-arrival of racking and an officer commented:

'My God, won't Dicky be wild?'

The author of the anecdote replied, asking, 'Who's Dicky?'

'Our COO and a cyclone in human shape if ever there was one. He's been cursing Didcot about that blasted racking for a month.'[31]

In time, Richards managed to achieve some measure of organization.

In early 1940, Bill was part of a visit to the BEF with members of the General Staff along with Sir William Rootes. The purpose of the visit was to see vehicles in action, but also to assess the support infrastructure. It was a wakeup call that tragically came too late, but which would feed into planning thereafter.

Following the report of this visit, the COS, Basil Hill, visited, and he reported on 6 April. Reading through his report, the points of note are criticism of the too-rapid unloading of stores which resulted in muddle, the poor condition of some vehicles, a lack of spare parts for guns, but overall satisfactory performance on Motor Transport and the successful adoption of Visidex except for some of the advanced depots. The name Visidex warrants a brief explanation. With the multitude of parts the RAOC handled, effective record-keeping was vital. Bill decided to use the manual Visidex system which could be used anywhere, rather than NCR mechanical accounting which was in no sense portable. Interestingly the practice of dry-cleaning uniforms set up in the First World War was being used to good effect.[32] Another echo from the First World War: some ammunition storage had insufficient space between stacks.[33]

The decision in London had been taken to invade Norway to try to avoid it falling into German hands as Denmark had done. Two points of attack were chosen: Trondheim and Narvik but the attack failed for a multitude of reasons and, in order to avoid total disaster, the force was evacuated on 1 and 3 May. The episode led to a vote of censure in the House of Commons that the government won, but which began the process that would install Winston Churchill as prime minister.[34]

Harry Whitaker was posted to the Norway campaign after only six months at Chilwell. Also on the doomed Norway campaign was Lancelot Cutforth, who would be heavily involved in personnel and training before joining the Ordnance team within the 21st Army Group in the run up to D-Day.

Whitaker was succeeded at Chilwell by Reddy Readman who, with his First World War experience of tanks and his career in the steel industry, would take the Centre for Mechanization from strength to strength in the course of the war with, predominantly, those other officers taken from industry. D.S. Robinson wrote of him:

> Most of us had little, if any, experience in the Army. Edgar, however, had served in the First World War and had continued his Army experience in the TA between the wars while establishing himself as a senior executive in the English Steel Corporation. He was, therefore, already an ideal amalgam of the businessman/soldier which so many of the younger men were required so quickly to become.[35]

Betty remained at Chilwell working first for Whitaker and then for Readman, and being available to support Bill on his frequent visits. She recalled how she acted as a 'listening post' as he talked through the problems he was facing.

Bill's focus was on Motor Transport. Six years later, in his farewell speech to the officers of COD Derby, he told how he negotiated the purchase of a second site for MT at Sinfin Lane at 'a very good price'. I infer that he probably did the same at Old Dalby which was also intended to be a Motor Transport depot, but which later became a depot for a wide range of armaments. On 7 April 1940, Bill had been appointed Director of Ordnance Services (Warlike Stores) for six months from 16 March 1940. This post included Motor Transport, but was very much wider covering guns, ammunition and much else besides. Bill would work alongside an experienced officer close to retirement, Major General K.M. (Joe) Body, who would have responsibility for all other stores and aspects of ordnance work.

This was very much for the future, for, as is recorded in many places elsewhere, in May 1940 the German advance through Belgium completely outclassed anything the British and French could offer. The result was defeat and retreat to Dunkirk which could so easily have ended in total disaster had it not been for the tenacity of the rear-guard action, the bad weather which gave some protection against air attack, and the Royal Navy and flotilla of 'little ships' which brought some 338,000 British, French and Belgian troops back to England.[36] For Ordnance, it was a loss of experienced men, either dead or captured, who had supported the rear-guard, but also a massive loss of equipment, not least precious motor vehicles.

Chapter 6

The Depots and the Motor Industry

June 1940 must have been truly a terrifying time.

Bill, only two months into his new job, with Geako, Cecil Haigh (Class of '22) and, former gunner, Maurice Lea-Cox as his deputies, had a massive task. There was a very real risk that Hitler would invade, and, so, what equipment there was had to be gathered, repaired and made available to the Home Forces. Air attack was expected, and so anti-aircraft batteries had to be supplied. Ronald Weeks had returned from Dunkirk with the 66th Division and had then been appointed Brigadier General Staff (Staff Duties) at Home Forces HQ where his role was to put forward the demands of home forces for what little equipment there was, all the time in competition with overseas forces such as those in the Middle East. This would prove to be a vital experience.

The name of Lea-Cox is significant, as was clear from the piece Bill wrote on his retirement in 1953. The three branches which came under the Director of Warlike Stores had previously been within the remit of the Master General of Ordnance (previously responsible for the production, procurement and supply of warlike stores) and so a transfer to come under the QMG required careful management. As Bill writes, the man selected to manage these three branches should come from the Royal Artillery and should have Staff College training to enable him to handle relationships with both the Ministry of Supply and the General Staff at the War Office. Lea-Cox was such a man.

Of at least equal importance, an Ordnance team had to be built from men of very different backgrounds. D.S. 'Robbie' Robinson, who was very much at the sharp end, later wrote this of Bill:

> He foresaw in 1938 the impact on the supply services of the coming war. When still a Colonel and Chief Ordnance Officer at Chilwell, to prepare the Corps for it, he embarked

upon a campaign to encourage business men in various walks of commercial and industrial life to join the Army Officers Emergency Reserve and be ready, as and when war broke out, to put on uniform. When that happened and we found ourselves in the Army, he ensured that we were given work to do for which our civilian training and experience had fitted us. He pressed us to the limit of our abilities in a new and strange environment, inspiring us by his own energy and force of character.

There are many men, 1 am sure, who will be forever grateful to him for the opportunity he gave us to fulfil a wartime role to the utmost of our energies and capacity and, in so doing, to contribute a quick and purposeful share to the war effort.

The wartime performance of the RAOC was undoubtedly enhanced by the capacity of General Williams, first as DWS and then as COS, to weld his new intake with his small establishment of regulars. History may prove that this was not an unimportant factor in keeping at bay the overwhelming superiority of our enemies in the first place and then helping to build the supply organization which ultimately supported the drive for victory.

He was unrelenting in having his orders carried out, uncompromising in criticism, but generous in appreciation.[1]

Those first months in the War Office saw unrelenting work despite the Blitz which was going on all around. Betty's album picks up the story again on 5 December 1940 with the dinner menu card recording when General Sir Walter Venning, the Quartermaster General, visited the new depot at Derby, then commanded by Robinson who had moved across from Chilwell.

It is worth again taking a step back to see quite what the depot work encompassed.

For Bill, with Warlike Stores, there was, of course, Chilwell and the new depot at Derby. There were the embryonic armament depots at Donnington, Greenford and Old Dalby. There was the nineteenth-century arsenal for small arms at Weedon and, of course, Woolwich. Ammunition was stored at Bramley, but with the new underground depot at Corsham under construction. Betty included in her album a newspaper report on a 'secret' massive underground ammunition depot. Someone had written on the cutting the word 'Corsham' for that was the place, just outside Bath, where this was. So much for secrecy. Corsham is a name that appears in the accounts of a number of people in this story. It started life in 1936 when Brigadier Verschoyle-Campbell (who had commanded an ammunition train in the early months of the First World War, and who was very much an ammunition guru) and Colonel Stokes (who had served on the committee which designed the ordnance officers' course) were charged by the War Office to find underground storage to supplement CAD Bramley. The barracks at Corsham were named after the then Controller of Ordnance Services, Basil Hill.

For General Body, clothing was dealt with in a former pickle factory at Branston near Burton upon Trent, to which it had moved from Pimlico in Central London. Harold Crosland, a businessman and TA officer from Berkshire who had won an MC in the First World War, would command the depot at Branston for the duration of the war. Bulk stores were kept at Didcot, on a key railway junction, which had been 'built on the cheap' in the First World War and had developed systems quite different to those at Chilwell. There was then the Corps HQ at Hilsea, which had been overwhelmed by the numbers joining on mobilization. There were the command depots and there was the Training Centre also then at Hilsea, but also Chilwell and Bramley, under the command of Jack Omond.

The opening of Donnington, described as a 'new Woolwich' somewhere in the Midlands, was the subject of a further set of press cuttings in 1941, although the event written about had occurred in that grim summer of 1940. Charles de Wolff had returned to oversee the construction of the brand-new armaments depot and work was proceeding, but not fast enough. Following the retreat from Dunkirk, the War Office rightly anticipated air attacks on London and that the arsenal at Woolwich would be vulnerable. Accordingly, the decision was taken to move the contents of Woolwich, together with such arsenal employees who would go, to Donnington. It was a massive operation clogging up the railways for days. Even de Wolff took his jacket off to help with the work. It was reported that the concrete floors were barely dry when the Woolwich equipment arrived. Clerks would work in warehouses with no heating all through the ensuing winter. The depot was surrounded by tented camps where the troops working at the depot lived.

Above left: Mildred Mercy Williams.

Above right: Alfred Hamlyn Williams.

Right: 32 Trossachs Road, Dulwich.

Above: Alleyn's School c.1908, Leslie Williams is fourth from the right in the third row looking to the left.

Left: Bill Williams (indicated with an x) at Mombasa Station, with the Marquis of Stafford whom he had met on the voyage from England, 1911.

Above left: Bill Williams, Rivers Macpherson, Charles de Wolff and Cyril Cansdale (sitting).

Above right: Bill and Betty at Mombasa Station, 1944.

Right: Lieutenant Bill Williams, 1914.

The Duke of York's visit to Hilsea, 1922. Top row: Lt. A. Symons, Capt. A.R. Valon, Capt. J.H.D. Sheppard*, Capt. D. Manuelle*, Major W.M. Stokes, Capt. G.W. Palmer*, Lt. A. Knox-Wilson, Capt. H.R. Skinner. 3rd row: Capt. G.R.S. Love*, Capt. A.M. Hidden*, Capt. L.H. Williams*, Capt. J.S. Omond*, Rev. G. Heaslett, Capt. C.F. Cansdale*, Capt. W.K. Dines, Capt. W.W. Richards*. 2nd row: Capt. W.E.C. Pickthall*, Rev. J. Kelly, Major F.S. Smith, Major A.C. Gibson (Equerry), Major J. Asser, Capt. E.R. Macpherson*, Capt. D.R. Smith*, Capt. C.F.T. Haigh*. Front row: Capt. C.W. Bacon, Lt. Colonel H.L. Wethered, Colonel R.S. Hamilton, Major-General Sir John Stephens, HRH The Duke of York, Lt. General Sir Travers Clarke, Major-General Sir H.D.E. Parsons, Colonel H.S. Bush, Lt. Colonel Jasper Baker. (Class of '22 indicated with *. RAOC officers in the Class of '22 but not in the photograph: Capt. P.W. Kidd, Capt. L.H. Aste.)

Secretary for War Captain Margusson, Major General Williams, officers and ATS at COD Derby, 1941.

Brig. Readman,
Secretary for War
Captain Margusson,
Major General Bill
Williams and QMG
Sir Walter Venning at
COD Derby.

Delegates at COO Conference, 12 March 1942, listening to Colonel Hiam. Brig. G.T.W. Horne (DDOS WO), Lt. Col. Coles, Col. C.H. Carne (Bramley), Col. G.W. Palmer (Bicester), Lt. Col. Bateman, Col. K.C. Johnson-Davies (Greenford), Brig. H.P. Crosland (Branston), Mr G. McOnie (Civil Adviser to DGAE), Brig. E.P. Readman (Chilwell), Brig. D. Brown (DDOS WO), Major General R.M. Weeks (DGAE), Major A.J.M. Hunt (Bill's eyes and ears), Major General L.H. Williams (DWS), Major General K.M. Body (DOS), Brig. H.R. Shillington (Didcot), Brig. R.F. Johnson, Brig. C.E. de Wolff (Donnington), Col. H.T. Bell (Weedon), Col. D.S. Robinson (Derby), Col. A.H. Allen (Corsham), Col. Hurst (Nesscliff), Col. R.C. Hiam (Old Dalby), Lt. Col. Hewett, Col. Wilson, Lt. Col. S. Lewis-Lewis. (Reproduced in the *Picture Post*)

Above: Colonel Hiam addressing the COO Conference.

Left: Major General Bill Williams and Brigadier Palmer at the COO Conference, 1942.

Above: The King and Queen with Major General Bill Williams and Brigadier de Wolff at COD Donnington, 1942.

Right: Cartoon, 1942. Top from left: Sir Walter Venning, Major General Bill Williams, Brigadier Readman. 2nd row from left: Colonel Hiam, ATS ?. 3rd row from left: Colonel Robinson, ?, Colonel Coleman.

Major General Bill Williams, General Riddell-Webster QMG, Brigadier de Wolff, COD Donnington.

Major Generals Geake and Williams with Colonel Hunt in Italy, 1943.

Miss Perks, Major General Bill Williams and the staff Humber, December 1943.

Dicky Richards and Bill Williams in lighter mood

Major General Bill Williams, K.T. Keller (President of the Chrysler Corporation) and Miss Perks, 1943. (Photo US Ordnance Corps)

San Francisco press interview with Major General Williams, 1943. (Photo courtesy US Ordnance Corps)

Generals Simpson and Williams with Ingrid Bergman. (Photo courtesy US Ordnance Corps)

Visit to the *Daily Mail*, 9 March 1944. From left: Bob Pew, Alexander Clifford (war correspondent), Miss Clifford, Sydney Hine, Major General Williams, Miss Perks, Stanley Bell, Brigadier Palmer and Mrs Palmer.

Sir James Gregg, Secretary for War, at COD Bicester.

Oliver Littleton, Minister of Production, at Bicester.

Colonel Commandant Major-General Sir Basil Hill inspects COD Bicester.

Bill by Brock.

COO Conference, March 1945, with Miss Perks.

Major General Cansdale hosting a dinner at BAOR, 1945.

Ladbroke Hall invitation.
(With permission from
Rootes Archive Trust)

Geneva Motor Show, 1949.
(With permission from
Rootes Archive Trust)

Major General Sir
Leslie Williams (front
row, second from right)
marching in the King's
funeral procession.

Bill Williams,
Sir William Rootes and
Jinx Falkenburgh on
Coronation Day. (With
permission from Rootes
Archive Trust)

Bill Williams, Emile Bustani and a Humber Pullman. (With permission from Rootes Archive Trust)

Colonel Commandant Major General Sir Leslie Williams at COD Chilwell, 1952

Sir Leslie Williams, Master of the Worshipful Company of Carmen, welcoming Sir William Rootes. (© Keystone Press Agency)

Humbers and the Middle East Mission, 1953.

Her Majesty the Queen's visit to Deepcut, 1959.

Funeral procession for Major General Sir Leslie Williams, Seer Green, 1965.

Charles de Wolff takes up the story once the depot was in full operation, writing first of the scale of the operation, but also his pride in his creation. By 1943, he was commanding 15,000 British troops, including 367 officers, 3,200 women of the Auxiliary Territorial Service (ATS) and some 2,000 Italian PoWs. There were also 4,000 clerks all in one massive building. De Wolff was a soldier first and foremost, and took immensely seriously his other role as Garrison Commander in the Mid-West District where he had battalions of the Oxfordshire and Buckinghamshire Light Infantry, the Lincolnshire Regiment, the Duke of Cornwall's Light Infantry and the Worcestershire Regiment based in the garrison with three regimental bands. He prided himself on his approach to discipline; as he put it, 'there is a considerable difference between discipline and regimentation. Discipline and efficiency go hand in hand'.

One significant issue was the blending together of soldiers and temporary officers coming from industry. Robbie Robinson, who was very much at the sharp end, later wrote this of Charles de Wolff:

> With many others, I found myself posted to Chilwell from the Army Officers Emergency Reserve, in the first week of the war, and, because of the inevitable explosion in the size of the Corps, was promoted to Lieutenant Colonel within less than two years' service, catching up in rank regular officers who had taken twenty years or more to achieve similar rank. It was not that popular with some, quite naturally, and there was a certain amount of feeling between the trained soldiers and temporary gentlemen.
>
> De Wolff, who suffered almost complete deafness, was unstinting in encouraging an acceptance of the usefulness of those of us coming into the service with the benefit of industrial and management training which was, of course, what we were wanted for.[2]

Another issue which came close to de Wolff's heart, I would suggest much to his surprise, was that of the ATS. As with the previous war, the army saw a need for women to carry out jobs that had been undertaken by the men who had been mobilized to theatres of war. The ATS stood for the army alongside the WRENs for the navy and the WRAF for the air force. They undertook a whole range of duties to great effect and many thousands worked alongside men of the RAOC. De Wolff tells how a decision, seen at the time to be revolutionary, gained publicity in *The Star* of 12 January 1943 under the title, 'The Fence that Went'. De Wolff told them that

> early in the war, a barbed wire fence was put up round an ATS camp in the South to keep the troops away. The troops immediately began to gather round the fence trying to find a way of speaking to the girls. The situation became so impossible that the officer took down the fence in despair. At once the soldiers lost interest.

He explained that he had followed the same principle at Donnington allowing men and women to mix as freely as in their home towns. 'They dance, go to the cinema and theatre and go for walks together.' The result was, of course, that 'behaviour has never been better'.[3]

De Wolff's openness is also revealed in his attitude to communists. MI5 compiled dossiers of communist sympathizers working in depots, and, presumably, in other war-related establishments. MI5 officials visited Donnington and de Wolff was asked/ordered to keep the identified soldiers under a watchful eye and to enter details of any suspicious behaviour in the dossiers, which were kept securely in the depot safe. After two years, no entries had been made and, when challenged, de Wolff declared that he had full confidence in the men. He added that they carried out their duties in an exemplary way.

In relation to the ATS in particular, he started all manner of classes to further their education. He lists them, and one immediately senses attitudes of the times: the making of wooden and soft toys, lino-cuts, poster work and modelling, but also courses in languages and clerical work. Education more generally was made widely available, for de Wolff was shocked at how many men and women arrived at the depot with no literacy skills. He set up a school.

De Wolff was the only chief ordnance officer to write at length about his depot, but there are surely many features in common with the others, not least size – they were all massive. The provision of education was a thread throughout. Kenneth Johnson-Davies ran the Greenford depot, with his wife, Anne, as welfare officer. Together they instituted a very broad education provision, including a series of lectures drawing on Kenneth's contacts industry and the law. A not dissimilar regime operated at Derby under Robbie Robinson, who saw it essential for his men and women to understand the context of their work. He also championed education and effective relaxation, given the very long hours worked.

The benefit of good industrial management practice was not one-way traffic. De Wolff writes of visits by managers at ICI to learn from what was happening at Donnington. At Old Dalby, run by Dunlop manager Bob Hiam, a delegation from Dunlop visited and went away clearly impressed. Chilwell had become a beacon of good practice for the motor industry.

Major General Sir Basil Hill retired as Controller of Ordnance Services in January 1941 and took up the post of Director of Hand Tools at the Ministry of Supply from 1943 to 1945. The intervening period saw him much involved with the rationalization of vehicle supply and the formation of REME, of which I say more below. For the RAOC, the post of Controller was discontinued and Major General Joe Body was appointed Director of Ordnance Services and Senior Serving Officer of the RAOC.

In Betty's album, there was a clear focus on Chilwell, evidenced on 7 February 1941 by the menu for a guest night at the Chilwell officers' mess. There is then a 'red letter day' marked by photographs and press cuttings recording the visit of the Duke of Kent to Chilwell on 7 March 1941. The motor vehicle theme continued with Bill attending, with some 200 others, the annual luncheon of the Commercial Motor Users' Association. Bill was certainly nurturing the relationship with the motor industry. Betty later hinted that this may have had a spin-off in paving the way for Bill's career when he left the army. I think there was still more to it than this. Bill was a 'petrol boots'; he loved the motor car. I have already noted that he had owned a Model-T Ford, an Austin, a Sunbeam-Talbot and one of the first Jaguars. Of course, he would want to get to know like-minded men in the motor industry.

The role of the motor industry in supporting the war effort cannot be overstated. As well as motor vehicles of all kinds, they were manufacturing aircraft and aircraft components. They were manufacturing guns and ammunition cases, steel helmets and jerrycans; design departments were devoted to developing weapons not least the tank, particularly by Vauxhall and the Nuffield companies.

In June 1941, Cecil Haigh was posted to India, and John Hildreth moved from Donnington to the War Office as Bill's deputy. Hildreth had served in Aden in the mountain artillery. In 1931 he was thrown from his horse which left him with a fused joint and 'so lame that the army proposed that he be invalided out'. Hildreth was made of sterner stuff and transferred in to the RAOC in 1935. He then served at Didcot before being posted to Donnington to serve under de Wolff.

Betty writes how John 'took a tremendous load off Leslie's shoulders'. He knew if he delegated any task to John it would be done quickly, thoroughly and without any risk of mistake. Evidence of John's arrival is in the National Archives where June 1941 was the first monthly *War Diary* of the Director of Warlike Stores in the records. The monthly diaries provide an often-fascinating overview of the work being undertaken, and I refer to them in a number of places.

Many years later, Sir John, as he became, would write Bill's obituary for the *RAOC Gazette* and he recalled those early days:

> At all times and through long and difficult days under bombs and doodlebugs, I worked directly to him. 1 saw him in all moods. Perhaps I thus got to know him as well as anyone ever did and to me, he was a very great man. Without him and his drive and determination I doubt whether the RAOC would exist today. Many things went wrong in those early days, enough certainly to daunt the spirit of a lesser man, but not Bill Williams. Many people, Corps and Regiments wanted to take over for themselves those stores and equipment of their peculiar concern. Some to a limited extent succeeded. It was only Bill Williams's audacious determination, first to put right what had gone wrong and second to hold the Corps together as a successful entity, that prevented the wholesale distribution of our job to others.[4]

The more I look at Hildreth's appointment, the more I think I see the hand of Ronald Weeks who had been appointed Director-General of Army Equipment in March 1941. Within his remit came the RAOC and I am sure that one of his first meetings would have been with Bill. The man, Weeks found, was clearly able but surely overloaded and inadequately supported. Weeks knew from his industrial experience that effective support is vital. To find a right-hand man in the person of John Hildreth made a massive difference.

Gerald Horne, RAOC officer, was appointed Weeks's deputy and on 16 March wrote to Dicky Richards. Horne had been out to visit Richards to gain an understanding of the issues being faced in the Middle East. I tell more of this in Chapter 7. Here it is the first part of Horne's letter that is revealing. He welcomes Weeks's appointment, adding that there could be no one better. Weeks was clearly seen to be a man of great and appropriate experience, with his service in the First World War, his time in the territorials and his hands-on industrial experience at Pilkington. Nevertheless, in his *History of the RAOC*, Fernyhough writes of the disappointment of members of the RAOC that Basil Hill had not been appointed to the post Weeks got. Sir Basil, though, would play a vital role as Colonel Commandant to both the RAOC and the newly formed REME, acting as the glue that perhaps only an illustrious sportsman could bring.

Away from the strides being taken in the depots, a standing committee on army administration had been set up on 6 August 1940, and on 23 August a sub-committee was added to investigate the workings of the departments under the QMG. Ordnance services were reviewed, recommendations made and largely implemented. There remained, though, the ordnance services concerned with motor transport. COD Chilwell, which was regarded as the pioneer of the new ordnance system of accounting, was visited and 'much knowledge of the workings thereof acquired'. Then, in order to review the overall systems for the maintenance and repair of motor transport, the Finch Committee was set up in September 1940 with the particular remit of exploring the benefits and drawbacks of transferring the whole of repair and maintenance from the RASC to the RAOC.[5]

At this point it is important to acknowledge the significant role of the RASC in mechanization. One of its key roles was transport, and, from the mid-point of the First World War, the petrol-powered truck began to take over from the horse-drawn carriage. In Chapter 4, I told of the mobile workshops set up to maintain vehicles and of Wilfred Collings's experience with RASC MT in Basra. By 1940, the RASC operated and maintained half the vehicles in the army; the other half, principally armoured fighting vehicles, were supplied and maintained by the RAOC.

At the same time as the Finch review, a committee under the chairmanship of Sir William Beveridge was set up to study the issue of the acute shortage of skilled mechanical and electrical tradesmen, with the remit of making better use of the army's technical skills. A third review was set up following Ronald Weeks's appointment when he was asked to review the place of the RAOC in the War Office. To me, the existence and demands of three reviews addressing ordnance services go a long way to explain John Hildreth's comments on the pressures facing Bill in those early years of the war.

The first monthly *War Diary*, that for June 1941, reports that funding had been approved for the new WS depot at Bicester which would deal with the whole range of Warlike Stores from MT to small arms. Geoffrey Palmer, another of the Class of '22, was appointed COO and he gathered a small team at premises in Long Eaton to oversee that project. Betty's brother, F.A. Perks, served at Bicester as a lieutenant colonel. I have evidence of Bill's personal involvement in the building of Bicester from a telephone conversation I had whilst researching. Cecil Pinchin of Bicester told me that he remembered, as a young boy, Bill lodging on occasions in their terraced house. It was a place where he could escape. He lodged alongside two young RAF men, whom Cecil remembers were somewhat in awe of him. The three lodged with Cecil's mother; Cecil's father was away each night manning the fire station. Cecil told me of 'this big man with flat hat and shiny boots carrying him around on his shoulders'.

On 3 July, there is the first record of a speech by Bill, which he makes to the officers, men and women of COD Greenford to thank them for the £2,000 they raised for the purchase of a tank. Such fundraising was going on right around the country.

A week later there is an extensive piece in the *Daily Sketch* on 'The Greatest Firm in the World', that is the departments that come under the Quartermaster General, and there are photographs of five men: Sir Walter Venning (QMG), Major General L.H. 'Bill' Williams (Director of Warlike Stores), Major General K.M 'Joe' Body (Director of Ordnance Services), Major General R.M. Weeks (Director of Army Equipment) and Major General M.J.H. Bruce (Director of Mechanical Maintenance). The article covered the huge range of supplies made to the army, most of which at that time were destined for the Middle East and the build-up of the Eighth Army.

The first evidence of Bill's long association with the Worshipful Company of Carmen comes in the form of a lunch menu for 24 July 1941. Significantly he sat next to E.E. Coxhead, who would become a great friend. Coxhead had been Master in 1933 and Bill spoke of this in the speech he gave, proposing the toast to Coxhead as Master in 1944:

> I remember Ernest always telling me the story of the time when he used to carry his master's bag to the Grocers' Hall, and looking lovingly at the City men who were about to enjoy one of the big city luncheons or dinners which were given in those far distant days, and of the pride with which he himself entered the Grocers' Hall in 1933 as the Master of this Company.[6]

The Carmen had no hall of their own and always had to use the halls of other companies. That first luncheon Bill attended was in the Vintners Hall, as was the second on 28 October, when Bill made a speech to which I refer below. The lunch of 6 October 1944 was held at the Tallow Chandlers Hall. I am unsure whether Bill had known that his great-grandfather had been a tallow chandler, albeit in the City of Westminster rather than the City of London.

In a later album there is an article on the Worshipful Company of Carmen in *Everybody's Weekly* of September 1944, tracing its origins from the thirteenth century. It was then the organization that regulated the use of carts in the City of London. The article quotes one record of its activities in 1297 when it ordered that 'no cart serving the City with water, wood or stone should be shod with iron'. It notes that the modern use of rubber on wheels addressed the same issue. Within Bill's archive there is a book on the history of the Carmen which tells rather more, and, in particular, why a busy man like Bill might want to devote time to it. Historically, City Livery companies were the place where masters of trades could meet, and the companies, or rather their Courts of Livery, had powers to regulate the conduct of their trade. The Carmen seem to have been something rather different. As the history states in the first chapter:

> The History of the Worshipful Company of Carmen, a history of incessant struggle to maintain itself in being as a body corporate, is a fascinating record of the persistence

of tradition in the life of the city, and of the never-ending efforts of men to solve economic problems in that life, which have indeed existed from time immemorial.[7]

The Carmen went from being a loose fraternity of men who carted goods to a group aligned with wood-mongers, whose fortunes deteriorated with the coming of coal as a preferred fuel. In 1668, the Carmen became a fellowship, but only with powers of regulation among its members. In the nineteenth century it became a livery company, but one at risk of extinction because of a lack of people wishing to join it. Its emergence, as a force within the City, came when it invited members from the rail and motorized transport companies to join. It began to grow from the first decade of the twentieth century and eventually received its Royal Charter in 1946.

Bill's relationship with the Carmen had a number of purposes. It fostered contacts with the motor industry, essential for the RAOC which needed to be assured of supplies, particularly of spare parts. Surely, it also in part realized his childhood dream of being in the City of London. His speech about Ernest Coxhead has echoes in his own past. This is borne out in the next lunch on 28 October, the menu for which is filed alongside the text of the speech Bill made at the lunch as the reply to the toast of 'The Guests'. In the speech he acknowledges that he is speaking under 'false pretences' since, not only was he a member of the company, but also in his job very much a Carman. He goes on to outline the extensive vehicle-related activities of the RAOC. The speech was reported in the *City Press* of 31 October 1941:

> The Carmen in the army are the people who do this job on the battlefronts. But you Carmen are the people who have to do a lot on the roads and railways of Britain. Incidentally the Ministry of Supply and the War Office have done their best to help you in your problem by allotting a definite proportion of the output of new vehicles and spare parts to civil transport. ...The Carmen of Germany are good. But I believe that the Carmen of Britain – both in and out of the army – will do the better job. We shall in the end go further, our staying power is greater, and we shall go on until victory is ours.[8]

Another theme that stands out in the albums is the record of visits by representatives from Allied nations. On 26 August 1941, there was the first visit by Polish officers to Chilwell which the *Nottingham Journal* reported at length. Bill and the RAOC would have significant involvement with the exiled Polish Army; after the war Bill would be appointed Knight 2nd Class of the Order of Polonia Restituta.

Of greater significance was the lunch given by Lord Beaverbrook, Minister of Supply, on 10 September, for invitees to meet Major General Charles Wesson, Chief of the United States Army Ordnance Corps. It was a lunch for some thirty guests of which Bill was one, but also William Rootes and future prime minister, Harold Macmillan. General Wesson repaid the hospitality with a lunch at Claridge's on 30 September and this was reported by the *Evening Standard* on 1 October. It is worth noting that this was before America entered the war.

There was much else going on. In the war diaries, for the latter part of 1941, the focus was on one issue: that of parts. Reader, before you glaze over, let me explain. Ordnance 'factories', as Bill called them, had the task of not only supplying tanks, guns and radios, but of fitting them with many hundreds of additional parts in order to prepare them for use in the field. The point was simple: if any part was missing, the whole piece of equipment could not be issued. I infer that units were complaining about the slow delivery of what they needed. My suspicion is that Bill and his team had been 'firefighting' such complaints for well over a year. My suspicion is, again, that John Hildreth, with fresh eyes, was saying to Bill, 'Let's explain the problem to the QMG', who would be the recipient of the war diaries. He went further, though, and set up a monthly booklet entitled *DWS News* which was sent to the commanders of all units and so could explain to them what the issues were. The first edition of *DWS News* began with these words:

Never Enough in War
Until the war ends everything we want will be in short supply. The very day it ends, we shall have the most monstrous surplus the army has ever known.[9]

Future editions would outline issues, suggest how units and formations could help and set out the types of equipment available. This last point brings me to a lecture that Bill gave in January 1942 to the officers on the ordnance officers' course. The text is filed with the *War Diary* and is revealing for Bill speaks of the Warlike Stores organization as a business. He, although he doesn't say it, is managing director. He has three deputies: John Hildreth as general manager and then two 'sales' managers, one handling MT and the other the remainder of Warlike Stores.

Betty Perks was appointed Bill's PA in September 1941. I know this because she kept all her pocket diaries and, on Thursday, 11 September, she noted her interview at the War Office. This was followed on 15 September by her record of writing her acceptance of the offered post. She reported to the WO on Monday, 29 September 1941. To find a PA in the person of Betty must have been a lifesaver: she would have known the issues he faced from their frequent conversations on his returns to Chilwell and she also knew how he worked.

Possibly the most significant piece of paper in any of Betty's albums is that of 27 October 1941 in which the QMG declares that the RAOC is now a combatant corps. For many years the Royal Army Ordnance Corps had been classed as non-combatant, so that its officers and men would not be called up to fight. However, for some time, officers and men had fought alongside their brothers in arms; now it was official. It is difficult to assess quite what the impact of this may have been. My overriding impression, from reading various accounts of Ordnance in both world wars up to this point, is that Ordnance was the poor relation. With ordnance men now trained alongside other fighting troops and charged with the defence of their depots, it may have been reasonable to infer that they were more warmly accepted. I suspect though that the proof of the pudding was in the eating, and the experience of seeing better-trained ordnance men in action would have earned respect. Interestingly, Bill's war diaries offer a different viewpoint on the declaration, and it was about time pressure and priorities. Clearly, as combat troops, particularly if called upon to defend a depot from attack by paratroopers, the RAOC men would need regimental military training. This though took them away from their departmental duties which could mean that essential issues of equipment, for example, fell behind. It was a constant balancing act.

On 7 November 1941, Bill visited Old Dalby, Derby and Chilwell to thank the personnel for raising money for tank funds, and he handed the cheques to the Secretary of State for War, Captain Margesson, or to give him his full title, the Rt. Hon. The Viscount Margesson, Secretary of State for War – a member of the War Cabinet. He had served as a captain in the 11th Hussars in the First World War. The visits, which also included General Weeks and the QMG, are recorded extensively with photographs and were reported in the local press. One conversation that might have taken place between Bill and his fellow visitors was progress on the Finch Report.

The Finch Committee would report that December. Reading the minutes, the proposal that the RAOC should take over the supply and maintenance of all vehicles had, not surprisingly, met with stiff resistance from the RASC. A number of senior officers, including General Humphrey Gale (who will reappear in Chapter 8) argued that the RASC had a proven track record of operating and maintaining their own vehicles and, more to the point, they did operate around about half of the vehicles used by the army. Gale also argued that the RAOC workshop system was untested. I have to admit that I find this latter assertion hard to understand, given the long experience in the First World War, the developments in the interwar years and the experience in North Africa.

Bill's colleague, Major General Bruce as Director of Mechanical Maintenance within the RAOC, had, following his appointment, effected a number of changes to improve the effectiveness of the RAOC repair service and he gave evidence to the committee on a number of occasions. Bill attended the committee on 3 September 1941 and argued strongly that 'by making the RAOC responsible for all vehicles, stores and spare parts, a considerable saving both of personnel and of stores holdings could be achieved'. A subcommittee was formed to explore this latter assertion, and the conclusion reached was that the case for savings was unproven.

The Beveridge committee had, meanwhile, reported to the Secretary of State for War that skilled men were to be found in every part of the army, with their skills largely unused and that, in particular, vehicle repair workshops were run by each of the RAOC, RASC and Royal Engineers, adding that those of the RAOC were the most efficient. The committee recommended that:

> Men should be enlisted not for this or that Corps, but into the Army as a single Service. On being received, examined and sorted at centres common to the whole Army, they should be posted from those centres to a definite Corps only

when it is clear that they fit the requirements of those Corps and that any scarce skill posed by them will be turned to full account.[10]

This focus on the best use of skills resulted first in some 50,000 men being combed out of the army and returned to industry where their skills were most needed. The committee's recommendation ran into difficulty in Cabinet with the expectation of stiff opposition from the War Office which would have seen itself criticized for lack of attention to the use of skills. Through Margesson, it argued that it was more important that the army was an effective fighting unit than efficient in civilian terms. The Prime Minister became involved as the report was amended over Christmas.

What happened next becomes clearer from a paper addressed to the Army Council by General Riddell-Webster who was then QMG in the Middle East. One argument that he put forward was to view the RASC as a vehicle operator, with lorries, like the Tank Corps was with tanks. There was no logical reason why the operator should also be the supplier and repairer, these latter tasks being specialist and better focused on a single corps serving the whole army. A further paper in the archives suggests that the three reports – that of the Finch Committee, the Beveridge Committee and Weeks's review of the position of Ordnance in the War Office – should be considered together by the Army Council. It was with them, after all, that the buck stopped and any new structure would need to be operated by them. The beginning of 1942 would see, or rather not see, discussions going on behind closed doors. The Beveridge Report came to Cabinet in January 1942.[11]

COD Greenford, under its COO, Colonel Johnson-Davies, was host to Bill at its first guest night on 1 December 1941. Just one week later, Bill was visiting the Polish Army at its bases in Scotland. That was followed by a guest night on 18 December at Weedon to say au revoir to Colonel McVittie, who had served in Salonika in the First World War and had returned to the RAOC in 1939, but had reached a final retirement.

The conversation would surely have focused upon an event that took place on the other side of the world, on 7 December 1941: the attack on Pearl Harbor by the Japanese. This had the effect of bringing the USA into the war on the side of the Allies both against Japan and Germany. Unlike the situation in the First World War, the US Neutrality Act had prevented US companies from supplying arms up until that point. From then on, the USA would become key to the Allied war effort. The Japanese offensive against Pearl Harbor was followed by attacks on Hong Kong and Singapore where McVittie's son, also an RAOC officer, was taken prisoner along with thousands of others, notwithstanding the RAOC officers and men living up to their new combatant status.[12] The younger McVittie would, after the war, rise to the rank of major general and become a colonel commandant of the Corps in the 1960s.

There are then pages of Christmas cards from nearly all overseas ordnance unit and home bases. A Special Order of the Day, dated 23 December 1941 and signed by Bill, said this:

> Christmas 1941 sees the war spreading to all corners of the world with the never ceasing call for more munitions of war. Tanks, guns, weapons, vehicles, wireless, ammunition, RE and signals stores are being produced in vast quantities at home and in America, with the consequent ever increasing load on the Royal Army Ordnance Corps.
>
> The highest standard of efficiency reached by my depots and War Office branches, together with the devotion to duty shown throughout our organization, is contributing in no small measure to the successful prosecution of the war.
>
> A great deal remains to be done, we are by no means perfect, and there are doubtless mountains ahead which we must face and overcome, but I have absolute confidence in the ability of my magnificent team of officers, other ranks and civilian employees to cope with it all.
>
> I thank you all for your devoted service and the splendid work you have done during the past year and wish you a Happy Christmas and New Year as we can hope to have under present circumstances.[13]

In Betty's album, the new year begins with a visit to the vast marshalling yards at Paddington Station, emphasizing the huge issue of transportation which would soon become an even greater issue with the shortage of rubber consequent on the loss of Malaya to the Japanese. The albums note steps taken to reduce the number of journeys by lorry, ensuring, for example, that lorries never returned empty. On a broader front,

Bill's old friend, Harold Kenward, as president of the Tyre Manufacturers' Conference, played a major role in setting up arrangements to avoid a 'tyre famine' during the war. Kenward would be appointed Distribution Director of Dunlop in 1943, but, before then, would, like so many, suffer a family tragedy when his son, Peter, was killed in the disastrous Dieppe Raid on 19 August 1942.[14]

Betty notes that there had been adverse press comment on the RAOC. The *War Diary* also notes this, and puts it down to disgruntled employees speaking to the press. Of greater concern, in September 1941, an incident had occurred which incurred the wrath of no less a person than Prime Minister, Winston Churchill. A number of tanks had been shipped to the Middle East, but had arrived damaged and, in particular, rusted by the ingress of seawater. Churchill demanded an inquiry. It transpired that the managing director of the manufacturers had asked a major general, over lunch, if the tanks could travel without company engineers, whose job it would have been to ensure proper care maintenance. It seems that the major general had been convinced by the managing director's arguments that he needed every man he could have to ensure production targets were met. Heads would have rolled, but for the untimely death of the major general (who remains unnamed).[15] Churchill, though, remained suspicious of Ordnance Services. Perhaps in defence, the *Picture Post* of 12 March 1942 carried a big piece on the conference of chief ordnance officers at Derby. This was repeated in *The Sphere* and elsewhere. It was headed, 'British Generals Meet to Speed Supply to Russia', and emphasized the excellent work being done, not least in supplying Russia, which had entered the war on the side of the Allies in June 1941 in response to the German offensive against them.

These conferences became a quarterly fixture, and would rotate round the depots. The host for each conference would prepare an information booklet on the depot, and Betty placed a number of these in her albums. Senior officers were encouraged to visit other depots on a regular basis to exchange ideas: continuous improvement was key. It is perhaps an appropriate place to quote words of John Hildreth on Bill's management style:

> He had an amazing ability to know in minute detail the procedure on which our Depots operated, and he knew exactly what each Officer and Man should do and how it

should be done. They were indeed procedures he had drawn up basically before the War for Chilwell. He expected all his Officers to know their subject equally as well as he did. He would not allow any Officer to call for a junior to explain any facet of the functions for which he was responsible. If he did not know the detail himself, he was 'out'!

As Hildreth says, 'there was a war to be won.'[16]

Ever present at the quarterly meetings was Dick Hunt; as Bill wrote many years later,

> he was at my side at the War Office and accompanied me on my visits to the theatres of war. His tact and qualities were such that, when things were wrong (as they often were), he was able to criticize and advise without antagonism.

In 1957, John Hildreth recalled, first, heated words from Hunt when Hunt visited Donnington in 1940, where Hildreth was then serving; the heated words were followed by Hunt laughing, and a compromise being reached. Hildreth went on to say about Hunt:

> From that time, I regarded him with respect, admiration and great affection. He was a tower of strength in those dark and difficult days. His cheery smile, his sense of humour and his deep and realistic knowledge of the Corps and its procedures helped and encouraged many of us through otherwise unsurmountable difficulties. From 1941 until the end of the war, we served together on General Williams' staff in the War Office, he rising to the rank of Colonel. We spent long hours together on many problems – day after day and month after month. I watched, with admiration, the way he tackled things, helped and led his staff, remained imperturbable in the face of doodlebugs, frustrations, long hours and angry seniors, brought humour and laughter into the grimmest situations and always got the job in hand done.[17]

Betty includes an invitation by Lord Nuffield to a lunch at the Savoy on 27 April, very much about relationships with the Ministry of Supply.

I am sure that contact was both frequent and regular. There is some evidence of the cordial nature of the relationships from a letter Bill received to congratulate him on his knighthood:

> The most noisy and hilarious congratulations on your KBE. Whether this award has been given to you for your work in Ordnance or as Chief Publicity Officer of the Army I do not know … when in Washington I saw nothing but your dhobie mark in every Generals' room.

On 7 May 1942, Bill spoke at the passing-out-parade at OCTU Foremark Hall, Derby. RAOC officer and other training had had to move away from Hilsea, because of the disruption by frequent air attack. Leicester was chosen as a base, and Foremark, which, after the war became the home of the preschool to Radley, offered the right sort of accommodation for officer training. Jack Omond, who had shouldered the burden of training from the start of the war, retired and moved to the Home Office, and F.G. Coleman took his place.

On 5 June 1942, there is an invitation to the opening of the officers' mess at Nesscliff, the new ammunition depot built to support Bramley and Corsham. Betty adds the words 'A New Baby' and the COO Colonel B.D.H. Hurst writes in Bill's invitation, 'I hope you can persuade Gen Weeks to come.' There is no record of whether he succeeded. In the photograph, Charles de Wolff can be clearly seen. V.O. Lonsdale, then Deputy Director of Warlike Stores for Ammunition, led the ammunition depots: Bramley, Corsham, Nesscliff, Kineton and Longtown.

On 31 May, Joe Body retired, making Bill the Senior Serving Officer of the RAOC. He was promoted to permanent major general on 28 June 1942. Body's retirement also made room for Clifford Geake to take the rank of temporary major general and fill the office of Director of Ordnance Services (Clothing and Stores). The photograph that follows is of Bill and others enjoying an evening of watching boxing at Greenford. There is then another photograph of a COO's meeting with General Geake now present.

Betty's unmistakeable green ink announces in July 1942, 'The Yankees are here,' with an invitation by the QMG to lunch at Claridge's. On 7 July, the new Senior Serving Officer visited Chilwell for a guest night and this resulted in a lovely cartoon of Venning, Williams, Readman, Hiam, Robinson (on his way to Feltham which had become an RAOC depot with the reallocation of responsibilities with the RASC on the formation of REME) and F.G. Coleman at the new Leicester Training Establishment. The other signatures are less easy to make out, but one is almost certainly ATS, underlining the growing importance of the role of women in Ordnance.

17 July was another red-letter day with the King and Queen visiting Donnington. Charles de Wolff had a number of lovely stories about this visit, but I think what made his day was that, in conjunction with his friend Dr Woods, Bishop of Lichfield, he had arranged the whole visit before Bill and the War Office had been informed.

The *RAOC Gazette* of October 1942 announced the creation of REME.[18] This coincided with Bill's promotion to Controller of Ordnance Services and marked a significant change in the army's approach to mechanical and electrical engineering. Earlier the Beveridge Committee had at last issued its recommendation:

> There should be established, in the Army, a Corps of Mechanical Engineers. The success of the Navy in making use of mechanical engineers is not due solely to the fact that the naval problems are simpler to those of the Army. It is due also to the fact that the Navy has had for so long an engineering branch of high authority and other technical branches specialized in torpedoes and electricity or ordnance. The Navy is machine minded. The Army cannot afford to be less so. The Navy sets engineers to catch, test, train and use engineers. Until the Army gives to mechanical and electrical engineers, as distinct from civil engineers, their appropriate place and influence in the Army system, such engineers are not likely to be caught, tested and trained as well as in the Navy; there is a danger that they will be missed by men whose main interests and duties lie in other fields.[19]

These recommendations had been approved by the Army Council, and a second committee had been charged with implementation. This committee's members included Lieutenant General Ronald Weeks, by then Deputy Chief of the Imperial General Staff; Sir Robert Sinclair, Director of Army Requirements who would go on to become chairman of Imperial Tobacco; and Mr A.W. Dunkley, director of the Anglo-Iranian Oil company and a member of the Petroleum Board. They proposed that the technical elements of the RAOC and RASC, with mechanical and electrical engineers from the Royal Engineers, should be combined in a new specialist corps: the Royal Electrical and Mechanical Engineers (REME), which in future would carry out all major repair work. The RAOC would take over all vehicle and spare part provision. The RASC would focus on its transport operating activities.

One immediate consequence for the RAOC was that the RASC vehicle depot at Feltham was added to the fold. Robbie Robinson was sent down from Derby to introduce RAOC methods. Among those working with him was Stan Preston who would take the expertise he gained out to India in support of the Fourteenth Army in the war against Japan.

The reorganization would impact on the RAOC and RASC in all theatres of war as well as the home base. In the Middle East, the DOS, Harry Whitaker, issued a Special Order in which he said:

> I fully appreciate that those who are being transferred must naturally feel regrets on leaving the Corps with which they have been for so long associated, and I would like to take this opportunity of welcoming all ranks of the Royal Army Service Corps who will be coming over to the Royal Army Ordnance Corps and to say that the RAOC look forward to their cooperation and assistance in tackling the important tasks of storage and issue of MT vehicles and spare parts.
>
> In this work, which is vital to the army, I know that the long experience of officers and men of the Royal Army Service Corps will be a very great value to the Royal Army Ordnance Corps.[20]

The change saw large movements in personnel from the RASC to the RAOC as well as movements from both to REME. Brigadier Baird was one of the RASC officers who came across to the RAOC and he joined an RAOC committee overseeing the transfer. The toast he proposed at Bill's retirement dinner at Chilwell, some years later, is revealing:

> [Bill's] service to the Royal Army Ordnance Corps was known not only to our Empire but to our Allies as well. But it was known to a very few, the personal kindness General Williams had shown to the Officers on the RASC who came to him on merger.

Brigadier Baird's dramatic toast was 'Gentlemen, not the soldier but the man – Bill Williams.'[21]

Longer term, most RAOC depots would have within them REME workshops. In spite of the division into two separate corps, the men on the ground continued to work closely and harmoniously for the duration of the war. Sir Basil Hill added to his role as Colonel Commandant RAOC that of Colonel Commandant REME – roles he held until 1947.

Back once more to Betty's album: there are then two programmes of visits by the QMG, first to Chilwell and then to Weedon. A much bigger visit to Greenford is documented by a number of photographs of different aspects of that depot's work. Kenneth Johnson-Davies was still COO and he produced a booklet for his team of 'a letter of guidance and encouragement from an elder brother to a man just joining the unit'.

The holder of the post of Director of Army Equipment changed from Major General Weeks to Major General Charles Murison, a former gunner who had served in the Royal Field Artillery in the First World War, and there is the programme of his visit to Weedon. Ronald Weeks had been appointed Deputy Chief of the Imperial General Staff, with a seat on the Army Council, to deal with organization and equipment problems. It is clear from Betty's albums that Bill and he kept in touch until Weeks's untimely death in 1960.

There then follow images of tanks at Chilwell, with the caption 'Tanks to Russia'. With the entry of the Soviet Union into the war on the side of the Allies in June 1941, Churchill saw the need to supply them as a high priority. It wasn't only Chilwell; supplies to Russia also came from Donnington.

A book of Longtown's history was produced for an ammunition conference held there on 4 September 1942. Interestingly, Betty then includes a photo of Tiny Stower, an old friend of Bill's from the First World War, now at the West Riding District. The photo shows him with RAOC and REME staff. I suspect that he and Bill found a little time to reminisce.

The next visit programme has Lieutenant General Riddell-Webster as QMG. General Venning had moved to Washington. I infer a good relationship between Bill and the new QMG, stemming, perhaps, from their involvement on the thorny issue of who supplied the vehicles.

On 5 November 1942, Major General L.H. Campbell, Chief of Ordnance for the USA visited Chilwell and then Old Dalby. Campbell had, like Bill, served in the First World War and had made a point of seeing all he could of USA Ordnance in the intervening years. These visits are followed in Betty's album by an article on how the RAOC and REME were working together and then two photographs show the efforts being made in packaging to save shipping. Effective packaging would become a constant theme championed by Bill.

The opening of Bicester is evidenced by an invitation to a guest night on 6 November 1942. In the RAOC archive there is a paper telling the origins of Bicester, and it suggests that Bill and other officers began their search for a suitable site back in the 1930s. Betty's reminiscence of Bill also speaks of a search for a site for a new depot but that Bill had homed in on Swindon as a suitable area with excellent communications.

Bicester had the largest workshop for the repair of tanks anywhere in the UK. With this theme, Bill attended a complimentary dinner to Sir George Usher organized by Lord Nuffield, industrialist Garfield Weston and others. The dinner took place on 19 November and Bill made a short speech in praise of Usher in his role as Director-General of Tank Production. Later in the albums there is a photograph of Usher's home, from which I infer a friendship. Tanks were a major part of Bill's work.

It seems that Christmas cards were set to get bigger for Betty kept an A3-size Christmas card from Bob Hiam at Old Dalby. Other cards, including those from Polish and Russian allies, follow as does a record of a significant event in the history of the RAOC: the leaving of their headquarters at Hilsea.

Bill was awarded a CB in the New Year's Honours List and there is, in his archive, a file of congratulatory letters really from all corners of the army and war establishment in the UK, and USA and Canada. Sir Harold Macintosh, Chairman of the National Savings Movement, wrote on 4 January 1943 with his congratulations, adding, 'I am full of admiration for all that has been achieved at Chilwell; it is a magnificent show, combining as it does the best of industrial and military experience.'

Representatives of the Polish Army visited the Army Equipment Exhibition at Greenford, now commanded by Alfred Goldstein. This visit was followed by an invitation to cocktails with William Rootes and another with the Soviet ambassador. All the time, Bill is building relationships: networking, we would call it now. It is interesting that the relationship with Russia is mirrored in Charles de Wolff's memoirs and was evidently strong. The King and Queen visited Chilwell on 3 March 1943 and Betty writes the names of the Allied nations in a horseshoe above the visit programme which has on its cover the corresponding flags. King Peter of Yugoslavia visited Greenford on 12 March 1943 and Chilwell on 8 May 1943, underlining the role of the RAOC in supplying Allied nations.

Chapter 7

The Middle East and Africa

Dicky Richards didn't have Betty to compile tidy albums of his activities. He did, however, leave to the Imperial War Museum two large boxes of files, which their archivist describes as holding 'low level correspondence'.[1] That may be the case, but by reading them it is possible to gain a sense of the issues he faced. I am hard pressed to decide who had drawn the shorter straw: Bill, with the massive task of building a depot infrastructure which could efficiently and effectively supply a modern army, or Dicky, who had to take a depot structure built in the Middle East for peace, and transform it into something capable of supplying a whole new style of mobile warfare.

The first piece of 'low level correspondence' is a letter from Dicky to his boss, Basil Hill, Controller of Ordnance Services, essentially reporting that he had arrived in his 'old stamping ground'. Surely, Hill had selected him for the job given his previous experience in Egypt. The letter otherwise sets out requests for all manner of equipment. Dicky had gone out with a handful of officers and a few hundred other ranks. His second in command was also one of the Class of '22, Leslie Aste, who later took on the demanding role of Ordnance Officer for the Lines of Communication, which in desert warfare, would stretch to breaking point.

The next letters are to Joe Body as Director of Ordnance Services, and Dicky tells him that the situation was much worse than previously reported with stores being issued as soon as they were received with no possibility of building reserves and indeed a real risk of shortages. It is then clear from a further letter that Major General Verschoyle-Campbell, who, as I tell in Chapter 11, had become DOS India, had visited to explore what needs India could meet. A later note, from the time of El Alamein, sets this out in some detail and the numbers, particularly of uniforms, run into the tens of thousands. Notwithstanding this, local manufacture would become almost a defining feature of ordnance supply in the Middle East.

There are then a good number of letters to one of Bill's deputies, Gerald Horne. I have already mentioned the contents of part of a long handwritten letter from March 1941; the remainder concerned the situation in the Middle East and followed a long liaison visit Horne had made. The first point concerns Dicky's need for a deputy, presumably since Leslie Aste was then running Lines of Communication. He says in the letter that Geoffrey Palmer was only able to serve in the UK (without saying why) and suggesting either Harry Whitaker or Ernest Tankard. The records show that they both went out at some point. Basil Cox and George Heron, also of the Class of '22, were with Whitaker at 5 BOD, the massive depot at Tel-el-Kebir (ten miles from Ismailia) and Tankard, at 4 BOD, Abbassia (near Cairo).

Horne's next point, which he underlines as the most important, is about manpower. The government had stated that it needed to retain skilled men for war production and so the availability of such men, 'will dry up by July'. He ends though by saying, 'hurry up and get the "Wop" out of Africa.'

There are two reports on lessons learned covering two key periods of the campaign. The first from December 1940 to February 1941, against the Italians, highlights, what to me seem like, some pretty basic shortcomings:

- The original plan was for the advance to be by train, as of course it had been in the First World War. This clearly failed to provide enough of what was needed when it was needed, and so an ad hoc system of motor vehicle convoys was introduced. This worked and would be developed further.
- There were no bespoke tank recovery vehicles, and so local purchases were made of powerful lorries and tractors, which were then converted. In time bespoke recovery vehicles began to arrive.
- Water was in short supply; the allocation of water wagons was wholly inadequate. Some 5,000 gallons of distilled water per week was required for vehicle batteries, radio sets and tank radiators.
- As the line of communication to the advancing troops grew, so too did the number of pairs of clean underclothes needed, until ultimately five per man were required. Water shortages made laundering very difficult. The RAOC purchased additional local laundry equipment and were cleaning 90,000 items a week

A series of advances and retreats covering many hundreds of miles characterized the desert war and perhaps typify what a mechanized war was now like.

> In March–April 1941 the Italians, with decisive support of German troops under Rommel, drove the British 370 miles to the east. At the end of 1941 a British offensive forced Axis forces 340 miles back again, but in two stages, from January to February and in June 1942, Rommel reached Alamein after an eastward advance of 570 miles.[2]

By September 1942, Dicky had been promoted major general as Deputy Quartermaster General Army Equipment in the Middle East and Harry Whitaker was signing off war diaries as Director of Ordnance Services.

The second report covers El Alamein (24 October to 20 November 1942) and many of the shortcomings noted in the first report were not repeated. Repair, not least with the presence of REME for the first time, was more effective. There was a focus on salvage, and the report admitted that it simply was not possible to salvage all the scrap metal on the battlefield. Captured German artillery was of such a wide variety, that their supply problems, in getting the right ammunition to the right place, must have been even more challenging than that of the British.

The reports were acted upon to a degree, but, as is clear from a further report by Colonel Dan Warren from Chilwell, who went out for three months to explore why spare parts weren't getting through, tried and tested systems simply were not being applied. This was particularly the case in planning the quantity and type of spare parts needed. There is correspondence between Dicky and Cyril Cansdale on the need to appoint an Inspector RAOC Overseas who would ensure that proper and common systems were in place throughout. This appointment would take another year, but Robbie Robinson was appointed to the post in the run-up to D-Day.

In the period running up to El Alamein, the Commander-in-Chief, General Claude Auchinleck, was coming under pressure to attack Rommel. Much criticism was being levelled at the 'tail of the army' pointing out that, of the 750,000 army personnel, only 100,000 were fighting troops. The remainder were in support, and, of course, these included RAOC and REME. One of Dicky's officers was J.K. Stanford whom Dicky appointed as Inspector of Army Equipment Eighth Army and who later wrote a book entitled *Tail of an Army*. He tells of much wastage, not least in the habit of cannibalizing vehicles for spare parts, but also for wholly inappropriate uses. It seems that from the early days of shortages, army supply had grown 'like topsy'. Stanford writes of Tel-el-Kebir as being a massive hutted camp, all with electric light and neat gardens made from taking soil from the Nile.

In August 1942, General Auchinleck was posted to India as Commander-in-Chief, and General Alexander took command in the Middle East with General Montgomery taking over the Eighth Army. A separate Persia and Iraq Command (PAIC) was formed. In this period there is frequent correspondence between Dicky and Brigadier King who was DDOS Eighth Army. I think that, working with King, was Jim Denniston, something I infer from a sentence written on Denniston's retirement that he had 'marched with the Eighth Army'. A constant issue was the shortage of petrol, meaning that great care was needed when planning journeys to ensure the return journey wasn't wasted. The same was being done in the UK to save rubber. Another veteran of the First World War, Brigadier T.C. Clarke, was DDOS to the First Army in the invasion of French North Africa, where he could bring lessons learned in Norway, but also himself learn lessons for D-Day. Among the Christmas cards filed each year, the name Terry Clarke was ever present. After the war he became a Conservative Member of Parliament.

Betty records a short piece from the *Observer* of 8 November 1942:

> Some talk of Alexander – and rightly. Some of Montgomery – with no less justice. All talk – and duly – of 'all ranks'. But we should not forget, in our tribute to the 'world's great heroes', the men and women who made and delivered 'the stuff'. The 'stuff' was there, abounding. The battle of Egypt had been won in factories and ships and the offices of the QMG as well as in the sands of the desert. Also in America, whose tanks have been the toughest.[3]

Dicky Richards served in the Middle East and North Africa right from the campaign against the Italians through El Alamein to the invasion of French North Africa. The obituaries written on his untimely death in 1961 add rather more about this remarkable man, who surely was as significant on the battlefield as Bill was at the home base.[4] Bill wrote:

A law unto himself, he covered the name of our beloved Corps with glory and helped to give it a reputation throughout the Middle East as the Corps that gets things done regardless of all difficulties and obstacles, and that service to the Army as a whole comes first before everything.

Colonel McEwan, who served with him in North Africa, added:

I had much to do with him from the 'Gates of Egypt' until the Eighth Army reached Messina. He had an unerring instinct as to what was required in the Forward Areas, and with his enthusiasm, concentrated drive and sense of purpose, he imbued others to think and act alike. Deliver the goods at the right time and place, to link with operational plans, was his aim and purpose always.

His frequent visits to the Forward Areas encouraged all. He made promises with assurance. We often suspected that rear installations would encounter greater trials than we did! An optimist, but also a realist. No small canvas for him! Action, combined with pressing buttons A to Z simultaneously.

Brigadier Mayhew, who was COO of 4 BOD before Tankard, had a similar experience, again writing from the early days in Egypt:

All changed with the arrival of General Richards and we very soon learned (sometimes rather painfully) what was expected of us. I think I can truthfully say that Dicky Richards got out of us, veterans and greenhorns alike, all that we were capable of giving. I valued and have never forgotten the lessons he taught me.

He was a hard man but a fair one. He made Middle East Ordnance Services work. We were proud of him and what he did, and the Staff had confidence in him. His methods may have been a little rough and ready at times, but he got the results.

Colonel Meadows, who was Richard's right-hand man from 1940 to 1948, wrote that the best tribute he could pay to him was that he had collected more 'rockets' than anyone else in the Corps, writing, 'I always had the greatest respect and admiration for him, for his gift of seeing ahead, and for his leadership.' He wrote this about Dicky's side-lines in the Middle East: 'His Rubber, Mine Filling and Deceptive Devices Factories, the flow of spares from the South African engineering industry, his Clothing Factory, and the Alexandria installations.' The UK simply did not have the capacity to meet all the supply needs in the Middle East, and so Dicky improvised to great effect.

In February 1943, Dicky returned to the UK to take up the War Office post of Director of Clothing and Stores, previously held by Clifford Geake who was appointed DOS at HQ Middle East Forces and, later that year, as DOS AFHQ North Africa and subsequently moved with it to Italy.

In April 1943, Bill made the first of his visits to the RAOC overseas, in this instance North Africa and Gibraltar. Problems were being reported with shipments and he decided to see for himself what the issues were. Three years later, at his leaving dinner at Donnington, the then Chief Ordnance Officer, Gordon Hardy, another of the Class of '22 who had led the ordnance element of the British Army in Washington, wrote this:

> General Williams is a born traveller – before he was 21, he had lived in East Africa and Malaya. His duties as C.O.S. took him into every theatre of war, and, for at least three months of every year, he visited ordnance installations overseas, both at base and in the field. Only thus could the efficiency of his organization be tested, and the knowledge gained on the spot contributed in no small way to its success.[5]

The travel arrangements were basic. On 3 April, Bill, accompanied by Dick Hunt, took off from Hendon in an American aircraft to Marrakesh via Prestwick. They slept on the steel floor of the aircraft. The itinerary began at Marrakesh where they stayed at the Mamounier Hotel, formerly a sultan's palace. They travelled on to Algiers where Bill met with General Humphrey Gale and, one of the Class of '22, Wallace Pickthall. Gale was then Chief Administrative Officer to General Eisenhower's Allied Forces HQ; Wallace Pickthall was appointed Director of Ordnance Services at Allied HQ and would gain a priceless insight into Allied workings for a seaborne invasion. Alan Fernyhough was serving in North Africa and so could see at first hand the qualities of the man whom he described in his history of the RAOC:

> Brigadier Pickthall was not the man to shirk this task even though he was shrewd enough to know that it was

likely to get him more criticism than credit. He had all the knowledge and experience of Ordnance work necessary for the appointment, but his chief qualification was that he had qualities of personality and character most needed at that time. His transparent honesty, integrity, friendliness and sense of humour ensured the maximum co-operation. The Americans liked and trusted him. Even those who prided themselves on being hard-bitten, 'Vinegar Joe' types found difficulty in keeping up the act. His loyalty to his own staff evoked from them respect, admiration and a determination not to let him down. He lacked that element of ruthlessness which must be available in such a ruthless war. Later in the war he came under severe and unfair criticism, though not from his own Corps, where his qualities were appreciated. He felt this very deeply and his health suffered.[5]

Colonels MacCausland and Warren had flown out from Chilwell to address the specific concerns over shipments and Bill met with them at 1 BOD in Algiers. Over the next ten days, Bill visited just about all the RAOC units in North Africa and spoke to a good many of his officers and men in the field, in workshops, Field Parks and depots. He began at Constantine and the Sixth Army workshops, then Le Kroub where he met with the corps commander, then to First Army HQ and HQ 18th Army Group. More Field Parks followed, and a meeting with the Americans. From there to No. 1 Railhead (handling 200 tons of ammunition a day), V Corps Ordnance Field Park and No. 4 Ordnance Beach Detachment. Eventually he returned to Algiers and a debrief with General Gale. The visit gave Bill both a clear impression of the campaign in North Africa, and also an insight into field experience of seaborne invasion. Bill's trip finished up in Gibraltar where he stayed with the Bishop of Gibraltar and met old friends from his time there in the 1920s.

Operation Torch, which had begun with the Allied landing in French Morocco, finally reached Tunis on 12 May 1943. Ordnance in the Middle East would continue to play a significant role in the war effort. For now, Bill had learned a massive amount from seeing ordnance men in the field at first hand. All the lessons learned would need to be brought to bear in the preparations then beginning to get under way for the Allied landings in northern Europe.

Chapter 8

Bill, Betty and the USA

The significance of the USA to the British war effort cannot be overemphasized. In headline terms it was the Sherman tank, the Jeep and, of course, the DUKW, but also heavy transporters. The phrase 'spare parts' will appear more than once; the US tyre companies were vital, not least with synthetic rubber, but also US battery manufacturers. Bill had learned that personal relationships with his UK suppliers had paid huge dividends. In May 1943 he left for a longer visit to the USA, accompanied by Betty. His primary objective was thus to establish good working relationships. In the back of his mind must have been the experiences of his mentor, Tom Leahy, who had served in Washington towards the end of the First World War, and General Tom Bridges who had been part of the British Mission smoothing the supply of US arms to the Entente countries.

I would say that a question high on his list was just how to make sure that a seaborne invasion had with it the spare parts it would need, clearly identified, protected against damage and readily transported. He went with ideas rather than answers, and was very much there to learn. Betty produced a report of the trip with separate detailed reports of each visit.[1]

His trip followed a visit from 1 November to 21 December 1942 by his friend Sir William Rootes (Chairman Supply Council Ministry of Supply), which itself continued on from a mission led by Sir Oliver Lyttleton (Minister of Production), and which included General Weeks. Sir William Rootes reported on the British organization in Washington, which to a degree mirrored that in London with a Ministry of Supply Mission, headed by Director-General, Sir Walter Venning and a British Army Mission led by Commander, Lieutenant-General G.N. Macready. The issues to emerge were first the sheer volume of army supplies which, when combined with those of Canada, were at least equal to home production. Following this came the question of just how the two

British organizations could work more effectively together. Possibly most telling, Sir William recommended visits to the USA and Canada by British civil servants and industrialists to learn from new American ways, but also trips to the UK by British staff based in the States who all too often found themselves isolated.[2]

Betty compiled two albums, one with pages of her wonderfully personal diary with accompanying photographs and memorabilia.[3] The other has mainly press cuttings.[4] There is a third, given to Bill by his American hosts, largely with group photographs of the people he met.[5] Placed side by side, the albums measure about one foot. It is an astonishing record. The first section of the diary, though, is about the journey, which, as will become clear, is something that today would never be repeated.

Monday, 17th May, 1943

I got up bright and early on the Monday morning, and met the General down in the Hall, all baggage packed and ready for off.

Betty was aged 24, had never been outside the British Isles and had never flown. She admitted to excitement as she and Bill boarded the train at Paddington.

It was a lovely day, the sunshine was brilliant, and I thought how marvellous it was to see our dear old England looking at its best. It was as if England was saying, 'Don't forget I'm very beautiful, you are going abroad for the first time in your life, you will see many beautiful and thrilling sights, but don't forget my beauty.'

The route taken appears now distinctly tortuous. Betty includes in her album diagrams of the route. The train went from Paddington to Bristol Temple Meads, from where they were taken by coach to the airport. I will let Betty describe what happened next:

Here we met Red Tape with a vengeance. We were all weighed with our baggage, then our papers were censored and our passports and ration cards examined. It amused me to see the General as 'Mr Williams', he certainly had not realized that a poor civilian just has to wait his turn. A General can get a bit of priority, and a few red tabs and flashes of gold lace help a lot.

Red Tape survived, they boarded the BOAC 24-seater, which 'seemed very luxurious'.

> We all boarded the plane, gosh my tummy felt strange inside, but it was all so thrilling … then came the take off. I was so afraid of feeling ill at this juncture, and crossed my fingers hard … thank goodness it didn't affect me, I only experienced an enormous excitement.

The first stop was Shannon, and then an afternoon in the grounds of Dunraven Park, 'the prettiest countryside with its ruined castle, just the sort of castle described in fairy tales; the sort of castle that is really a castle'. At 9 pm, they took off again in

> a beautiful seaplane called The Flying Ace. The take-off from water was a delightful sensation one immediately feels the freedom and lightness of the air. … We had to draw the blinds of the plane; I suppose this is in case any of the passengers are spies, and on the look-out for gun sites etc. However, being me, I made up my mind I'd look out, so I peeped behind the blind. We taxied quite a long way on the water, till we came to a good long stretch in the estuary. Then the engines were rev'd up and we speeded up. The plane went at such a speed on the water, before taking off, that the water sprayed up each side like terrific wings, and then – we were up. Peeping though the window blind, I saw the tiny Irish farm houses, looking so sweet and peaceful nestling by the sea shore.

Once fully airborne, Betty observed her fellow passengers:

> I had for some time been watching the other passengers. They are a very mixed crowd. The ones which particularly strike my imagination being a Swedish girl, who is apparently a

newspaper reporter, a young American engineer who seems to rather follow her about, and a middle-aged woman with a French name, who is as English as I am, and who is travelling up to Bathurst to take over a government job at Dakar. She constantly clutches a mandolin which she is taking with her. If I had a very vivid imagination, I should be able to make up a story about her. I'm sure she must be carrying all sorts of secret papers in her silly old mandolin, the care she is taking of it. Then there is a peculiar old Norwegian Doctor, a scientist I think, very intimately concerned with explosives etc. He seems rather intrigued with the Frenchie. There is also on board an American of the worst type, a loud mouthed objectionable man who constantly chews gum. The other passengers are all American, and I'm sure they are all American soldiers or officers returning home on leave or something of the kind. They don't strike me as being particularly impressive.

They landed at Port Lyautey in northern Morocco, which Betty described as 'ugliness itself, the back of beyond'. Betty also had her first experience of American food.

> We had coffee, wheat cakes and maple syrup. Believe me, I didn't like it. We had to drink the coffee out of the most awful cups I have ever seen, about a quarter of an inch thick, without exaggeration.

The General (as I shall call him here, since she does) took matters in hand and found two seats in a car which a couple of American war correspondents (*Chicago Tribune* and *New York Times*) had arranged to take them to Rabat. Betty writes that

> they were most charming men who had accompanied the American forces throughout the North African Campaign. One, Jack Thompson of the Chicago Tribune, had actually made a parachute jump with the Americans in their advance. The driver of the car was an American sailor, how typical of the sailors we see on the films. A real 'tough guy', and so funny in some of the things he said.

She continues:

> The road to Rabat from Port Lyautey was a rough, dusty road, made of stone – no asphalt. Our car – such as it was – was an American army car, an open one with rather un-upholstered seats! However, it did make the journey unforgettable. The scenery and vegetation are also unforgettable. The road was lined with Eucalyptus trees, and the surrounding country so barren in parts, and covered with cactus. The natives had cultivated parts of the ground, and scraped a meagre livelihood from the produce of the poor parched earth. The farmers live in tiny mud huts, which appear to be half ruins. They must be terribly dirty inside, as there is no sanitation or water supply whatsoever. Their water comes from wells.
>
> I was horrified to see the great fat Arab merchants and farmers travelling along the road on the backs of tiny donkeys, kicking them to make them go faster. It is a wonder that the poor little animals can move along at all.
>
> A roadside is always the most interesting place on earth to watch life and the world, and this Moroccan roadway was one of the strangest: it is here where the east and the west meet – on the road, all kinds of methods of transport are seen, donkeys, lorries, horses, cars, and even carriages and pairs.
>
> Before reaching Rabat, we drove through the ancient Moorish town of Sale (pronounced Sally). This is a city of the ancient days of pirates and hidden treasure.

Rabat itself was initially 'unimpressive', however, as they drove further into the town through the French residential quarter, Betty delighted in the modern-style houses 'painted cream or white with roofs some red, some green and some blue. The gardens were beautiful, filled with lovely shrubs, Bougainvillea and Morning Glory. Stately palm trees line the roads, and, in colour and sunlight, one can imagine fairyland'.

It was obviously a wonderful trip, for Betty writes, 'however far I travel in this world, and I hope I shall be fortunate enough to travel far and wide [as indeed she was], I don't think I shall ever forget my first glimpse of a truly Arab quarter.' She continued with her description:

> What variety of wares were being sold in that busy eastern street: shoes, sweets, vegetables, clothes, meat, baskets and brassware ... we saw a tailor in his shop, sitting cross legged sewing some poor soul's ragged coat, trying to make it look respectable again. The shoe-maker was there busily stitching at his goatskin sandals ... all of them, whatever trade they followed, were bargaining with their customers ... The man I shall never forget in this market was a tall wiry Arab – a water-carrier – who ran hither and thither through the streets with a goat-skin full of water on his back, selling his water to the buyers. This was almost a Biblical scene, the only thing which made it modern was the presence of Europeans.

The journey back to the boat was hot and tortuous, but 'the General had managed to scrounge some oranges on shore, so we made pigs of ourselves in the plane with them before going to bed'. The flight was again overnight to Bathurst in the Gambia. This time the General decided to plan ahead and so contacted the British Army Area commander, Brigadier Venning, a cousin of Sir Walter Venning whom Bill would meet with in Washington. Venning ensured an agreeable short stay which clearly made an impression, for Betty wrote:

> But the most delightful thing to me, in spite of all the wonderful and strange things I have seen [she had seen a monkey run across the road in front of their car just after passing through a mangrove swamp 'most eerie, snarled and twisted trees growing in a 'Walt Disney' fashion] was to see England, or part of it in this outpost of Empire. The English men, the troops, the organization and the efficiency of our Colonial organization is wonderful. How proud I am to be English, to see fine clean English boys of the Royal West African Frontier Force.

Venning also gave Betty a rose from his garden when they left. The rose, pressed, is in the album.

I think she was proud too of the well-run ordnance depot with Gambians and Englishmen working effectively side by side in the unbearable heat. She was entranced by the scenery:

> Before we left to return to the air-base, we walked onto the balcony overlooking the sea. What a lovely sight it was. On each side of us the cliffs formed a beautiful bay, and below the cliffs, which were covered with a brownish-yellowish grass, stretched the beautiful golden sand. We often read books describing sand as 'golden', but I have always thought sand to be a most uninteresting colour. The sand there along the water's edge was truly golden, it had that tinge of pink in it which gold sometimes has. If only I could paint, to show the browny cliffs, the golden sand, the clear green sea edged with white foam surf, and the clear azure blue sky, what a picture it would make. It is a picture I will always remember.

There is a wonderful notebook kept by an RAOC driver in the North African campaign which has his handwriting on the left-hand pages and his watercolours showing the scenery on the right. It is in the Imperial War Museum and is a delight.[6]

A longer flight this time took them across the Atlantic to Trinidad. Betty once again peeped round the window blinds to see destroyers and aircraft carriers floating proudly in the harbour. The land 'bathed in the early morning sunlight, the sun glistening on the sea, giving it the lights and fires of a sapphire'.

'Would the General object to Government House being told of his arrival?' they were asked. Indeed, not! First, though, the business of registering at the Queen's Hotel in Port of Spain and then breakfast. I have to smile at the next passage knowing, as I do, the importance for my mother of regular meals. A bath and a freshen-up and then

> what a lovely breakfast room. It had no outer walls, the roof was supported by pillars, and the outer walls were just lovely shady verandas. Everything had been done to make the hotel as cool and as habitable as possible in the terrific heat of the island. Breakfast began with Pau Pau, a most

peculiar fruit, something like melon, then we had fried egg
and bacon and then of all things, bananas!

There was then the drive through Port of Spain:

> We could see evidences of the early days of Port of Spain,
> the days when it was a pirate stronghold. Old buildings
> dating back to 1785, guarded by cannon. This part of the
> town too was full of life, busy, business-like and different
> in every way to the more modern shopping centre. Daddy
> would have liked it down here, some good old Harbour
> smells and little ships being loaded up. The spirits of the
> good old pirates still live there, I am sure.

Lunch at Government House with Sir Bede and Lady Clifford was
clearly a delight. The dining room was

> lovely, very spacious, and overlooked beautiful rolling
> lawns, and magnificent trees. On the walls hung two
> beautiful pictures, one of King George V and one of
> Queen Mary. These pictures reminded me of the great
> tradition there is still in the British Empire. The King is
> the head, and he appoints his representatives to administer
> his colonies. I feel very proud when I think back on that
> day in Trinidad.

The General was shown the island's defences. Betty continues:

> When our business was finished, we drove by car through
> the hinterland of the town. How lovely it was, climbing all
> the time through the densely wooded hills. We saw banana
> trees, mango trees, pau-pau trees, palm trees of every
> description, including the Royal Palm cocoa nut palm.
> I saw cocoa beans growing, oranges, limes and lemons.
> I saw breadfruit trees and in fact all the tropical vegetation
> you can think of. The colours, the sounds, and sweet scent
> are never to be forgotten. Greens, yellows, browns, reds,
> the swish of the palm leaves and suddenly the sound of

the Cigale beetle, a shrill whistle caused by the little insect blowing up its tummy and then scratching at it with all its might.

Before leaving, Betty was presented with two gifts: a spray of orchids and a 'lovely bunch of bananas'. Back on the plane, 'my bananas were unfortunately distributed round all the passengers, so I only had two! I felt like crying'.

The next stop was New York and Betty wrote of her thoughts as the plane approached:

> I opened my eyes that morning and suddenly realized that in a few hours I would be in New York, America. America, the country I had longed to visit ever since I have been old enough to long to visit anywhere; America, the land of skyscrapers, the Rockies, cowboys and Indians, the land of nightclubs and gold rushes.

Imagine, then, her disappointment when they landed at the sea-plane base at La Guardia, with no view of the New York skyline. It wasn't all bad for, on reaching the terminal building, Mr Williams and Miss Perks were called forward to have passports and baggage checked over. Then they were met by two brigadiers, 'Nobby' Clark and, old friend from the Class of '22, Gordon Hardy. 'There they stood, as happy as sand-boys seeing their chief ... as tickled pink as two schoolboys seeing a couple of faces from dear old Home'.

'Both Brigadiers had a big fight in stopping a huge crowd of Newspaper men from mobbing the General'. Betty later learned the techniques of how to handle the press, for they would be ever-present on the tour.

A 40 horse-power Buick took them into New York:

> We eventually drove into the busy part of the city, past blocks of flats and tenement buildings, just like the pictures, and then into the heart, down the enormously wide streets, glittering with neon signs, crowded with people, and lined with shops full of the loveliest things, cinemas, restaurants, and, what was most amazing, decorated by the most colourful taxicabs one could ever imagine. They were green, blue, indigo,

yellow, orange and red – in fact the colours of the rainbow! I thought they were fine, they add colour to the streets, but of course take away any dignity the city might possess.

We passed Times Square, the American equivalent of our Piccadilly Circus, teeming with people; then by 42nd Street, Broadway as we all call it; by Fifth Avenue, where all the wonderful shops are. All the buildings in the heart of the city are skyscrapers, tall, majestic, a little bit frightening in all their splendour. The streets are so wide, however, that the buildings look in keeping. We passed by America's Hyde Park, Central Park, and eventually came to 7th Avenue, the Hotel Avenue, and what hotels, enormous places, every one of them a Palace in its own right.

They stayed at the Pennsylvania Hotel, opposite Penn Central Station:

Stepping out of the car into the busy street, I felt quite dazzled by it all: the bright lights in the shop windows, the colourful taxis, the beautiful women, in fact by everything. It was as if we had been thrown right off the earth into another world.

The hotel was so different to anything I had ever seen before, so light, so big, so full of life and colour, an enormous lounge in the centre of which masses of flowers and shrubs were growing in cleverly concealed pots. People, people everywhere, coming and going, chatting, laughing, smoking, drinking. I felt a bit like one of the 'orphans in the storm', coming from a rather drab and war-weary England, into this land of light and laughter.

The General was straight to work, discussing with Hardy the issues they faced in Washington. Food, though, was never far away and I shall let Betty describe dinner at The Barberry Room owned by the 'high-class bootlegger' Jim Moriarty:

We had avocado pears, stuffed with a peculiar but very tasty mixture of crab meat and vegetable, followed by an amazing steak – not a steak as we know it or a fillet steak – but a huge chunk of meat roasted, and carved into portions like a joint.

Then came the unforgettable, they call it Angels Food, and it certainly tastes like it. It is a lovely fresh fruit salad, all kinds of fruits, orange, grapefruit, melon, apples, cherries, pineapple, in fact everything, then dressed with just a touch of Kirsch, a very fiery liquor! but oh boy! wasn't it good. Even the coffee was 'different', a small cup of black coffee, into which a spot of brandy is poured and a little nutmeg grated in. I have never tasted anything as good. Jim Moriarty, being a bit of a connoisseur, produced a lovely bottle of claret to drink with the meal, followed by some lovely liqueurs all-round. To use some American slang 'we did ourselves proud, buddy!'

Then came the bill paying.

The Brigadiers [Betty, in her notes, begins to refer to them as the Boys] insisted that it was all on them, but the bill came along minus any charge for the wines. On enquiry we were told these were on Mr Moriarty. We heard the waiters talking about it to themselves, and one witty bounder said to his pal, 'Say, that's just a bit of lease-lend.'

There was a little time to wonder at the New York shops, before taking the train to Washington, and Betty stood in awe at both Penn Central and Washington stations. Once in Washington, the General was straight into a meeting with General Anderson, the Deputy Quartermaster General (DQMG). Mr Churchill was there at the same time, 'but unfortunately we didn't see him'.

They took a stroll after dinner, and Betty wrote:

There doesn't seem to be a war in America, no fear of air-raids, plenty of fruit and really good food, enormous newspapers, each about forty pages, instead of the two-page English ones. They are so far away from it all.

After breakfast, Betty had this to say:

American tea is terrible stuff. Instead of warming the teapot, putting the desired quantity of loose tea leaves into the pot, and pouring freshly boiled and still boiling water on it, they bring onto the table a cup of hot water with a small muslin bag containing about a teaspoon full of tea, and expect you to immerse the teabag in the hot water and get tea. You can imagine what the result is.

On 24 May 1943, Betty and the General went to the Pentagon, for the General to meet his opposite number, General Campbell, and for Betty to arrange with Campbell's PA the itinerary for the General's tour. Betty was clearly impressed with the Pentagon, and just a little jealous of her opposite number's office accommodation:

> I must say the Pentagon is pretty good. The offices themselves are most luxurious. The PA's room was furnished with beautiful walnut furniture, a lovely thick green carpet and was about 20' by 16' in size. When I compared it, in my mind, with my funny little cubbyhole of the War Office, I felt a bit sick! That is one thing I do like about the Americans, they don't do things by halves, like we do. They go 'all out' on a thing.

Sir Walter Venning organized a cocktail party for Bill to meet many high-ranking American officers. Betty was not invited.

All the time that the General was in meetings, Betty and Captain Darby, Brigadier Hardy's PA, were working on the detailed programme for the trip. It runs to nine pages and covers some five weeks. It is in the album and I follow it.

A couple of days later, they set off, first stop Aberdeen, Maryland, in a Lockheed Lodestar which had been loaned to them for the tour by General Campbell. The Aberdeen Proving Ground was impressive, and they saw all manner of weapon demonstrated. This visit prompted the first of a great deal of newspaper coverage of the visit. *The Pittsburgh Post Gazette* of 12 June declared:

> *Briton Gets Some Yankee Pointers*
>
> Major General Charles T. Harris Jr, Commandant of the Aberdeen Proving Ground, points out to Major General L.H. Williams, British Army Ordnance Chief, some of the fine points of a 90mm gun. General Williams is in the

United States repaying a recent inspection visit to England by Major General Levin H. Campbell, American Chief of Ordnance.

The General took the salute at a march-past of 10,000 men from the nearby training school which he also visited; he made a speech telling them what an important job they were doing. They then flew the 70 miles to Philadelphia, 'quite different from Washington or New York, still an "old town"'. A police escort was provided from the airport. The hotel they stayed in was the Bellevue on Board Street, a 'terrific building'; Betty was amazed to hear it was forty-two years old, 'it is quite as good as our best hotels in England'.

The Chester Tank Depot run by Ford (dealing with tank repair, modification and preparation for shipment), the US Signals Corps HQ and the Frankford Arsenal (the oldest in the US Army dating from 1815) occupied the next day, followed by a train journey to New Brunswick and the Raritan Arsenal, a depot storing small arms, artillery and ammunition. All the time Betty's report picks up on detail for action, mostly with a focus on packaging.

Then back to New York and a weekend break in Katonah, New England. Sir Harold Mackintosh had introduced Bill to Mr Sturtevant who lived in a 'delightful house of the colonial style'. Betty had compiled a list of contacts of influential Americans from introductions provided by Sir William Rootes and many others, including Mackintosh. There were other weekend guests, and a very enjoyable time was had. The Sturtevants would become good friends. Betty did have a little time on her own and tuned in to the wireless:

> The Americans have a most peculiar system for broadcasts. Firstly, there is no licensing fee, and all the programs are 'sponsored' or in other words financed by some commercial firm such as the Palmolive soap people or Ovaltine etc. The news bulletins are given by a group of men, who just give their own opinion about the news. There is no strict control as there is in England. I found it a very annoying system; I much prefer the BBC. How I long to hear an English voice.

The weekend was followed by an inspection of the New York port of embarkation. Next came Canada and the Longue Point Depot specially built to handle stores from Canadian Production which had been bought by the Allies … it should have been an efficient place … but it was not … we gathered that a number of issues prevented 'its easy and smooth running management'.

From Betty's report, it seems that the depot was full of spare parts, but with inadequate records of what they were. Bill met a number of senior officials including Major General J.V. Young, his opposite number, to urge action to identify and release these vital supplies.

Travel to Toronto by train was 'terrible', hot, and they were only just able to find seats. On arrival, all was forgotten as they were met by a railway official whom Betty thought must have 'mistaken them for the King and Queen'. The serious work was at General Motors of Canada which Bill found very receptive to suggestions. As elsewhere, they were taken to the boss's home and entertained regally.

Niagara came next, in a Ford Lincoln, Betty writing, 'I had always imagined that the Niagara Falls would be wonderful, but I had not visualized anything as wonderful as this.'

Back to the USA, Cleveland and Mr Hoover, 'rather elderly, but very shrewd and wise'. He had under his care some eighty children evacuees from England living with employees of the Hoover Company. He provided a Buick which took the General and Betty to the rubber plants at Akron: the Goodrich Tyre Co., Goodyear and the General Rubber Company, each of which was producing weapons in addition to tyres. Finally, a tour round the Hoover plant itself which had redirected its production to all kinds of sub-assemblies for the war effort.

The *Akron Beacon Journal* picked up on Betty's presence: 'Girl is aide-de-camp to visiting army officer'. The article goes on to quote Bill as saying, 'Akron-built treads for half-tracks are not only superior to anything the Nazis have developed but out-do the corresponding product of the English.'

Next stop, Detroit, but in an old converted Douglas bomber. The General had a meeting with General Glancy (a former industrialist), visited General Motors and saw their new amphibian truck. The following day was Chrysler and the Tank Arsenal where both the General and Betty were given a ride in a Sherman tank and where Bill was impressed by their packaging procedures.

There then came a 'heyday' of all days with a visit to the Ford organization: 'The River Rouge plant alone was enormous ... the whole of the manufacturing of a car is done in this one plant.' There was then the Willow Run bomber plant, but then a summons for the General to return to Washington to meet with General Somervell, US Commanding General, Services of Supply. Of the Ford Willow Run bomber plant, *The Detroit Free Press* reported Bill as saying it was the 'most inspiring sight that I've ever seen'.

Sunday, 13 June 1943 was the General's fifty-second birthday, and marked by a stiff fight with the Americans over the question of spare parts. Betty produced a detailed note of the meeting which set out what was, in effect, the packaging blueprint for D-Day – the Carton Unit scheme. The focus was on the soldier in the field unit receiving the spare parts; packing was to be in logical sets, in the order of likely needs, in packaging that could withstand inevitable rough handling, clearly and indelibly labelled, and packed in cases not exceeding 70 pounds (unless the spare itself weighed more – such as a complete engine).

The return to Washington meant more meetings between Bill and British Generals Venning and Macready on the subject of spares, and Betty gained the impression that they were not being supportive of Bill's position. A further meeting seemed to resolve matters, and the meeting with General Somervell was swift and amicable.

Back to Detroit and Champion Sparking Plugs. Then on to Kentucky and the Indiana Ordnance Ammunition Works. From there, to the Tank Training Centre at Fort Knox and some US Ordnance field installations, and the Rock Island Arsenal by the Mississippi. On to Salt Lake City and then to San Francisco, the Ford plant, the port of embarkation and the Richmond Tank Depot. Betty recalled 'the sun setting behind the hills and the water between the arms of the harbour made dazzling sheets of flaming gold. Now I know why it is called the Golden Gates.' Betty clearly fell in love with this 'Queen of Cities'.

The next stop was Los Angeles, and a press conference and trip to the port of embarkation. This was as nothing compared to the visit to the Warner Brothers Studios. Betty, as a child and a teenager, had been film-mad, 'I never dreamed I would be able to see it all for myself.' At the studio that day were Ingrid Bergman and Flora Robson; sadly, for Betty, Errol Flynn was not working that day. He did though sign a photograph for her. The following day at MGM, she saw Gladys Cooper.

Flying on from Los Angeles, they crossed over the Grand Canyon, 'a great chasm, full of colour and beauty'. On to Fort Worth, where the General found that a poor tired newspaper man had been waiting to interview him. Although then midnight, he gave an interview. 'Just like him – always thinking of the "other fellow".' On to New Orleans and another port of embarkation, before returning to Washington and a whole series of meetings.

They arrived home on 2 July. The punishing schedule had Betty laid up ill more than once, and Bill had been in for a check-up at the Ford hospital. Nevertheless, mission accomplished. Betty's report of the whole trip did not appear until December, by which time most action points had been addressed.

Chapter 9

D-Day Before and After

In February 1943, Dicky Richards returned from the Middle East to take up the position of Director of Clothing and Stores. He was also to chair a Standing Committee on Ordnance Field Operations, bringing his experiences of mobile warfare. He would work with Brigadier Cyril Cansdale, a fellow Class of '22, who became Bill's Deputy Controller of Ordnance Services with line responsibility for Field Operations. These key changes were made in preparation for D-Day.

However, as I believe will become clear from Bill's Christmas message to the Corps at the end of 1944, the RAOC job was the supply of a two-pronged invasion of Continental Europe: the Eighth Army fighting its way up through Italy, and the 21st Army Group carrying out the D-Day landings and then fighting its way across northern France to Germany. Bill had many talented soldiers at his command; the key was to choose the right people for the right job. John Hildreth recalled that he had

> found it exhilarating to serve someone who really knew his job and mine, and most other people's, and who also knew what he wanted done, how and by when. He was a great leader, probably the greatest the Corps has known. Some found him harsh and he had to be, for we were at war and only the best was good enough. But he was never unfair. I saw at first hand many instances when Officers, who had shown themselves inefficient or incapable in a specific job, were given another chance in the same rank on different work. Most of them accepted the challenge and succeeded for, as Bill Williams used to say, he always looked for the best in everyone. He was always prepared to listen, and it was one of his maxims that, no matter how much you knew yourself, you could always learn something from somebody else.[1]

It can only be inference, but I suspect that Bill, in conjunction with the QMG, who had served with Dicky in the Middle East, decided that they needed Richards' drive for D-Day and that Clifford Geake's talents could be better used in the Middle East and then in Italy. As was clear in Geako's letter to Bill on his retirement, there were no hard feelings. Neither was it a question of one being better than the other; it was picking the right man for the right job.

Brigadier Neville Swiney, also of the Class of '22, had been in the initial team planning for D-Day, but his place was taken by Brigadier Jim Denniston with Lancelot Cutforth as second in command. I found a photograph from 1943 showing Denniston sitting in the middle of the front row of the staff of the RAOC Training Establishment at Leicester. I suspect it was here where his working relationship with Cutters had begun; they would make a formidable team. Like Geako, Neville Swiney was posted to the Middle East. Swiney's appointment, with its focus on the Eighth Army, was thus every bit as important as Denniston's; again, it was horses for courses. Fernyhough points to the different characters of Richards and Geake: one the go-getter and the other the diplomat and conciliator.[2] It is clear to me, also, that for Bill there were two wars to worry about. Victory in Europe, for which all the planning was reaching a conclusion, but also Victory in Japan for which planning was a work in progress, and for which the Middle East would play a key part.

So, of that core group, as I termed it, in the Class of '22, Dicky Richards was now working alongside Bill as Director of Clothing and Stores, Cyril Cansdale was directing Field Operations, and Charles de Wolff and Alfred Goldstein were running the key armament depots. Geoffrey Palmer was running the massive all-purpose depot at Bicester, and Gordon Hardy was in the States hurrying spares. 'Picky' Pickthall had returned, sick, from Africa and was serving with Northern Command, but all the lessons he had learned had been passed on.

Less than a week after arriving home from the USA, on 8 July, Bill chaired the Central Depots Co-ordination Committee meeting at Bicester. It is interesting that all the photographs of these meetings have twenty or so middle-aged men and one twentysomething woman. Betty was an ever-present source of support.

On 14 July, Bill attended a lunch at the Goldsmiths Company, wearing his Carmen hat. I feel sure that he would have spoken of his American trip; he would have been circumspect about the massive preparations that were already under way for the invasion of northern France. It is likely he would have remained silent on another trip that was being planned, to India, in preparation for a land war in the Far East. I write of that trip in Chapter 11.

Bill's *War Diary* records the extensive preparation in hand for the invasion. The most serious issue facing all depots was an acute shortage of manpower. The three armed services were seeking able men and women, as were the war industries. The RAOC already understood the pool of talent within the ranks of the ATS. This was exploited further by recruiting women to undertake technical ordnance duties, for example, with ammunition, but also in waterproofing vehicles ready for an amphibious landing. Bob Hiam had written a report on the way depots and the field organization should work more closely together, and steps were taken to implement its recommendations. A great deal of covered space would be needed for waterproofing work, and RAOC construction units were set up to erect Romney huts. Existing space was also requisitioned, for example, at the White City Stadium.

Preparations for D-Day were being made across the nation, and a cutting of 31 July 1943 from the *Derby Evening Telegraph* showed pupils from Bemrose College packing MT spares. Armed with the Carton Unit scheme agreed on the US trip, a massive exercise in packing was under way: some 300 million items had to be packed and there simply were not enough pairs of hands in the depots. Everyone joined in from WI groups to off-duty firemen. Training was a key part and, on 20 August, Bill took the salute once again at Foremark where D-Day training was well in hand. Also in August 1943, the Queen visited COD Greenford, which was then under the command of Alfred Goldstein preparing for the key role it would have in supplying the D-Day force. Her Majesty was accompanied by the Princess Royal and took particular interest in meeting the many ATS working there.

An invitation by the Lord Mayor of London to lunch at the Mansion House on 16 September 1943 must have drummed up memories of Bill's chance meeting with Churchill at the same venue all those years before. Also present at the lunch was C.R. Attlee, the deputy prime minister.

The new ammunition depot at Nesscliff had featured before, but Betty now includes the 'New Boys Guide', giving all the essential detail. Photographs of the visit follow, with the wonderful one of Bill and Dicky off duty in party hats.

For Bill and Dick Hunt, the autumn of 1943 was taken up in a visit to India which I describe in Chapter 11. Betty did not accompany them. On their return, the new year started with a visit to Donnington, with the QMG, an invitation from the Soviet ambassador and a visit to the *Daily Mail*. All over the country, preparations were under way for the invasion.

Bill made a second visit to the USA from 20 March until April 1944. In addition to Betty's diary of the trip, a further piece of evidence underlines both its purpose and importance. John Hildreth's obituary of Bill had this to say:

> When, before Normandy, spares for American tanks could not be obtained from that country because the policy there was to provide tanks in priority over spares, he went there and talked to the factory workers of our difficulties in maintaining their tanks in battle. He asked for, and got, additional production effort from the workers which, not only maintained the output of tanks, but gave us the spares as well. He is reputed while over there to have persuaded Mr. Kaiser to build an extra ship to carry the spares over in and I can well believe that he did, too.[3]

They set out on 20 March 1944 and Betty, now the seasoned traveller, writes that 'it was the old, old story, a long wait. The weather [at Hendon] was a bit dull, and I expect that was holding operations up a bit'. En route to Prestwick, it was not the secretive peeping through the window blinds, but being given 'very interesting and important briefs' to read by the General.

'The "no females" rule still prevails at Prestwick', so Betty ate supper alone in a little back room. Then more waiting until a 'kind' airport staff member cooked her some breakfast at about midnight. They eventually took off at 1 a.m. heading for the Azores. They hit bad weather and the pilot rerouted to Casablanca. Betty delighted, as before, in seeing 'white houses and little square fields which the natives were trying to cultivate'. On landing they made the mistake of declining the offer of American food, for, in Casablanca itself, all the restaurants had sold out. They ended up in the Union Jack Club, 'run by a group of French women and filthy'!

Back to the airport, only to find a further delay and so to the best hotel, the Transatlantique. Again, Betty puts it in a nutshell, 'if that was the best, heaven only knows what the worst is like'. They made the most of it by visiting those parts of the city that weren't out of bounds to service personnel, and then dining at the American Officers' Club where 'the General renewed a number of acquaintances'. The next day they were delayed yet again, and Betty watched the life of the city, the place where east meets west:

> A group of American soldiers fooling about outside the HQ office block. A tiny, dirty, hungry Arab boy, scuffling around them, being boot black. They stood there, entirely unaware of their surroundings. Then the traffic, first a huge American army lorry came trundling along the dirty, smelly streets, that might be followed by a horse and carriage, and following along behind a filthy fat old Arab on a tiny donkey.[4]

The next day, they did manage to take off for the Azores. They landed at 5.30 p.m. on a tracked landing ground: 'the land had been levelled and track laid by our engineers in an incredibly short space of time after Portugal's agreement to our using their islands as our bases'. A meal in an American mess: 'I think the word mess must have originated in America! The food they produce is just a mess – or so it seems to me.'

A breath of fresh air came from a gallant RAF officer who escorted them to tea with Air Vice-Marshal Bromet. 'Here we had tea! What a luxury, what a joy! How strange it is that a little thing like that can mean so much for an Englishwoman away from England.'

They took off again and slept for a short period until woken to take oxygen as the plane had to gain height to avoid bad weather. Landing at Newfoundland, the mess was 'tip-top', as was the whiskey and soda which 'went down well'. Airborne again, they flew over the wild desolation of Labrador and eventually circled for what seemed like an hour over New York, where 'we had some good fellows for pilots and we made a perfect landing' at La Guarda.

Am I allowed to laugh at the difference a year makes, for, now, Betty writes, 'I must admit I do like New York. It has a strange fascination and charm. It is like London, the very essence of life.'

They travelled by train to Washington and met up again with the Brigadiers Hardy and Clark. 'It was good to see them again. I bet they felt it even more than we did, when they thought that we had been in dear old England, such a short time ago.'

The next day the routine started, meetings with the brigadiers and then General Anderson, Sir Walter Venning and General Macready. Dinner in Hogates seafood restaurant: 'Boy oh boy, what a feed!' Betty mentions Mrs Reynolds as being kind to her. This, I think, was Digger Reynolds's wife, Jane, whom my sister and I met when we visited Majorca as children. She and Digger had retired there. The following day was Saturday, and was spent in meetings at the Pentagon, with Generals George (Chief of US Air Transport Command), Somervell, Clay and Campbell. Sunday was a half-day off and a visit to George Washington's home. The remainder was final planning for the tour. Dinner was a late snack at a drug store.

The itinerary for the following week shows that it was spent in Detroit with meetings, first with the Chief of Ordnance Detroit, and then with motor manufacturers to urge the production of vital spare parts; so Ford (with Henry Ford II), General Motors, Chrysler and Continental. The spare parts which had been shipped had arrived without vital, fast-moving items, and beach maintenance packs, which would be needed on the Normandy beaches, were lying incomplete. There was also a particular shortage of spares for Sherman tanks such that tanks were being lined up unrepaired; the same was the case with Diamond T Mack transporters, essential for the advance across northern France. I believe that the message was clearly received. The week ended with a meeting at the Detroit Scales branch where Bill expressed horror in learning that the Carton Unit scheme had not been implemented in Canada, because of failure of communication. He instructed that immediate steps be taken.

The weekend was spent with the Hoovers at Akron, with visits to follow at the tyre manufacturers, Firestone and Goodrich. Then back to Washington for more meetings, and on to Philadelphia and Ordnance Chief Jared Ingersoll (whose wife Agnes became my godmother). There were visits to the Chester Tank Depot and Exide Battery Plant. The weekend offered an opportunity to witness the Easter Parade on 5th Avenue, of which Betty wrote: 'New York and His Wife going to church.' After Easter, it was back to work with a meeting with Sir Ashley

Sparks of Cunard; there was little point in urging the production of spares if they couldn't be shipped. Back to Washington and an exhibition of jungle equipment, giving more than an eye to the war in the Far East which would follow on from victory in Europe.

They returned to the UK on 15 April, landing at Prestwick at 3.30 p.m. to find everything in hand. Bill had chosen his team and would have trusted them to get on with the job. Shortly before D-Day, the BBC broadcast a piece by journalist, Hugh Searight, who tells the story of Bill's overseas visits, but also the major role played by volunteers in packing all that was needed for D-Day. Close working with the American allies clearly mattered, for there is a photograph of a presentation box of glasses given to Eisenhower's Chief of Staff, General Beddell-Smith. There is then his letter of thanks.

On 23 May 1944, some fifty officers of the RAOC and the Canadian Ordnance Corps gathered in the Debating Hall of the Royal Empire Society in London to listen to Bill, Dicky Richards, the QMG and Brigadier Jim Denniston. In Chapter 1, I quoted some of what Denniston said. Here are some short extracts from the other speeches.

From Bill:

> I think we have a well developed team spirit not only within our field units, but between units and formations, between the War Office and your headquarters, and between the main base element in the organization and the field force. I'm sure that the home-depot organization in this country and the ammunition central depots will give you their very best, will always stand firmly behind you, resolved to give you the most efficient and most speedy service possible.

Dicky added:

> For those of you who have operated in the Middle East, North Africa and the Central Mediterranean, don't forget that you have shorter lines of communication. We control the sea. Our aircraft, I am confident, will control the air, and with this cover, stores will have every chance of getting to you quickly.

The QMG, General Sir Thomas Riddell-Webster, picked up what was surely a well-worn but none the less vital theme:

> Now, it has been my experience that Ordnance officers are a little inclined at times to plough a lonely furrow, and that they don't take their difficulties and their troubles sufficiently to the staff, who are responsible for the policy and co-ordination of maintenance of the Army. Please remember that the position of the staff is primarily this. They are the commander's oilcans which carry the oil round to the creaking joints of the army. If they don't know which joint is creaking, they cannot apply the oilcan in the proper place; and, it is most necessary for Ordnance officers to be in the closest touch and cultivate the very best relations with the QMG's branch of the staff.[5]

Just what Bill did on D-Day itself, there is no record. Betty included in her album the piece from the *Evening News* of 6 June 1944 for the report on D-Day. Surely, he and all those around him would have carried a huge weight of worry: a seaborne invasion on this scale had never before been attempted and effective supply would be fundamental to its success.

For Bill, on 9 June 1944, there was a guest night at COD Feltham for the head of Canadian Ordnance, Major General Young, with whom Bill was, in effect, sharing some of the responsibility for D-Day supply. The British and Canadians were working together in Normandy. The invitation was from the relatively new Chief Ordnance Officer, Arthur Sewell. Betty notes that Bill visited France in the week following D-Day, but there are no photographs or details. A week later, Bill visited Austin and thanked them for their great contribution to the invasion. He warned them, though, that a land war with Japan awaited. Later in the albums, there is a poster signed by Bill thanking the motor industry more generally.

Betty includes a feature in *Autocar* magazine entitled 'Motor Agents to the Army' and a report on an invasion-eve visit to an RAOC Vehicle Reserve Depot where transport was massed for the assault on France. This is some of what it said:

> Today the RAOC is operating and controlling the supply system which sent the British and Allied invasion armies

across to France with every type of vehicle human ingenuity can devise, from Staff Cars, similar to the humble eights and tens we drove in peacetime, to amphibious behemoths capable of carrying twenty ton tanks. Working in close accord with the motor industry, these 'backroom boys' of the army also keep units in the field supplied with every conceivable spare part needed, from a dipstick to a differential. This alone seems a prodigious task when one bears in mind the numerous types and makes of vehicles in use today – 300,000 parts are handled, an ever increasing figure as new types come into service – but the RAOC are equal to it and the methods they employ ensure rapid dispatch of the correct parts to the right units at the time they are needed [with permission, *Autocar*, 16 June 1944].[6]

She also cut out an article from *The Star* dated 12 June 1944 and with the headline 'Supplying the Beaches'. It continues:

For four years Major General L.H. Williams, Controller of Ordnance Services, has been organizing stores for the invasion. Now, at last, he is shipping abroad to our men on the beaches all the hundreds of thousands of stores, arms, ammunition and secret weapons which he has been accumulating all this time.

He talked to me about his job today in his room in the War Office. There were no precedents to guide him; no friendly port was available equipped with modern machinery for handling heavy tanks and guns.

'From what ever angle we viewed the problem, it was fantastic,' said General Williams. 'The needs were fantastic, the variety of articles fantastic. And through it all was the need for speed. Our men must land from barges on the open beaches and they must have sufficient heavy weapons to hold them and push on.

'We learnt a lot at Norway when we landed there.' Afterwards, General Williams went to Africa, Syria, Iraq, Sicily and Italy. Each successive landing taught something.[7]

There is a full-page article on ammunition for the invasion from *Sphere* magazine of 3 June 1944 by Charles Graves entitled 'In Praise of the RAOC', and which began with this:

> As with the Corps of Military Police and the Royal Army Service Corps, so with the Royal Army Ordnance Corps. This is an all-in war, and men of the RAOC are finding themselves right up in the forward area of the battle instead of being well behind the frontline.
>
> When our troops return to the Continent, the first flight of the maintenance organization will be landed on the beaches while the first assault brigades are fighting for an initial foothold. This is the Beach Group, which includes an Ordnance Beach Detachment, and which goes in with the assault troops and establishes the beach dumps of ammunition and stores. It holds ammunition, complete wireless sets, small arms, clothing, spare parts and accessories for armoured fighting vehicles and trucks, together with engineering and signal stores and a limited range of expendable stores. This detachment will be situated at first in the beach maintenance area.[8]

Bill travelled to Halifax to speak on 6 July 1944 as part of Salute the Soldier Week. His *War Diary* had told of the strain which this vital initiative had placed on RAOC resources. The initiative was arranged by Sir Harold Mackintosh, Chairman of National Savings, to attract savings for the increasingly draining war effort. This is some of what Bill said in his speech:

> I am deeply conscious of the honour of being asked to open the 'Salute the Soldier' Week for your great Town. When my good friend Sir Harold Mackintosh and your Committee asked me to do so, I said, 'Yes, certainly, I will do anything to help.' Perhaps you would call it a selfish gesture, as the more money you save the easier my job becomes.
>
> As Controller of Ordnance Services, I handle practically the whole of the equipment with which our Army fights. It is your money that buys that equipment, so I act as your agent.

It is rather like an enormous industrial concern; you are the shareholders and I am the Director of the firm responsible for placing orders and delivering the goods to the customers. The customers are the Army, every unit; every soldier to me is a customer to be clothed and equipped.

My Corps, the Royal Army Ordnance Corps, incidentally is one of the oldest Corps in the Army, as in bygone days it was responsible for supplying the Army with bows and arrows and armour for the men at arms, in fact, I believe in the early stages of our history we planted the yew forests, from which the bows were made.'[9]

Bill broadcast to the staff at COD Derby on 16 July, and thanked them for their efforts. He accompanied Sir James Grigg, Secretary of State for War, when the latter visited Greenford and Bicester on 23 June 1944. Bill then spoke at another Salute the Soldier event, this time at Knaresborough on 22 July.

Bill visited France and the 21st Army Group, Second Army, 15 BAD, 17 AOD and Canadian units from 2 to 5 August. The 21st Army Group comprised the British Second Army and units from the Canadian Army. They each had their own embedded ordnance officers, with Jim Denniston and Cutters at Army Group level and Terry Clarke with the Second Army. They were supported by supply infrastructure including a number of Base Ammunition Depots (BADs) and four Advanced Ordnance Depots (AODs) numbered 14 to 17. 16 AOD and 17 AOD had set up at Vaux-sur-Aure and began supply at the beginning of July. 14 AOD was to set up at Caen, but, with the delay in taking that town resulting from stiff German resistance, it set up outside and, under the command of Bob Hiam from Old Dalby, began issues. A gruelling fight across northern France followed, supported by mobile Ordnance units supplied from Caen. Antwerp was eventually taken in early September. Over the following weeks 15 AOD set up in the former German depot outside Antwerp. 14, 16 and 17 AODs later joined it all under Bob Hiam's command to supply the final hard-fought push into Germany itself. By this time, Robbie Robinson was well into his role as Inspector Overseas and he certainly would have visited France. He had worked alongside his long-time Dunlop colleague in preparing 16 AOD for the invasion. The four AODs clearly worked closely, for, in the post-war period, they held joint annual reunions.

The significance of the USA is again underlined with a photograph of a presentation of an RAOC flag by an officer in the British Army to his opposite number in that of the USA. On the reverse side, all is revealed: the British officer is Gordon Hardy DOS British Army Staff Washington, and the recipient is Major General Levin H. Campbell Chief of US Ordnance. The event took place on 2 September 1944 at the Armed Service Forces Training Centre (Ordnance) Aberdeen Proving Ground, Maryland, in front of 10,000 troops. The article adds that the RAOC flag had been made by 5 BOD in the Middle East under the command of Brigadier Tankard.

Amid all the hard work, there was for Bill some space for much-needed rest and recuperation. This is evidenced by photographs of Bill staying at Aldbar Castle, in Scotland, with Bob Chalmers of Tecalemit and Gordon Richards of Solex. Aldbar Castle had been in the Chalmers family for four generations and Bob was managing director of Tecalemit. Gordon Richards was a Londoner whose business was part owned by the French Solex Company of the Velo-Solex fame and which manufactured Solex, Zenith and Stromberg carburettors. These two men, who would remain friends with Bill long after the war, offered a wonderful distraction from the labour of war, although they both contributed significantly to the war effort. In Gordon Richards' case, he had contributed much more personally in losing his eldest son, Charles, in a bombing mission over Germany in December 1943. Richards' first wife Juliet died barely six weeks after the war ended.

Images in the album from the Middle East and Italy are evidence of a further trip, as is a menu of a dinner with Major General Geake at Pontecagnano in September 1944. An order of service for the dedication on 19 August 1944 by the Bishop of Lichfield of the Memorial Church of St Martin and St George must have taken place on the same trip. This was in remembrance of those who died in the landing in 1943. The Bishop was Dr Woods, who had been de Wolff's friend and had helped with the Donnington royal visit. During the trip, on 26 September 1944, Bill was granted an interview with the Pope.

As the author of the official RAOC history puts it,

> late in the war, Brigadier de Wolff moved to an important but less exacting appointment as DDOS Lines of Communication in Italy. But by then, the main difficulties

[with Donnington's work] had been overcome and to him must go the credit for this great achievement.

Gordon Hardy had returned from Washington to take over command at Donnington. For Wolffy, Italy was a return visit, for, in his Malta years, de Wolff had travelled widely in Italy and had witnessed the harsh stamp of Mussolini. He tells how

> from one end of the country, length and breadth, extracts from Mussolini's speeches and slogans were painted on the walls of every town and village. Private houses were not spared, and woe betide anyone who dared to remove them.[10]

The *City Press* of 13 October 1944 reported Bill's address to the Carmen dinner at the Tallow Chandlers Hall in praise of Ernest Coxhead, as I related in Chapter 6, and also of Churchill. This is some of the report:

> Major General L.H. Williams, in proposing the toast to the Company and its Master, said that transport was the lifeblood of the war we were waging. It had enabled us to follow the enemy in huge advances made by Montgomery in France and Alexander in Italy. To keep the vehicles on the road was a great problem. During the last two months he had visited the two great theatres of war. When he arrived in Normandy what struck him most was the amazing way in which we had dealt with transport, for we landed on the beaches. It was one of the greatest achievements of the war to see the 'ducks' working between the shore and ship and was a great sight. It was a fine piece of work. We had lengthened the lines enormously, and success was due to transport, the tenacity of our fighting troops and the leadership of Montgomery and Mr Churchill.[11]

I feel certain that any RASC officer or soldier listening would have been just as affirmed as a member of REME or the RAOC. The troops of whom he spoke had fought their way across northern France. They had attempted the audacious attack on Arnhem, Operation Market Garden, in which men of the RAOC played a full part.[12] The failure of Market

Garden meant that there was no quick way of winning and the RAOC was key in making sure the advancing army had the tools they needed.

A piece in the *Depot Digest* of 28 October 1944 offered space for Bill to reflect. He recalled that the Chilwell site had been very near to being sold in 1935. It was the occasion of a visit by the QMG when he offered his congratulations and thanks for all that had been done under the leadership of Brigadier E.P. Readman. To mark this visit there is a cartoon of Chilwell with Bill, Lord Belper, QMG, Reddy and 'the sheriff of Nottingham'. Lord Belper was Deputy Lieutenant of Nottinghamshire whose son was serving in the army.

Possibly reflecting a shift in Bill's focus, there are photographs of an exhibition and reports from *The Motor Trader* about the work being done on packaging at Feltham with Colonel Sewell. Those photographed included Israel Sieff of Marks & Spencer, with some officers from the Greek army. M&S had been one of the companies which had helped in the early days. In Bill's archive there is a letter to Simon Marks to this effect.

Bill wrote his Christmas message to the Corps on 28 November. Here is some of it:

> 1944 will be recorded in history as a year of wonderful achievement. Our heroic invasion army, this time last year, scattered throughout Great Britain and the Mediterranean is now battering its way through the last line of defence to the Ruhr and Germany itself. The gallant Eighth Army has fought a tough but brilliant campaign from the Toe of Italy almost to the Brenner Pass. Greece has been liberated, and, in the Far East, our men are proving themselves masters of the Jap. I would especially ask you at this Christmastide to remember this Army fighting in the jungle, swamps and hills of the Far East and who have held, no, more than held their own against a ferocious and fanatical enemy. To those of our Corps I send special greetings and assure them that we do not forget them.[13]

Bill had no intention of forgetting them, as he set out on his next long overseas trip.

Chapter 10

The Middle East and Africa to VE Day

Neville Swiney had been posted to Egypt in late 1943, first to take over command of 5 BOD from Basil Cox, and then to take up the post of DOS Middle East. I suggest that this role had a quite different purpose to that of his predecessors: they were building up; he was managing a reduction to release resources to other more active theatres of war.

With this background, Bill and Dick Hunt, this time accompanied by Betty, set out on a major trip to the Middle East and Africa. We again have the benefit of Betty's diaries to help us gain a sense of the trip.

On Friday, 24 November, 1944 their driver, Sergeant Smith, drove them to Waterloo Station where they took the train to Christchurch, only to discover that their flight had been postponed because of bad weather. Betty took the opportunity to visit a relative in Bournemouth, and was shocked to see barbed wire still along the promenade.

They eventually took off on Sunday afternoon and flew south, passing Portugal with Betty delighting at the gleaming lights of Lisbon. She writes that 'the plane was most comfortable but at one point the heating was too intense'. This was in sharp contrast to earlier bitterly cold flights.

They arrived in Rabat where they had stayed the previous year on the way to the USA (see Chapter 8). The hotel this time was one requisitioned by the RAF and was 'cold and not very clean'. The following morning it was pouring with rain, but the plane took off again and headed over the desert. This is how Betty described what she saw:

> It looks like a dried-up sea. The land, scarred and cut with traces of streams and rivers, ranges of hills and knife-edged ridges, could easily have been the basin of the Great Lakes. There are still tiny streams of water as they reflect the sun like a mirror. The great dried scars must have been rivers, for parts of them have been laboriously cultivated and all

the way along you can see these patches of dark brown well-tilled soil. But what a hard life! It can hardly be an existence for these hardy people.

We flew over miles and miles of this type of country, then eventually sighted the sea. We approached the coast at a point in the Gabez Bay near Mareth, the famous battleground. I have never seen such a beautiful sight as the blue of the Mediterranean Sea near the shore. It is the colour of turquoise, clear and bright and shimmering. We flew for miles and miles in line with the shore and I just lapped up its beauty. I could see the date palm trees below, and the blue-green of the olive trees and the brilliant shining green of the orange trees. The General pointed all this out to me and said 'remember this for your diary.'[1]

They landed at Castel Benito aerodrome as a halfway stop, but then took off again towards Cairo. They saw Tripoli, in fact the whole route was the reverse of that taken by the Eighth Army. They passed Benghazi and Tobruk into the sunset of which Betty wrote:

How can one write a sunset? I cannot paint it. The words are hard to find to describe the beauty of the sunset tonight. The sky a deep purple blue, lit by a solitary but brilliant star, and then on the horizon ten thousand rainbows rolled into one, red, orange, indigo, blue, purple so blended together that the sky looked like a little bit of heavenly painting – a miracle of beauty and splendour.

Betty then makes a note of some of the fellow passengers. Two other women, both going to Russia, one working for the Ministry of Information and the other a journalist. Several RAF boys, a couple of airways pilots, a couple of civilians and a Foreign Office man.

They landed at Cairo and were met by General Geake. The night was cold and they shivered as they drove through the desert in the moonlight. Two pyramids came into sight as they arrived at the hotel. Betty's bedroom overlooked the desert and, waking up the next morning, she delighted in the early sun.

Straight to work, and the first visit was to GHQ to discuss with General Geake the problems in Italy. They were also met by Brigadier Gaisford and his PA, Miss Johnston, 'a very nice and capable ATS Junior Commander'. Time and again Betty gives the name of the senior officer bracketed with that of the PA, which to my mind emphasizes the two essential and complementary roles. Brigadier Gaisford was another of the Class of '22.

Old names keep cropping up, for it was Ernest Tankard (4 BOD Abbassia) who took them to lunch before meetings with US General Olmsted, a soldier with a strong reputation in logistics. The next visit was to the Tura Depot where ammunition was stored in caves hewn out of the rock. Following two further meetings at GHQ, there was a cocktail party and a meeting with the DOS Middle East, Neville Swiney.

That, though, was nothing compared with the sight of the Sphinx by moonlight, 'the shine of the Alabaster on the top of the second pyramid, the stillness and coolness of the night, the brightness of the moon and stars and the black of the sky, are "never to be forgotten" memories'.

Following further depot visits, Swiney took them by car the 120 miles across the desert to Alexandria, one of the three main depots in Egypt:

> The desert, endless and flat, was scattered with empty petrol tins, a crashed plane and other signs of the great army which last year camped there. Little plants grow along the roadside, some of them known as camel-thorn, and the desert looks rather like a wood of miniature trees, trees as small as those planted in an English rockery.

The depot was some miles outside Alexandria:

> The smells and filth we saw and experienced all around was indescribable, horrible. The poverty endured and the cruelty inflicted on anything and everything by the native is hateful. We saw all this driving further through the town to the clothing repair factory. This was a marvellous place. Hundreds of native women work here and mend and sort socks, uniforms, pullovers and indeed do a wonderful job.

Betty describes one activity in the depot:

> The teasing of cotton which the local people do by a method
> which has been used for centuries. A kind of one stringed
> musical instrument is used; the operator twangs the string
> and the vibrations 'fluff up' the solid blocks of cotton. The
> teased cotton is used to stuff officers' sleeping bags which
> are also made in the depot – sewn by workmen who bring
> their own sewing machines and get paid rental for them.

The Motor Transport stores were next to the quayside and clearly were
overflowing. In Betty's formal report of the visit, it is clear that there
was over capacity, but also that work being carried out was ineffective.
Bill's conclusion was that Alexandria should be drastically shrunk. As
for the unnecessary tasks, one was the stripping-down of vehicles for
spare parts. Unfortunately, no thought was being given to the need for
particular spares and, so, much work was done simply to produce piles
of spares which no one wanted.

Robbie Robinson, as Ordnance Inspector Overseas, had visited and
briefed Bill on the issues; it was then down to Bill to give the orders. It
will be apparent from Betty's description that the depot had become part
of the industrial infrastructure, as it had been during the First World War
where it supplied all the activity in the Middle East. Dicky Richards had
made a point of local sourcing as much as possible. All of that would
take some dismantling. Neville Swiney, with his attention to detail, was
clearly the man for the job.

The next day was a trip to the major depot at Tel-el-Kebir and Betty
describes the scenery on the route: 'indescribably pretty: palm trees,
tamarisk trees, orange groves, vegetable fields – cabbages bigger than
I have ever seen.' The depot, commanded then by Brigadier Brown, was
'very well run'.

This trip was followed by yet another cocktail party and further
familiar faces including Betty's old boss at Chilwell, Harry Whitaker,
who by then was leading central provisioning for the Middle East.

The next day was a conference on the provision of stores for the
Middle East and the General addressed a gathering of the whole staff
in the garrison cinema. This was followed by a trip round the native
market,

an amazing place, a blaze of colour, buying and selling, bartering and bargaining going on all the time. The streets swarming with people, old, young, strong, weak, blind and crippled.

Then a much-needed cup of tea at Shepheard's Hotel. They flew to Lydda near Jerusalem, flying over Tel-el-Kebir and seeing the increasingly cultivated countryside. The General and Colonel Hunt visited the depot at Haifa with Brigadier Swiney.

An evening walk demonstrates perhaps the easy relationship that was growing between Betty and the General, and involved 'scrumping' in the orange and grapefruit groves. Betty observed that she could tell that the General had a lot of experience in 'scrumping' (stealing fruit). She adds, 'we laughed like billio and especially when we hid behind the orange trees to prevent children seeing us.'

The next visit was to Baghdad in a converted Wellington. Out of the windows, Betty watched as the fertile country gave way to something more barren where 'one could easily imagine the Shepherds watching their flocks'.

They were met by another of the Class of '22, Colonel Heron. This is a name that may ring bells for readers of *Ordnance*, for his father was the man who conceived the plan of laundering thousands of uniforms and blankets each winter in the First World War. Another link to the Great War comes up in Betty's diary where she describes the colourings along a riverbank:

> fawn of sand, yellows and olive greens of the vegetation, palm trees and a delicate blue sky, streaked with grey reflected in the still river. This was near the site of a battle during the last war, where the Lancashire Fusiliers had fought so bravely. A small memorial had been erected to them.

Of Baghdad itself, Betty's memories seem to be mostly of animals:

> The sight of a handsome Arab on a prancing steed was not uncommon here. The horses were absolutely lovely, but my heart ached for the poor overworked, cruelly treated, little donkeys. Mixed flocks of sheep, goats, donkeys and cattle! Brown, fawn, black – the colour of Arab rugs.

By train to Basra and first the ammunition depot and then the BOD 'commanded by a piece of human dynamite, Colonel Snook'. Clearly, improvements had been made since the General's visit the previous year. 'Labour of all kinds worked there: British, Indian, Arab, Iraqi. The General gave the officers a pep-talk in the mess.'

Sunday, 10 December was the opportunity for a visit to Jerusalem.

> We drove through the lovely hills, past the supposed site of David and Goliath's battle, and strangely enough a small memorial to German airmen who were killed in Palestine in the last war … eventually we arrived in Jerusalem, the Christian shops were closed and the Mohammedan and Jewish shops open – rather a strange sight.

They drove to the Damascus gate, the Mount of Olives, the Garden of Gethsemane and the Church of the Ascension. Clearly an emotional visit. But a need to press on to Bethlehem and the Church of the Nativity, passing 'Rachel's tomb, built before the wandering of the Jews from Palestine into Egypt'.

A return to Cairo and the Shepheard's Hotel, and more meetings between the General and General Dowler, GOC East Africa. They then set off on the next leg to Khartoum via Luxor, where they managed a very quick visit to the palaces of Tutankhamen, and Wadi Halfa where they rested in a house previously used by Gordon and Kitchener. Flying on, they covered mile after mile of desert and high mountain ranges, great canyons and cuts in the land.

They approached Khartoum over the junction of the Blue and White Niles. More meetings at Gordon's Tree Ordnance Depot, but then a drive to the place where the two rivers meet, at sunset: 'the sky was just one mass of glorious colours, mainly flaming red and grey and blue. Looking at the river we could see the Blue Nile, actually blue, and the White Nile flowing into it looking quite white in fact.'

The following day, they took a flight first over uninhabited mountainous country but then over lake country with its native habitations. They landed at Port Bell near to Kampala, driving to Kisumu where they were met by another officer/PA partnership, Brigadier Primmer and Miss Crabb. Whilst the soldiers talked, Betty and Miss Crabb went walking among the jacaranda, plumbago and Bougainvillea, returning to the hotel just before rain came. 'It poured and thundered and lightninged … I had to share a room with Miss Crabb. During the night we heard all kinds of insect life, crickets and all sorts of other little whistlers.'

They journeyed on into East Africa, and to Nakuru which was the home to a group of remarkable ordnance factories. Bill was given a book setting out the history of the factories with illustrations of the work carried out. That book by now should be in the archive of the RAOC. This is a much-shortened version of its story.

In the mid-1930s, investigations had been made to assess the possibility of setting up industrial production in Kenya to remove the necessity of importing so many manufactured goods. The place chosen, Nakuru, was conveniently located on the Kenyan communication system both for the collection of raw materials and distribution of finished goods. With the coming of war and the entry of the Italians in 1940, Nakuru was mobilized to produce what was needed to defend the northern frontier. There was a tannery capable of producing five tons of leather a month, a whole plant for the manufacture of blankets, shoe machinery and a soap plant. Much of this production would have found its way into Dicky's local sourcing.

Next on the itinerary was Nairobi, and, en route, Betty delighted at the zebra, gazelle and ostrich. The residential areas of Nairobi had houses 'quite buried in Bougainvillea, Plumbago and Jackoranda'. They stayed at the Norfolk Hotel.

The next morning, they boarded a de Havilland Rapide for Mombasa. From the aircraft Betty saw the snow-covered peaks of Mount Kenya and Kilimanjaro. The pilot asked if they would like to see some game and so descended from 19,000 to 2,000 feet, from where they saw herds of buck, giraffe, zebra, rhino, elephants and buffalo. On landing, the General spotted and pointed out for Betty a small green insect, a praying mantis, rather like a huge grasshopper. A quick visit to the ordnance depot and off to the Mombasa Club for 'gin fizz … Sitting on the veranda of the club, we saw an Arab Dhow sailing magnificently into the harbour. It was one of the fleet of the Sultan of Zanzibar and was most picturesque'. After dinner, they walked for a few minutes outside of the hotel in darkness, and saw the stars as

> stars should be seen, just near the Equator, on a lovely still tropical night. And so to bed where I am labouring at the moment writing this. It is so hot and I am fascinated by the tiny lizards on the ceiling, catching moths and flies and eating them. These are real lizards – not imaginary ones or 'gin' ones.

From Mombasa, an Anson took them to Zanzibar where they stayed in the Residency, meeting the Resident, Sir Guy Pilling. It was 'an amazing house, white stucco walls, a bright red tiled roof, inside half panelled walls and a wooden floor covered in Bokhara rugs'. A visit to the ordnance depot and then the Sultan's palace and a walk through the narrow streets; 'the beauty of the buildings lay in their heavy doors decorated with brass'.

Bill had wanted to see the Africa Hotel where he had stayed as a young man. Where I referred to this in Chapter 3, the then older Betty was pretty straightforward, in her diary as a young woman, writing that 'it had deteriorated and it is now only a low native pub'.

Betty went sightseeing with Lady Pilling, who told her of the lot of the native people and their difficulties in wartime, how 'the growing of rice had caused a great increase in Malaria and how only a few years before an old man had died, who remembered, as a child, being bought in the market as a slave'.

The next morning, they were off again and arrived at the airport to await the plane from Dar es Salaam back to Mombasa where the General inspected the docks and Vehicle Assembly Unit. He posed for a photograph where one had been taken of him thirty-three years earlier when he had gone out to Portuguese East Africa to trade.

They then flew back to Nairobi and a further inspection. Retracing their steps further, they flew over ground they had covered before on land to Kisumu. A group of carol singers came to the hotel; it was, after all, 22 December. Back to Khartoum on 23 December and a lovely hotel on the Blue Nile. There was a dinner dance on and 'the General and I had a few dances'.

Christmas Eve, and a visit to Khartoum North Depot and the Sudan Government Stores and Ordnance Depot. 'Quite a good depot and workshop but rather old fashioned and "bow and arrow-ish".' Then further inspections and the tyre storage depot at Omdurman, 'the largest native city in Africa, crowded with children, donkeys and goats'.

> After dinner the General returned accompanied by one Mr Jack Morris who is a District Commissioner in a trading post in Abyssinia. He was a very interesting, entertaining and cheerful old man; I rather judged him to be a bit of a lad. Terrible though it may seem, the General and he had returned

early on the excuse that the General had work to do. They both in truth wanted to dodge a carol service being held that evening in the cathedral. Mr Morris had an amazing story to tell of how he had been caught up in the Italian invasion of Abyssinia and of his escape by canoe in the middle of the night on their declaration of war against England.

Christmas Day, and Betty rose late to find the General and Colonel Hunt deep in conversation about the Sudan Defence Force. This was cut short by the arrival of Mr Morris who took them round the palace and zoo, the latter with birds and animals free to roam. The King's Christmas message was broadcast at 4 pm and they 'listened in the shade of the veranda overlooking the sunlit Nile and bright Blue sky. A Faluka was sailing majestically along the river as we listened'. They were entertained to dinner, but first went to the cinema to see Walt Disney's *Bambi*.

Boxing Day had more retracing of steps back to Cairo and a stay at Shepheard's Hotel this time. The following day, there was a another visit to the clothing factory and further meetings with General Dowler and Brigadiers Swiney, Brown and Tankard. On the way home they had to sleep in tents at Djerba! The flight back over France was uneventful. Over the northern coast they saw the Mulberry harbours being dismantled. They arrived back in London at 10 pm on 29 December in a real pea-souper. Sadly, Betty's report on the trip is not in Bill's archive, although his efforts at releasing resources would show signs of bearing fruit in the campaign against Japan.

The New Year brought Bill's appointment as a new Colonel Commandant in succession to Major General Jasper Baker, alongside Representative Colonel Commandant, Sir Basil Hill.

The Bishop of Lichfield's dedication of the new church, built entirely from salvage, at a West Midlands camp was reported at length in the *Border Counties Advertiser* of 10 January 1945. The place, I infer, is Donnington and the long article tells how men and women from all parts of the camp had worked together to create the building for the camp. The church is built round an army 'Nissan' hut with 'a buttressed tower, Gothic chancel and belfry and the interior panelled from salvaged wood'. The article adds that the Bishop had just returned from two months with the Eighth Army in Italy (which ties in with the other dedication I mentioned above).

On 19 January 1945, the Central Depots Co-ordinating Committee met at Chilwell, and it was followed by a guest night. Betty's album has the seating plan for the night with the signature of each of those present. Dicky Richards was there, seated alongside the two other major generals: Bill and Reddy Readman. Brigadiers Cox and King were both back in the UK following their postings in the Middle East, with Basil Cox as COO COD Didcot working alongside J.S. Crosland with Dicky on clothing and stores. Controller Violet Falkner, CO of the large Chilwell ATS contingent, was on the top table. The guest of honour was unable to attend. He was local businessman Edward Herbert, who was later knighted and became chairman of Short Brothers.

In February and March 1945, Bill and Dick Hunt visited India for a second time and I write about this in Chapter 11. At the same time the Allied armies were advancing towards Germany and crossed the Rhine on 23 March 1945, an amphibious operation said to have been as complex as D-Day.[2]

Bill was back in the UK in time to chair the last Central Depots Co-ordinating Committee of the war which met at Branston from 13 to 14 April 1945 with Brigadier Harold Crosland as host.

Victory in Europe was achieved only a month later, on 8 May 1945, and there is a message from the QMG noting that 'never before had British Armies been so adequately maintained under such difficult and varied conditions'. Bill's victory message paid particular tribute to the non-regular officers, women of the ATS and civilians who worked so hard and well with regular officers and men. He welcomed the even closer links welded with the Ordnance Corps of the British Empire: India, Canada, Australia, New Zealand and South Africa. He ended by encouraging renewed efforts for the war against Japan.

He sent copies of this, the Royal Army Ordnance Corps Special Instruction of 10 May 1945, to the King, to the US Ordnance and to the Ordnance Corps of Australia, Canada and New Zealand. He may, of course, have sent it to India and South Africa as well, but their reply is not recorded. For the King, his private secretary, Tommy Lascelles, signed the letter of thanks. Generals Somervell, Campbell and Lee responded from the USA. Major General Young responded from Canada; sadly, I cannot make out the signatures from Australia and New Zealand.

The Institute of Automobile Engineers victory lunch was held at the Connaught Room on 11 May 1945 with Bill on the top table. Bill was part of the group accompanying General Montgomery on his visit to Paris from 24 to 26 May 1945. Bill, and Betty, also visited Germany and Belgium. For the album, Betty has press cuttings from VE Day. There is a long article in the *Commercial Vehicles Users Journal* entitled 'Mechanizing the British Army', with photographs particularly of Bill and Reddy Readman. Also, the RAOC itself produced a commemorative booklet of its activities with advertising from its many motor industry suppliers. On 1 June, there was a dinner at Feltham hosted by John Hildreth in honour of the officers of the Central Ordnance Depots for Warlike Stores.

On the same day, there was the first of many annual invitations from Sir Ronald Weeks to a reception at Claridge's. In 1949, Ronald Weeks published three lectures he had given on *Organization and Equipment for War*, drawing on his unique wartime experience. As Deputy Chief of the Imperial General Staff, his duties had been wide-ranging, but he does mention Bill individually in the context of 'wading', that is the need, in a seaborne invasion, for vehicles to be able to drive through water, and he praises first Sir Claude Gibb at the Ministry of Supply but as ably assisted and abetted by Major General Sir Leslie Williams and Major General Sir Bertram Rowcroft (Director of Mechanical Engineering). The second reference in the book is to the RAOC itself and the mammoth challenge it faced with spare parts when he writes: 'I have listened to more angry words about spare parts than almost any other subject; we even got at loggerheads with our American friends; I have no doubt the R.A.F. had similar difficulties.'[3]

Bill's focus was, though, now on the Far East, although he had been preparing for some time.

Chapter 11

India and South East Asia to V-J Day

Brigadier Verschoyle-Campbell, RAOC veteran of the First World War, was appointed DOS India in 1938 and then, with promotion to major general, DQMG, transferring to the Indian Army until his retirement in 1941. Clearly, there was a very close relationship between the RAOC and the Indian Army Ordnance Corps, but the latter was an integral corps within the British Indian Army and not part of the British Army in India. It was therefore responsible to GHQ in Delhi and not the War Office in London. In the early months of the war, India provided troops and then, increasingly, equipment, particularly clothing to the Middle East. With the entry into the war of Japan, it had a major role in supplying the army in Burma. Advanced Ordnance Depots were established in north-east India, notably at Dimapur and Limphat in order to support operations in Burma.

In June 1943, General Sir Claude Auchinleck succeeded General Sir Archibald Wavell as Commander-in-Chief in India with responsibility for the prosecution of the war against Japan, until, later that year, when Admiral Louis Mountbatten was appointed to command the newly created South East Asia Command. Auchinleck set up the infrastructure for the 11th Army Group, and established home Base Ordnance Depots and lines of communication to supply the Fourteenth Army. He saw shortcomings in existing ordnance services and, in response to his request, Bill and Dick Hunt travelled to India to investigate and report. The trip lasted from 18 October to 11 December 1943 and they went via North Africa, Italy, Sicily, Egypt and Persia to India and Burma. Betty did not go so there is no diary of the trip. However, from the photographs in her album and from other notes, it is possible to trace the itinerary.

They began at Marrakesh and inspected outside storage of thousands of engines and other stores. This is significant because Bill's emphasis on spare parts had shifted. There was a phenomenal amount of army equipment in and between bases, and producers were suffering from shortages of raw materials from which to produce new weapons. The key was to care for and maintain what there was, and identify, secure and label all available spare parts. Attention also needed to be given, in conjunction with REME, to the scale of spares required. In the reports he wrote on his visits, he placed great emphasis on the procedure concerning reconditioned engines. Later, he gave a talk on the subject which was reproduced and widely circulated, with a foreword by his REME colleague, Major General E.B. Rowcroft as Director of Mechanical Engineering.[1] He emphasized the need for the Carton Unit system and the particular importance of careful packing of spares destined for tropical climates. There are photographs of Cairo, the storage caves at Tura, Williams Way (which was named after Bill) and the ancient mason's mallet that was presented to Bill.

They then travelled on to India: Delhi, Bombay and Calcutta. At this point there is a typed itinerary. They arrived on 2 November and spent three days in meetings at GHQ in New Delhi, with the DOS IAOC Major General G.L.S. Hawkins. They then flew to Calcutta for meetings at Fourteenth Army HQ. There was then a three-day visit to the ordnance installations in the Bombay area. They then went on to Poona, Cawnpore and Agra. There is a record of a dinner on 30 November 1943 with General Sir Ronald Adam and the guests included Brigadier Cecil Haigh (of the Class of '22) as DOS of the 11th Army Group.

Bill wrote a report on what he found in India.[2] There were ordnance bases spread right across the sub-continent from Bombay in the west to Calcutta in the east, and Madras in the south to Chaklala in the north, with Delhi, Agra, Jubbulpore and Cawnpore in the centre. Bill's first point was that this spread was fine for general stores and ammunition, but for all other warlike stores (except complete vehicles) a single base depot, where all such stores are concentrated providing access in one place to all that is available, is the most efficient. Experience in North Africa had exposed the weakness of some stores being held at base A and some at base B. His recommendation did not completely follow, given the nature of India, and was for the Panagarh Calcutta base to form the main depot, but with a further base ordnance depot at Avadi near Madras. The space requirements would be considerable, with 2 million square feet of covered storage at Calcutta and 1.5 million at Madras. A related recommendation was that ancillary stores should be retained as part and parcel of the main equipment, and he gave the example of guns being held complete with fire-control instruments.

His report then looked at the personnel, and he noted the high quality of IAOC officers but also shortages in experienced officers, and a reliance on poorly paid civilians. He recommended increases in pay to attract the right skills. He advised that officers should be selected on the basis of their experience in man management and, ideally, have a business background. He also provided two key officers to set up the new depot at Avadi, which became known as 206 BOD. The officers were Colonel Browne, a Chilwell veteran who brought his experience as second in command at Greenford, and Lieutenant Colonel Stan Preston who brought packaging expertise from Feltham. They both had backgrounds in industry. The third strand of the report was the need for modern office and storehouse equipment. He added that a modern ordnance depot is similar to a large commercial organization.

During his visit, Bill met Norman Speller, a man who had served in the ranks in the East Surrey Regiment right through the First World War until 1932 when he was commissioned in the RAOC at Aldershot. After serving in the War Office, Didcot and the Middle East, he was posted to India. Bill later wrote this on his death which adds some colour to the picture:

> I saw a lot of the wonderful work which he did in India during my visits to that country when we were reorganizing and preparing the bases for the invasion of Burma. Those who served out there with him will remember the wonderful work he did at Cawnpore, Dehu Road and Panagarh, the latter being the great modern General Stores Depot which we created in the Calcutta area to deal with the supply of general stores to the 14th Army. His intense efforts resulted in a final breakdown in his health, from which he never really recovered. He retired as an honorary Colonel with 100% disability in November 1947. In addition to the MBE, he held the 1914 Star and other war medals of the First and Second World Wars and the Croix de Guerre.[3]

Norman Speller's son, Major General Norman Speller CB, would become DOS in the 1970s.

During the visit, Bill was called upon to address officers of the 11th Army Group on the issues faced by Ordnance Services. John Hildreth recalled, in the obituary he wrote on Bill's death, that speech Bill gave in Delhi:

> He had been asked to visit India and to advise on the best way to reorganize the Ordnance Services there – a prodigious task for one unacquainted with that country. Nevertheless, he picked the wood from the trees and clearly and succinctly told Field Marshal Auchinleck and his Staff exactly what must be done to put things right.[4]

In 1955, in the *RAOC Gazette*, a colonel, who had been in the audience when Bill spoke, recorded the scene. First, he set the context of an India, where home rule was being sought, at that time, by peaceful protest. The colonial power was increasingly resented, and I infer that this resulted in a lack of communication within and between the armies to the serious detriment of all.

> The scene a commodious cinema in Delhi. The audience all 'brass': two past and present Cs-in-C India; a galaxy of Generals and Lt Generals; a shoal of Major Generals; a flood of Brigadiers; and an ocean of humble Colonels.
>
> Sir Leslie Williams came to talk to us.
>
> He was introduced and nodded a greeting. Then he stood quite still on the stage, and only the flickering reflection of the floodlights on his spectacles revealed a restless animation. He spoke quietly and without gesture or emphasis, and didn't use any technical terms.
>
> He told of the military adoption of whole industries in England; of his employment of the women of Notts County in their own homes packing cartons for the make up of 'beach packs'; of his visit to the USA, and how our cousins-in-arms had agreed to amend their logistical sciences to coordinate with our Ordnance systems, the result of stark trial and error.
>
> In contrast to the ordinary training lecture or 'kriegspiel', there wasn't a cough, the scrape of a boot or the splutter of

a match. We heard him in stock silence, everyone tense and rigid, and I think moved, profoundly moved.

Then Sir Leslie came 'nearer home'. His appreciation of what might happen when the struggle for survival moved eastwards shook many people that day. He then merely asked that all and every difficulty and misunderstanding which might arise should be solved on the spot and by the person it actually concerned.

This was the end of his seventy-five minutes talk. there were no 'questions', none of the usual cheerful chatter on the release of a compulsory audience, but I felt that everyone of us was impressed.

Sir Leslie on this occasion well and truly laid a considerable stone in the fabric of Ordnance and British History.[5]

A photograph of Bill with Geako and American allies marked the homeward trip as did taking in a visit to Italy.

Back in the UK, plans for D-Day were far advanced and Bill turned his attention once more to the USA and the need for spare parts. However, looking at the war diaries, there is more than an eye to the Far East. The RAOC was already short of officers, but it sent over one hundred out to India, along with Browne and Preston. The other work that was going on in preparation for a long jungle war involved packaging and this focused on Feltham. The *Sunday Despatch* of 26 November 1944 had an article on a packaging exhibition held at Feltham. For the war against Japan, effective packaging was vital. If spare parts had been the mantra of the war against Germany, then packaging would be it for the South East Asia campaign. Effective packaging was vital in jungle environments where even 'sealed' binoculars would develop growths of mould.

As I told in the previous chapter, on Friday, 24 November 1944, Bill Williams, accompanied by Betty and Dick Hunt, embarked on a trip to the Middle East and Africa. The war in Europe had become bogged down, and there was the very real prospect of a long and gruelling land war in the Far East. Bill needed to visit the depots overseas, particularly to get them to release essential stores, especially spare parts, that would be needed elsewhere. The whole network of depots demanded rationalization. They would also need to release manpower, and he was keen to identify jobs being done that were unnecessary. Robbie Robinson, as Inspector of Ordnance Overseas, had produced a report and Bill was keen to make sure his recommendations had been implemented. The reason for mentioning it here is that a key purpose was to release resources for the Far East.

From 11 February to 7 March 1945, Bill and Dick Hunt accompanied the QMG on a further trip to India to assess progress since his previous visit. It looks as if again the route was via the Middle East for, in the album, there are memorabilia commemorating the visit of King Farouk of Egypt to 4 BOD. King Farouk was given some beautiful gifts and was hosted by Neville Swiney as DOS and Ernest Tankard as COO.

The journey on to India followed a longer visit by Robbie Robinson, RAOC Inspector Overseas. Bill's report is shorter, but just as sharp as his first.[6] The first priority was ALFSEA (Allied Forces South East Asia). Bill saw, as the priorities, the further development of reserve bases (205 BOD at Panagarh, as well as 206 BOD at Avadi). These would be essential to support the advance. He recommended that young ordnance officers with enthusiasm should be selected for ALFSEA and that they should be thoroughly familiar with all the recently developed methods of supply and packaging. A third strand was, again, an emphasis on preservation, packaging and stencilling of stores sent forward to AODs. The fourth priority was the need for every unit to be provided with First Aid Motor Transport Outfits, in addition to fully stocked AODs and Field Parks. Finally, he reminded readers that ammunition going forward required careful examination before it left the issuing depot, given the ravages of the tropical climate.

The rest of the report would have made depressing writing, as well as worrying reading, since most of the recommendations of the previous report had to be repeated. Insufficient attention had been given to centralizing MT spares. The support for ALFSEA as a whole was woefully lacking. He recommended centralizing control of depots at GHQ, standardizing methods and procedures, and placing emphasis on more effective training. Ammunition storage was a concern, and Bill made arrangements to send out an ammunition expert from the UK. Engines for reconditioning were still being badly packaged and were being damaged en route to repair, if indeed they ever arrived. To do what he could to address these shortcomings, he planned to take his best officers from other theatres, as well as providing 350 other ranks to strengthen Ordnance Services in support of ALFSEA.

The other way he could help was to urge from the Americans the supply of what the army needed. Bill, accompanied by Betty, again visited the USA in June and July 1945 to talk with opposite numbers and suppliers. Their itinerary can be gleaned from a handwritten notebook which Betty kept.[7]

They flew from Bovingdon to Prestwick on 21 June, then to Meeks Field in Iceland, Stephensville in Canada (where they had a good meal and Canadian whiskey!), on to New York and finally touching down in Washington at 7.15 pm on 22 June. They were met by Brigadiers Abel-Smith and Clark; by this time, Gordon Hardy was back in the UK as COO COD Donnington.

The first business meetings were with General Campbell, but also fellow US Generals Harrison, Somervell and Smith. The following day, at the Pentagon, the focus was on packaging. They then travelled to Philadelphia and inspected the QM and Ordnance depots. From there, back to New York and on to Katonah to stay the weekend with the Sturtevants, with whom they had become friends. On Monday, it was back to New York, and a meeting with Sir Ashley Sparks, the chief representative of the Cunard Shipping Line in the USA. Bill was shown round the *Queen Elizabeth* and met the port commander.

They then flew to Detroit to visit the Ordnance offices and then, with Brigadier Clark, Chrysler and General Motors. The following day was Ford, the Kelsey Hayes Wheel Company and Continental Tyres. They travelled on to Cleveland, and stayed again with the Hoovers. The next stop was Akron and Goodrich Tyres, and then on to Firestone and Goodyear. Brigadier Abel-Smith met them at the next stop, Chicago, from where they flew via Omaha and Denver to Salt Lake City. They visited the Ogden ASF depot and General Service Command. From there, they flew via Reno, Sacramento and Oakland to San Francisco where the General spoke to Ordnance District employees. Bill saw a demonstration of landing vehicles on the seashore. They then travelled on to Los Angeles and Beverly Hills. All the time, he was urging one final effort to get the war won.

It wasn't all work. I had for some time wondered why, in the album, there was a letter from the actor, Ronald Coleman. It all comes back to Brigadier Abel-Smith, who had married into a wealthy American family. He had been invited to cocktails at Coleman's house. During the party, he telephoned Bill to say that Bill and Betty had been invited to dine with Coleman and fellow actor, Herbert Marshall. Of course, they accepted, and Herbert Marshall drove them to Romanoff's Restaurant, where they met Coleman and his wife, Benita Hume. The evening was completed with a nightcap at the Marshalls' house. Mystery solved! This evening was followed by a trip for Betty to the Paramount Studio where she saw Alan Ladd working on *Calcutta*, and Bing Crosby who was working on a new film with Billy de Wolff. She visited the property room and various sets. There was then more film exposure, this time at MGM where Betty saw Clark Cable and Greer Garson to whom she spoke. For a young woman, who had spent every Saturday of her teenage years in one or more of Long Eaton's three cinemas, this must have been a dream come true.

For Bill, there was a discussion with scientists at the California Institute of Technology, and an inspection of the Rocket Testing Centre. The following day he met Commander Hezlep, the landing vehicle expert. They returned to Chicago, then to Detroit and on to Toronto and General Motors where they saw a vehicle designed to wade in 5 feet of water (which Bill drove). All this would be vital if Japan was to be defeated. They travelled on for meetings with senior Canadian officers in Ottawa, and on to Montreal and the Longue Point Depot. They flew back to Washington and a packed day of meetings. Good progress had been made.

There were then the long flights back to England where they arrived on 31 July.

Back home, the final wartime visit was to Bicester, where Ernest Tankard had returned from the Middle East to take over command from Geoffrey Palmer. The Representative Colonel Commandant, Basil Hill, carried out an inspection. Barely a week later, on 15 August, Japan surrendered following the dropping of atomic bombs on Japan on 6 and 9 August 1945.

Betty pasted in her album the image of a British Tommy and, beneath, wrote in her distinctive green ink, one word: Victory.

Chapter 12

The Post-war Army

A chapter heading, the Post-war Army, betrays a massive subject, too big for a volume such as this. So, what I seek to do in this chapter is to look at a particular part of the army, the RAOC, and specifically from the point of view of those in our story. Those wishing a broader view of the RAOC post-war, need look no further than Major General Phelps's *A History of the Royal Army Ordnance Corps 1945–1982*. He, for whatever reason, does not appear to have had access to my own father's archive, which, of course, I do. So, I can perhaps shed additional light.

One week after the end of the war, Bill, Dick Hunt and Betty boarded a Dakota en route to Brussels. They were met by the Director of Ordnance Services of the 21st Army Group, Brigadier Jim Denniston, who would accompany them on their five-day inspection visit.

They travelled through war-torn Belgium and Holland and then through the devastated towns of Germany. They were driven in a Rolls-Royce by a Belgian RASC driver with whom they entered into conversation. He told them that his uncle had been shot by the Germans and his aunt had just returned from a concentration camp with her arm covered in burns from cigarette-ends applied in torture. With this fresh in their minds, they drove past a deserted concentration camp on their way to inspect the huge ordnance depot at Antwerp.

In Belgium and Holland, they waved at passers-by; in Germany, they had been warned not to smile. They inspected ordnance and ammunition depots. The driver had to be wary of mines, although the roads had been cleared. They passed mile after mile of bombed farms and buildings. They drove through a place called Gelden – Betty adds 'this was once a town no doubt, but certainly not now'. They visited the site of the Battle of Waterloo; the headquarters of the Base Ammunition Depot was nearby. It made sombre viewing.

On 17 August 1945, the first peacetime meeting of the Central Depots Co-ordinating Committee took place at Donnington with Gordon Hardy as host. The agenda, I suspect, focused on the massive clear-up operation that now fell to the officers and men of the RAOC. In Dicky Richards' area of responsibility of Clothing and Stores, it is clear from his monthly war diaries that the work rate remained high, for there was the massive task of demobilization. As Dicky said at one of his fortnightly meetings with the Ministry of Supply, whilst the ending of hostilities would lead to an immediate reduction in the need for warlike stores, the same was not the case with much clothing and equipment. Soldiers awaiting demobilization needed accommodation, most probably in tented camps. The committee chairman, Sir Cecil Weir, reported that British manufacturers simply didn't have the workforce needed to manufacture the tenting that would be required. He recommended that German manufacturers should be employed. Soldiers still needed clothing, and returning prisoners of war needed clothing and equipping until they too were demobilized. The planning for demobilization had begun in 1944 or even earlier; certainly in the summer of 1944 demob suits were being ordered by the thousand. It was a monumental task.

A massive area of work was that of disposals. Bill had once compared the supply route of equipment to an oil pipeline through which oil would only flow freely if it was full. In 1945, the supply pipeline to the Far East was certainly fairly full; more to the point, there was equipment in all the many places around the world where there had been military activity. The war diaries of the Director of Clothing and Stores indicate that Dicky's responsibilities had grown to include motorcycles and 'B' vehicles. The diary of April 1946 records the numbers of vehicles approved for disposal to date: UK 69,661, NW Europe 28,197, ME and PAIC 685, CMF 90,489 and India 20,129.[1] The diaries have, as an attachment, a copy of the procedure for the Disposal of Surplus Stores. This breaks down into fifty-four paragraphs and is complex. As well as disposals of stores and vehicles, previously requisitioned accommodation was being released. Again, there are figures. By April 1946, 7 million square feet of covered space had been released, comprising some 444 properties.

Looking at Bill's war diaries as Director of Warlike Stores, alongside those for Dicky, the picture fills out further with flows of all manner of vehicles back into the UK depots.[2] With the sheer volume of vehicles – the total for the army was an astonishing 1.4 million – one problem to emerge was a lack of drivers. Happily, returning PoWs were on hand and a sifting process was undertaken to identify trained drivers for the depots.

An issue that emerges time and time again is the desperate shortage of both labour and experienced officers. Temporary officers were keen to return to their civilian jobs; indeed, every soldier was keen to get home. Government was equally keen to restore the civilian labour force, but also to appease otherwise disgruntled servicemen. For most of the army, this was fine for they no longer had the need for anything like as many fighting soldiers. The same was not true for the RAOC, for it had the job of providing for demobilizing troops. It was handling the massive job of disposals and the far more dangerous clear-up of ammunition and warlike stores. The *War Diary* speaks of the need to use German PoW labour, but also of recruiting Pioneer Corps men and ATS.

Many officers were returning to their civilian roles. Feltham saw the dining out of Brigadier Sewell, and Harry Whitaker returned from the Middle East to replace Sewell as COO. 31 August 1945 saw a 'Fairwell to Reddy' dinner at the Chilwell Garrison Mess at Beeston near Nottingham. Reddy had run Chilwell since 1940, and so had been at the very heart of the Motor Transport activities of the RAOC. Geoffrey Palmer moved from Bicester to head up both Chilwell and, what was then, a vast Motor Transport organization. This was a challenging task, remodelling a massive organization to meet post-war requirements. Palmer retired in 1948 and was awarded a CB for his considerable efforts. A key farewell dinner was held at Donnington in September 1945 to say thank you to the Permanent Under Secretary of State (PUS) for War, Sir Frederick Bovenschen, underlining the close contact the RAOC had had with the Civil Service.

Amid the farewells, there was the serious job to be done as the *Daily Telegraph* reported in an article of 19 September 1945, of which this is a small extract:

> The greatest 'mopping up' operation in history is taking place in Germany, and we're seeing some astonishing things.
>
> Guns, tanks, vehicles and fantastically large quantities of other materials are being collected and sorted throughout the Reich. The work has already been in progress for months

and it will go on for a long time to come. Two big tasks are being carried out simultaneously: the Allies are steadily gathering their own property and they're taking away from the Germans every warlike article they possess.[3]

The article goes on to say how the task had fallen to the RAOC and how specially trained units had been formed and dispatched to the former theatres of war.

There were thank-yous too. The *Ford Times* reported a visit to Ford Dagenham by the QMG with Bill, hosted by Sir Roland Smith (Managing Director) and Sir Patrick Hennessey (General Manager and Director) of the Ford Motor Company.

Bill, accompanied by Betty, visited the British Army of the Rhine from 18 to 25 October 1945. By this time, Brigadier Jim Denniston had been posted back to the Middle East and Major General Cansdale was DOS BAOR. In the album, Betty writes, 'we passed through the quaint and picturesque town of Celle … and drove on to the ruins of Cologne, Essen and other Rhine and Ruhr cities.' In Cologne she observed that, 'in spite of the destruction, the Cathedral still stands as guardian of the city'. They journeyed on to Paris and enjoyed dinners on succeeding nights at the British Officers' Club on Rue du Faubourg Saint-Honoré (conducted by NAAFI) and then at the British Empire Club. I think it was only Bill who went to a cocktail party at the British Military Mission in the Hotel Gallia in Paris, and then on to the Tabarin at Rue Victor-Masse in Montmartre.

Major General Cyril Cansdale wrote to Bill on 5 November 1945, following the visit:

> To me personally your visit was a very special occasion in the long years of our friendship, and I count myself more than privileged to have served in the recent crucial war years as one of your deputies, service which gave me daily the perfect example of a single-minded leader getting big things done.[4]

Bill returned to go on a whole sequence of visits to depots. For that to CAD Nescliffe on 3 November 1945, a booklet was produced highlighting the volume of ammunition that had passed through the depot in the war years – some 580,000 tons. The following week, Bill was back at Bicester and then on to a dinner at Didcot hosted by the then new commandant, Basil Cox.

This was followed by the first post-war dinner of the Society of Motor Manufacturers and Traders, which had been part of Bill's life during the war and would become more so when he retired. The list of attendees reads like a Who's Who of the motor industry. Reginald Rootes proposed the toast and the President of the Board of Trade, Sir Stafford Cripps, replied.

Another overseas trip followed, this time to the Central Mediterranean Force (CMF) in Italy and Charles de Wolff as DDOS. The programme shows that Bill and Betty were driven round in a Humber Pullman, a shape of things to come. They began in Naples and then travelled to Rome, Florence, Venice and Padua. There is a programme for *La Bohème* in Teatro Reale dell'Opera in Milan. There is then a separate itinerary for a visit to 500 AOD in Graz and to Major General Geake, DOS GHQ CMF. Betty included some of Geako's poetry, probably from the previous year:

> The war is won. let's celebrate our victory o'er the Japs!
> Get out our nifty cameras and take one hundred snaps.
> The visit to the CMF of Bill and Dick and Polly
> is meant to prove conclusively that too much work is folly.
> The BOD's in Florence and the BAD's in Rome
> must certainly be photographed – to show the folks at home.
> The journey's end. The old home fires. The slippered Bill relaxes,
> and calculates, in peace and quiet, the cost to British taxes.[5]

I wonder whether Betty's nickname was indeed Polly?

The photographs in the album suggest that Dick Hunt was also on the visit, which then extended to Luxor and a Nile voyage on board the SS *Victoria* in December 1945. Neville Swiney is also in the photographs, as DOS Middle East. The visit is described as being to 1 BOD at the Citadel in Cairo.

The King's Birthday telegram dated 12 December 1945 was sent by G.T.W. Horne for the COS absent abroad. However, the New Year greeting is signed by Bill and is followed in the album by a great many Christmas cards, including one with a drawing by Feliks Topolski of Canterbury in *Wartime*, published by the London Polish Society. There is also a lovely pencil sketch of Bill from Cairo signed by Brock. I wondered if this was the illustrator H.M. Brock, but the signatures did not match. There were a number of artists and illustrators in the Brock family but I have been unable to find which, if any, made the sketch.

The 1945 Christmas card from Bill had a Shakespeare quotation and an image of Shakespeare's mother's cottage:

> This fortress built by nature for herself against infection and the hand of war. This precious stone set in silver sea which serves it in the office of a wall or as a moat defensive to our house, against the envy of less happy lands. This basic plot, this earth, this realm, this England.
>
> *Richard II*, Act 2, Scene 1

On 1 January 1946, Bill's name was among those listed in the New Year's Honours in the section KBE (Knight of the British Empire) (Military Division). Betty wrote the word 'congratulations' beside the newspaper cutting. In Bill's archive, there are two manila folders bulging with letters of congratulations. Betty filed them in alphabetical order and typed a contents list, essential since the signatures are very hard to decipher. There are letters from just about every part of the RAOC, but also Ford, Nuffield, Austin, Vauxhall, Marks & Spencer and Rootes, different sections of the Civil Service, Dame Leslie Whateley (ATS), officers of Allied nations, officers who had returned to civilian life such as Hiam, Robinson, MacKillop, Johnston-Davies and Readman, but also names from that first ordnance officers' course: A.M. Hidden (now at the Ministry of Supply), Rivers Macpherson (retired, photographed with Bill, Wolffy and Cyril Cansdale in the 1920s), Valon (retired) and Haigh (serving in Cairo).

The album has a good number of newspaper cuttings about the honour, and a letter from the War Office asking Bill which Christian name he wished to be used. Everyone knew him as Bill or Willy; he was, of course, Leslie. There is also an announcement that he was to be Representative Colonel Commandant of the RAOC for 1946. He would serve alongside the other two Colonels Commandant, Sir Basil Hill and Major General Joe Body.

The first invitation Bill received in his new capacity was from Ernest Tankard to a farewell dinner at Bicester in honour of General Sir Thomas Riddell-Webster, the QMG. Tankard had returned from the Middle East to take the post vacated by Geoffrey Palmer. The guest list is glittering and includes Chief Controller Dame Leslie Whateley, Director of the ATS, underlining the vital role women played in the work of the RAOC during the war.

This dinner was followed by a Central Depots Co-ordinating Committee at Corsham, with George Heron, also back from the Middle East, as Commandant. The quantity of ammunition handled through Corsham was 3.5 million tons in a depot covering ninety-five acres.

26 February 1946 was the date of Bill's investiture when he went to Buckingham Palace accompanied by Mabel and his mother. A proud day.

Bill and Betty again visited Cyril Cansdale in Belgium from 18 to 23 March 1946 and travelled on to Paris and dinner with Général de Brigade and Madame Regnault. Regnault was a distinguished infantry officer. Bill received honours from a number of Allied nations: from the French, Commandeur de la Légion d'honneur; from Belgium, Croix de Guerre avec lion en bronze; and from the USA, Legion of Merit Degree of Commander. Of course, it wasn't only Bill. Fernyhough's book records the British and overseas awards to RAOC officers and men. Of those in our story, the USA honoured Dicky, Geako, Victor Lonsdale, Alex Abel-Smith, John Hildreth, Dick Hunt, Gordon Hardy and Nobby Clark, and the Czechs honoured Dicky. Other RAOC officers and men were honoured by Norway, the Netherlands, USSR, Egypt and Greece.[6] By way of reciprocity, US Major General Campbell was awarded an honorary KBE.

In the album, there is an invitation to a rally to celebrate thirty years of the National Savings Movement with speeches from Prime Minister Attlee, Chancellor of the Exchequer Dalton, Anthony Eden and Violet Bonham-Carter. Bill had become good friends with the chairman, Sir Harold Macintosh, and had spoken at a number of Salute the Soldier events.

The first of a series of farewell events for Bill took place in the form of a dinner at COD Donnington on the Ides of March 1946. A report appeared in the *Codonian*, the weekly review of garrison news, on 22 March. The piece was either written by the COO, Gordon Hardy, or in conjunction with him, and quoted from his speech at the dinner. Hardy was, of course, one of the Class of '22, and so could recall Bill at Woolwich over a quarter of a century earlier. He said how Bill had stood out from the other brother students 'as a man with marked ability and energy'. In his career, and particularly with the creation of Chilwell in 1934, he was seen as a man 'who would cut tradition where tradition was useless', the article adds, 'and it was not surprising that he should be called upon eventually to plan base depots to be opened in the event of war'. The article continues:

> General Williams's new duties [after appointment as DWS] especially after Dunkirk, called for the development of a comparatively small organization and the story is one of continual progress. Under his direction, the strength of the Corps rose from 300 officers and 3,000 men in 1939 to almost a quarter of a million, in addition to thousands of civilian workers.
>
> On his desk, General Williams has a slogan – 'Thinking out plans will not amount to anything, unless the thought is followed by a determined will to succeed'. This has, without doubt, been one of the maxims of his life; his character combines, not only the genius of the planner, but the zeal and enthusiasm to see his schemes carried through to a successful conclusion. In 1945 he was awarded the KBE for services to his country and he will remain in the minds of all, as one of those men to whom Churchill did not turn in vain when the future was black.[7]

The card bearing the slogan is now in the RLC Archive.

There is then a visit to Bicester by another Frenchman, Général de Brigade Angenot, accompanied by Bill. A special booklet was produced for the visit. As well as a tour of the depot, the visitor inspected a scale model of the site. Bicester was something of a jewel in the crown.

Reunion dinners would become annual fixtures in the Corps calendar. The first Derby reunion dinner was held on 16 March 1946 with Robbie Robinson as president. Bill's speech, as principal guest, recalled his purchase of the Derby site in Sinfin Lane in the very early days of the war 'at a bargain price'. There is then quite a long poem which, I suspect, was read in full at the dinner. Just to pick up a couple of verses:

> So he sent for a young man named Robbie
> who was dealing in tyres, tubes and wheels
> and said come to Chilwell tomorrow, me lad
> and see how this uniform feels.
>
> So Robbie snatched up his dispatch case,
> placed it under his arm with a thrust,
> When the general gave him his orders,
> he cried, 'I'll do this 'ere job, sir, or bust.'[8]

There was obvious pride, amongst those gathered of the enormous task they had undertaken and completed.

Major General Richards' dining out for Bill was the main farewell event. Richards had succeeded Bill as COS and Dicky's words of thanks to Bill were printed in the *RAOC Gazette* on 29 April 1946:

> General Williams and I first met in France in [September 1915], and we both attended the first Ordnance Officers Course. We have watched the growth in responsibilities of Ordnance and we have watched our organization expand during the recent war years to an extent uncontemplated in peace. This expansion has thrown a heavy responsibility on the Head of Ordnance and we owe much to General Williams for his leadership, his organizing and administrative ability, and for his devotion to the interests of the RAOC.
>
> Ordnance Services have successfully survived the test of the greatest administrative war problems in world history, and this achievement is in itself a tribute to the work of General Williams.[9]

There was a 'Farewell from Chilwell' on 20 April 1946. Geoffrey Palmer said of Bill:

> We are going to miss General Williams and when I say that, I am taking the liberty of speaking not only for Chilwell, or

even for the Corps, but for the Services as a whole. We will miss his sound judgement, his leadership, his drive; but what is more, we will miss that kindly thought and consideration that he always had for the other man.[10]

June 1946 saw the great Victory Parade in London and Bill took part. His life, though, had moved to 'civvy street' and I describe this in the next chapter. He did keep more than one foot in the army camp. There is an invitation to an evening of boxing at Feltham. Then, in 1947, some more reunion dinners.

The RAOC Officers' Club dinner on 10 January 1947 had a glittering line-up of speakers:

- Senior Colonel Commandant – Major General Sir Basil Hill
- COS – Major General Dicky Richards
- QMG – General Sir Daril Watson
- Representative Colonel Commandant – Major General Joe Body
- Colonel Commandant – Major General Sir Leslie Williams

The Old Dalby Reunion followed the next evening, with president Bob Hiam, and Bill proposing the toast. This would be one of a great many to which Bill was invited right up until his death. I see it as underlining his commitment to those temporary officers who brought such vital expertise to the Corps.

A small booklet about 223 BOD Singapore, addressed to Bill, initially had me foxed. Bill had visited Singapore in 1913 on his way to the Malay Peninsula, but I could find no record of a visit during his army career. I needed to research further, and a newsletter of the 'Canbedoneans', a few pages later in the album, revealed all. The newsletter was a report on the first dinner of the 'Canbedoneans' at which Bill was present as guest of honour. The writer of the newsletter admits to doubts as to the wisdom of inviting such a guest, but he says that he took his hat off to Bill for his ability to mix with a crowd, many of whom he had never met. He then reported on the speech given by Stan Preston, their COO, who did indeed know Bill.

Preston said that he had first been drawn to the RAOC by the letters Bill wrote to business. However, the first taste of army life at Chilwell had knocked off all the rough corners. It was at Chilwell where he first heard Bill referred to by his nickname, 'Willie', apparently used throughout the Corps. When he first met him, the report goes on:

> He was amazed at the amount of detailed ordnance and accounting knowledge which the General possessed. He also described, to the amusement of all at the dinner, a subsequent meeting, which was in the Feltham Depot, where the General arrived for an unexpected inspection immediately prior to leaving for India. In the course of expressing appreciation for the amount of work which had been done, he applied his knobbly General's cane to the appropriate portion of Colonel Preston's body and, using the same cane, indicated a very dusty lampshade. According to Colonel Preston, that was just typical of the General, and showed that nothing was too large and nothing too small to be noticed and tackled, and, in fact, showed the true spirit of the 'Canbedonians'.[11]

Stan Preston had been at 206 BOD in India, as I told in Chapter 11, but had transferred to the newly formed 223 BOD which was set up in Hong Kong following the Japanese surrender. Reading between the lines, the task that faced them had been enormous; hence the vital attitude of 'can be done'. There is an album of photographs taken soon after their arrival. Appropriately, there is then the record of a reunion of the Old Felthamians with Brigadier Harry Whitaker presiding and Bill proposing the toast.

Dicky Richards had succeeded Bill as Controller of Ordnance Services on 21 April 1946 and served in that post until 17 July 1947. The post was then renamed, according to Phelps, in line with the American Chiefs of Staff system, Director of Ordnance Services.[12] Richards served from 18 July 1947 to 20 April 1948 as DOS. The focus of Dicky's tenure in both offices was essentially the managed reduction in the size of Ordnance, a massive task. Confusingly there were three other, but subordinate, Directors of Ordnance Services in the British Army of the Rhine (BAOR), the Middle East Land Force (MELF) and South East Asia. DOS MELF was first Neville Swiney, then Jim Denniston. Cutters Cutforth succeeded Cyril Cansdale as DOS BAOR. In South East Asia, the DOS was C.W. Bacon (who had been adjutant at Hilsea in that first photograph) with, amongst many others, Norman Speller in Hong Kong and Digger Reynolds in Japan.

On leaving the army, Bill moved with Mabel, Bill's mother and George Cook to a house he had found in comfortable commuter distance from his new civilian job, of which I write more in the next chapter. Long Grove House, which had been built before the First World War and had more than a few hints of the Arts and Crafts movement, was large, in need of tender loving care and surrounded by a seriously overgrown garden. George Cook began a love affair with the garden which would last very nearly until his death. The one thing the house wasn't, was happy. Bill and Mabel had grown apart, but Bill was unable to see any way forward. It was left to Frank Perks's solicitor, Sidney Littlewood, a man later to be president of the Law Society, to take Bill aside and ask the question which I suspect is obvious to the reader: whom should Bill avoid hurting, his wife or Betty, the woman he loved? (Betty had had to return to her parent's house near Chilwell to look after her sick mother.) The short story is that Bill and Mabel divorced, leaving the way open for Bill and Betty to marry, which they did on 16 April 1948.

In 1948, Major General Gerald Horne succeeded Richards as DOS and faced the challenge of continuing to reshape Ordnance for peace in a time of budget cuts. It was during his time in office that NATO was formed with a consequent knock-on for Ordnance Services. Of great practical import was the introduction of national service which again increased the workload of the RAOC with the need to equip a constant flow of new recruits.

It was Horne who announced Bill's first term as Representative Colonel Commandant for 1949, a role that encompassed a variety of ceremonial duties and which kept Bill thoroughly involved with the life of his beloved Corps. As a first task, Bill had correspondence with Buckingham Palace about the Australian Ordnance Corps adopting the badges and buttons of the RAOC. On 29 May 1949, the standard of the Plymouth Association of the RAOC was dedicated at the RAOC sportsground at Hilsea (the former headquarters) and Bill, as Representative Colonel Commandant, attended. The 1914–18 and 1939–45 War Memorial at the Minden Barracks at Deepcut was unveiled on Remembrance Sunday, 6 November 1949, and dedicated by the QMG, General Sir Sydney Kirkman, with Bill by his side.

On 14 October 1949, there had been the first reunion of the officers of 14, 15, 16 and 17 AODs. Gerald Horne as DOS replied to the toast, and Bob Hiam proposed the toast to the chairman with the reply by Cutters, present by virtue of his role in 21st Army Group. Cutters was then back in the War Office as one of Gerald's deputies. Bill was present as a guest. On 21 October 1949, Basil Cox invited Bill to a regimental dinner at Bicester. Bill then attended the Sovereign's Parade at Sandhurst on 15 December 1949.

His Christmas message to members of the RAOC was remarkable. This is some of what he said:

> It is a far cry from those early Christmases of the war, when we had our backs against the wall and were all working as a team, determined to win, in spite of all the difficulties and the handicaps with which we were faced.
>
> We had hoped, and most of us felt, that the results of our efforts would be to banish war for a long time to come and that it could only result, in the long run, in making this world a better place to live for future generations.
>
> In spite of these efforts, something has gone wrong, and we seem to be further than ever from our objective.[13]

Given Bill's very considerable efforts with India, it was appropriate that he should attend the Dedication of Memorials to Officers and Ranks of the Indian Army at Sandhurst in 1950.

That same year, Basil Cox was sent from Bicester back to the Middle East to Tel-el-Kebir. Cutters Cutforth wrote of this on Cox's untimely death in 1953:

> In 1950 he returned to TEK from which he had been invalided in 1943, and again set about the task in his old hunting ground with boundless energy and enthusiasm, ably assisted, in her proper sphere, by his wife. In the autumn of 1951, however, the troubles arising from the abrogation of the Egyptian Treaty began, and both as Garrison Commander and Commandant 5 BOD, he went through a period trying enough to affect the health of the strongest. He lost practically all of his civilian employees and more than half of his military strength, so that the whole organization he had built up was destroyed.[14]

Basil Cox was again invalided to the UK in 1952 and died a year later. In Bill's papers there is a letter from him to Bill reminiscing, but also picking up on Bill's comment in 1949 that 'something had gone wrong'.

Cutters was writing having taken over as DOS MELF from Jim Denniston who had held that post since he left BAOR. Denniston retired after a period in the Middle East which

> coincided with a difficult phase of economic re-organization which was made still more difficult by receding manpower, reduced estimates and a certain element of doubt and indecision. General Denniston met all difficulty with indomitable courage and unfailing cheerfulness.[15]

Cutters would have an equally challenging time.

On 17 July 1951, Brigadier Goldstein, the new commandant of Bicester, invited Bill, as founder of the depot, to a regimental guest night. It must have seemed light years away from their days at Woolwich in 1922. Goldstein was faced with a large wartime depot that quickly needed to be made suitable for a substantial peacetime role but also to equip those parts of the army committed to the Korean War. There were married quarters to be built, and four battalions formed at Bicester needed to have their regimental work integrated with technical duties. He set up activities and sports competitions, and a ladies' social club. On his retirement, he was succeeded as COO by John Hildreth who had first served with him in pre-war Didcot. Hildreth wrote of the apple-pie-order in which Goldstein handed over both depot and living quarters.

The holder of the office of Director of Ordnance Services had changed once more with the appointment of Neville Swiney on 21 April 1951. Swiney had previously taken over command of the MT organization at Chilwell from Geoffrey Palmer. If you go to Chilwell now, you will find a Swiney Way, as well as Williams Road, Readman Road, Whitaker Road, Body Road and Hill Road. There is, of course, a Palmer Avenue at Bicester. It was Neville Swiney who signed the letter appointing Bill as Representative Colonel Commandant for 1952.

The year began on a sombre note when, on 10 February, Bill, in his role as Representative Colonel Commandant, received a warning order from the War Office that he would be required to march in the funeral procession of the late king. Betty includes a full-page picture of King George VI from the front of the *Daily Mail* of 15 February, and many other press cuttings. There is a telegram of sympathy to the new queen from the Director of Ordnance Services; the king had been Colonel-in-Chief, as the new queen would become. Bill also wrote a letter of sympathy as Master of the Carmen, of which I write more in Chapter 13. There are then photographs of the procession. Betty notes that marching for that length of time was demanding for someone of Bill's age.

The remainder of the year proceeded as had his last as Representative Colonel Commandant, including, on 17 July 1952, a Buckingham Palace garden party. I suspect, though, he did rather less, given his responsibilities as Master of the Carmen.

In 1953 there was an Indian Army Ordnance Corps Old Comrades' Association reunion dinner on 9 May, and then, on 4 July, the Travers Clarke Sports meeting at Bicester. This annual event, which I remember for the tug of war, was named after the QMG in the First World War.

Bill was again appointed as Representative Colonel Commandant for 1954 and this year was busier, or at least, Betty recorded more activity. Bill visited the Leicester branch of the RAOC Association and there is a photograph of him with his wartime deputy, Brigadier Lea-Cox. Her Majesty the Queen approved the painting of a portrait of her for the Corps by Denis Fildes. In July, Bill was once again flying the flag for Chilwell when he welcomed the QMG there. A 'demonstration atlas' was produced for the occasion which set out the worldwide task of Motor Transport for both the RAOC and REME.

There was more than a hint of Britain in the 1950s, when Bill inspected the passing-out parade on 9 July 1954 of national service intake no. 5411. I tell in Chapter 13 of national service as it affected the Rootes Group. Two years in the services was not universally popular!

An invitation, with an echo from earlier times, came from Lord Mackintosh to visit the House of Lords on 20 July 1954 and was addressed to Bill and Betty with Mr and Mrs Sturtevant of New York. With the USA in mind, there was a sad moment for Bill and Betty when they received the *Newsky News* from Hoovers, reporting the death of H.W. Hoover who had been so welcoming on their trips to the USA.

In his Representative Colonel Commandant role, Bill attended two national events. The first was the Florence Nightingale Centenary at Westminster Abbey on 4 November 1954. Then General Marshall, chairman of the American Battlefield Monuments Commission, invited Bill to the dedication of the Cambridge American Military Cemetery 1941–45.

In 1955, Betty was diagnosed with cancer and had to undergo a major operation. By way of recuperation, they travelled to Algeciras in Spain. Needless to say, Bill took the opportunity to visit the RAOC presence in nearby Gibraltar.

Neville Swiney stood down as Director of Ordnance Services on 21 April 1955. His term had been eventful, with the Korean War, the troubles arising from the abrogation of the Egyptian Treaty and the subsequent run-down of the RAOC presence in South East Asia, the Middle East and Germany. He was succeeded by Cutters who appointed Bill Representative Colonel Commandant for the final time for 1957; the year began with a visit to Donnington on 7 February for which a separate album was produced.[16]

The portrait of the Queen, painted for the RAOC, was copied by the artist, Denis Fildes, and the resulting painting presented to the Junior Carlton Club where it was hung in the ladies' annex. It was unveiled by Lady Churchill on 15 May 1957. Bill attended.

One of Bill's last official engagements was to visit BAOR and the 4th Infantry Division Ordnance Field Park on 13 November 1957, in the company of the DOS BAOR Brigadier John Hildreth.

Bill wrote his last Christmas message to the Corps in December 1957, adding that,

> this has been a momentous year for our country and for the Services in particular. When the final reorganization is completed, I am sure that our great Corps, which earned such laurels in the last Great War, will be one of the most important and efficient in the army, and will, I hope, provide a secure and happy career for everyone concerned.[17]

On 1 January 1958, Bill was succeeded by Major General Cutforth as Colonel Commandant.

Bill's army connection didn't stop and, on 24 April 1958, he was invited to cocktails with the London Scottish. This was reported in the *London Scottish Gazette* from which I gleaned the information I included in Chapter 3.

A high point in Bill's army career must have been the visit by the Queen and the Duke of Edinburgh to the RAOC headquarters at Blackdown, Deepcut on 11 April 1958. Bill had first written to invite the Queen in 1953, so it had been a long wait. There is correspondence with Sir Edward Ford at Buckingham Palace first suggesting Bicester as the depot to visit, but eventually they settled on Deepcut. Betty included a transcript of the letter the Queen's private secretary wrote to Bill following her visit:

> The Queen wishes me to send to you an expression of her warm thanks for the arrangements which you had made for her visit to the Royal Army Ordnance Corps Headquarters at Blackdown yesterday. Her Majesty has long been waiting for an opportunity to visit the Corps, of which she is proud to be Colonel-in-Chief. In spite of the bitter weather, the programme which you had arranged for the Queen and the Duke of Edinburgh not only very greatly interested them, but was one which both of them very much enjoyed. From the very start of the day, when the Queen was received with a Royal Salute by a Guard of Honour which would have done credit to any Regiment in the Army, Her Majesty was impressed by the very high standard which was evident in every branch of the Corps' activities. Both Her Majesty and His Royal Highness realized the amount of trouble that had been taken to make the demonstrations effective and interesting in the short time allowed for each. Please convey an expression of the Queen's satisfaction and thanks to those concerned.[18]
> (© HM The Queen)

I see it as characteristically generous of Cutters to allow Bill the limelight for this visit. Cutters' term as Director of Ordnance Services came to an end on 21 April, just ten days after that momentous visit. During his tenure in the post, national service had continued to provide a steady stream of recruits for the RAOC, among them sports legends Henry Cooper and Bobby Charlton. There had been conflicts overseas demanding RAOC support: the Mau Mau operations in Kenya, the Enosis uprising in Cyprus and, most famously, the Suez crisis.

Cutters was succeeded on 22 April 1958 by Major General George O. Crawford who oversaw a shift to more modern weaponry such as guided missiles. He was succeeded on 22 April 1961 by Bill's right-hand man during the Second World War, Major General Sir John Hildreth, who would serve until 19 November 1964 and have to wrestle with yet more major reorganizations.

It seems appropriate that the final two items in Betty's albums are two letters from two brigadiers sending reports and good wishes from two reunions: the first from Stan Preston and the Canbedoneans, and the second from Robbie Robinson and the Old Derbyrians. There is also a signed menu card from the Old Dalby reunion, just a few weeks earlier. A handwritten letter signed simply R.F. dated 27 June sent good wishes from the many RAOC officers and men who had hoped to see Bill at the 1965 Travers Clarke Sports. Johnson added that the wishes came

> not only from the old-timers who served under you, and think of you as, after Parsons, the second founder of the Corps as we know it now, but also for the younger vintage, with whom the name of Bill Williams still rings a bell.[19]

Chapter 13

Civvy Street

In 1946 many thousands of men and women were leaving the armed forces and returning to civilian life. Six years of war had changed those who had survived in ways we would find hard to comprehend. Those returning to civilian life and work were surely many times more than six years older as a result of their experiences. War had offered people like Bob Hiam, Robbie Robinson, Arthur Sewell, Reddy Readman and Ronald Weeks a vastly bigger canvas to allow their skills to grow. Those skills would now be brought to bear in civilian life.

For the country, there was a massive burden of debt from the borrowing government had had little choice but to incur, as the Americans supplied so much of what was needed not only to wage war, but also simply for the British people to survive. Britain was no longer a major power; that role had been ceded to the Americans and the USSR. There were pluses. The Beveridge Report had won cross-party support, and its implementation by the Attlee government was leading to the creation of the welfare state, including, of course, the National Health Service. Another big plus was the legacy of technological developments 'which the war had directly or indirectly stimulated'.[1]

Significant events mentioned in the previous chapter had knock-on effects in civvy street. The Korean War knocked the balance of payments with a massive increase in defence spending. At the same time, the Iranian government seized the Anglo-Iranian Oil Company installations in Abadan which produced one-quarter of British crude oil imports. Oil, too, would be one of the victims of the Suez crisis. Nearer to home, rationing continued and, in some cases, became more severe after the war. Two financial constraints came to the fore that would blight the third quarter of the twentieth century for Britain: inflation and an adverse balance of payments. C.P. Hill explains the relationship between these two constraints.[2] During the war, people's ability to buy all they had wanted was limited by shortages and by rationing. With the coming of peace, six years of unsatisfied wants bubbled to the surface. The problem was that industry was not yet producing enough to satisfy the demand; classically too much money was chasing too few goods. Prices increased, but also more and more goods were imported. There was full employment as industry struggled to meet demand and so wages rose, once again increasing the price of goods, both for domestic buyers but also for exports which inevitably suffered. Successive governments would wrestle with this two-headed monster for many years to come.

The leaving parties held for Reddy Readman and Bob Hiam, evidenced by invitations in Betty's albums that I have already mentioned, indicate that these two returned respectively to the steel industry and to Dunlop. The same was true of Robbie Robinson and Dunlop, and Arthur Sewell and Tecalemit, although in his case at some point he moved to run Tecalemit in Australia. Following his term as Director of Ordnance Services in 1948, Dicky Richards took up directorships in the City of London with companies in the mining industry. Harold Crosland returned to civilian life but maintained a significant military involvement as an elected council member of the Royal United Services Institution.

Bob Hiam features twice in James McMillan's book, *The Dunlop Story*. The first is in the early 1950s when Hiam addressed the Birmingham Chamber of Commerce with a fervent defence of retail price maintenance, whereby a manufacturer could dictate the retail price at which its products were sold. His case was that tyre suppliers had to hold a large variety of stock and have to hand specialist equipment in order to serve their customers.[3] Bob Hiam was Sales Director of the Dunlop company which sold replacement tyres, that is tyres not sold with the original vehicle. The challenges here were great and Hiam's boss, Sir Reay Geddes, commissioned a report from American consultants, McKinsey, on the company's sales function. The report was critical and focused on 'the conflict between Dunlop's pride in combining employment growth and the iron logic of reducing employment to cut costs and meet competition'.[4] McKinsey recommended a smaller, better qualified sales force. Hiam concurred. This was the shape of things to come, but, for much of industry, it would take too long to be widely recognized.

Ronald Weeks took the top job as, initially, a non-executive director of Vickers but eventually as chairman. He retained a directorship of Pilkington, as well as adding non-executive directorships of the Hudson Bay Company and Massey Ferguson. He was appointed a government director of British Petroleum (to which the Anglo-Iranian Oil Company changed its name in 1954) and chaired the Finance Corporation for Industry.[5] The Vickers role would prove both challenging and demanding. In 1945, the company lost its chairman: Sir Charles Craven had died in November 1944 'exhausted by the demands of the war'. Scott, writing *The History of Vickers*, recognized in Weeks something quite special. He writes:

> by the end of the Second World War, Weeks' brilliance as an administrator had become recognized as something of a phenomenon. If his career and his personality had been designed for the chairmanship of Vickers, they would have differed very little from the actuality.[6]

Weeks was made chairman four years later when the company was in the throes of nationalization.

The Attlee government had embarked on an ambitious programme of nationalization with first the Bank of England, then coal, the railways and road haulage, electricity and gas, and perhaps most controversially, iron and steel. I have already mentioned the English Steel Corporation in relation to Reddy Readman and noted how it was owned between Vickers and Cammel Laird, the former having control. It was much more than a steel company; it was really an engineering company that used steel. Ronald Weeks was appointed chairman of English Steel in 1945 and for the next two years, led the argument that most of the company's production were not 'scheduled products' for the purposes of nationalization, but rather engineering products made from steel. Nevertheless, eventually the government argument prevailed and the company was sold into public ownership for, it has to be said, a fair price.[7]

The Conservative government was returned to power in 1951, and by 1953 the necessary structures had been put in place to return the steel assets to private hands. Sir Ronald Weeks was again involved and set up a committee to carry out a cold financial appraisal of the part of the business that had been English Steel to see if Vickers wished to buy it back and, if so, at what price. Again, a good price was eventually achieved, and ownership returned in time for an upturn in demand for steel. Reddy Readman would retire in 1958 and Ronald Weeks soon after.

For Bill, the route to civvy street was a little different. Were he to 'return', it would have been to the *Daily Mirror*. Too much had happened, not least he had acquired a whole new skill set. I would go further and say that he had pioneered and then advanced the whole support infrastructure for motor vehicles, learning very much at the sharp end. A long article on Bill appeared in *Scope, The Magazine for Industry*, in November 1944. It recorded his war experience but also aspects of his thinking. Towards the end he says to his interviewer, Olive Moore, 'About time I thought of making some money.' She writes that he grinned.[8]

Betty's notes indicate that he had conversations with a number of motor companies, including Ford and Rover. The conversation that attracted him most was with William Rootes, with whom he had worked so closely over the war years, but who was also a visionary very much like Bill. Looking more broadly at the motor industry, Graham Turner in *The Car Makers* paints a stark post-war picture for the motor companies. It must be remembered that these private businesses had moved mountains in supporting the war effort. One result was that car production for domestic consumption had dried to a trickle; Turner quotes a total production of 1,649 cars in 1943.[9] With the coming of peace and the need to restore the balance of payments, the motor industry focused on production for overseas markets. In many ways it succeeded. In 1946 total production was back up to 216,000 vehicles a year. In 1950 Britain was the biggest exporter of cars in the world, many of which went to Australia and New Zealand, but also to America which was the major manufacturing nation but with its focus on the home market. Turner highlights the cost of this drive for exports, firstly in terms of quality where Britain gained a bad reputation for the reliability of the vehicles it exported. The other cost, which he places at the foot of the drive for exports, was a failure to manage industrial relations. He quotes Rootes as having serious problems at its British Light Steel Pressings Plant in North London but that they opted to placate the 600 workers there, rather than risking a walk-out by their total workforce of 15,000. Notwithstanding these drawbacks, Hill is clear that the motor industry in Coventry, Birmingham, Luton, Dagenham and Oxford was one of the success stories of post-war British industry. It was into this heady atmosphere that Bill, fast approaching 60, set out on his second, or do I mean third, fourth or fifth career.

Bill joined Rootes in April 1946, and on 18 July he was invited to what must have been a great occasion. It was the opening, by the Minister of Supply, The Rt. Hon. John Wilmot MP, of the headquarters of the British Motor Industry at 148 Piccadilly, a fine town house built in the 1860s by Baron Lionel de Rothschild. It was to house an exhibition of the motor industry for some six weeks and then assume its headquarters role. There was also a jubilee banquet at the Dorchester Hotel, which Bill attended. Of significance to our story was the presence of Bill's old friend from Dunlop, Harold Kenward, as president of the Society of Motor Manufacturers and Traders, the principal trade association of the motor industry.[10] On 27 July 1946 the Rootes Group itself celebrated Britain's Motor Industry Jubilee, and Bill was photographed at the centre of a group of Rootes Group employee representatives.

Rootes was not the biggest British motor manufacturer. In his book, *Rootes Story: The Making of a Global Automotive Empire,* Geoff Carverhill quotes figures from 1950 when Rootes was ranked fifth of twenty-seven manufacturers with output of 90,000. Ford was largest with 185,000, with Austin second at 166,000, Nuffield third at 150,000 and Standard-Triumph at 112,000. Vauxhall came just below Rootes at 89,000. Of the total manufactured, 400,000 were for export.[11]

The job Rootes offered to Bill was as a general manager, but also with a seat on the Board of Directors. The particular general manager job could have been created specifically for him; it mirrored his acquired skill set so perfectly. It was to set up a whole new repair and maintenance depot for commercial vehicles, but also for domestic cars produced by the Rootes Group under the Humber, Hillman, Sunbeam and Singer marks. In his *Scope* interview, Bill had expressed his views on the post-war priorities for industry:

> It is obvious enough that our crying need after this war will be to expand our export. To expand it we have either to supply a better article or a cheaper article than our competitors; better still, a combination of both. Above all, we must give a really first-class maintenance service for everything we sell. I am speaking as the business man and not the Army man when I say in the majority of cases after sales service for export is not carried out to anything like the extent it should be or is in America.[12]

Ladbroke Hall would fulfil this ambition for the home market and provide a model for markets overseas.

The site was large – the former Sunbeam-Talbot factory in Balby Road, West London backing on to the Great Western Railway line – and so offered the right size of canvas. The 'paints' at Bill's disposal came from the early days at Chilwell, but then the imaginative layout of Bicester. The depot at Balby Road was, after all, a central ordnance depot in all but name, but, crucially, with the total integration of a civilian version of REME. In this regard, the massive REME tank workshop at Bicester must have offered a magnificent example. It wasn't just the UK depots; it was the US motor industry of which Bill had had an unparalleled view. So too, the other companies in the British motor industry; he had visited them all. His great friend Bob Chalmers's company, Tecalemit, knew more about garage equipment than anyone.

The result was described in a booklet entitled *Modern Truck Service*.[13] This explains to the commercial vehicle user the facilities offered by the new depot. At the heart of it was a massive sunken workshop which could service, at the same time, four of the largest vehicles produced by Commer or Karrier, the Rootes Group commercial vehicle companies. This takes the idea of an inspection sump to, possibly, its logical conclusion. The vehicles' wheels were driven on to steel girders and the engineers could work without crouching, addressing all the needs of the underside of the vehicle. Before this, the vehicles were thoroughly washed both above and beneath. In the sunken workshop, there were airlines, but also lines for lubricating and gearbox oils. There was a drainage system for spent oil, and overhead cranes powerful enough to lift cabs to facilitate work on engines and to lift whole bodies to enable work on chassis. The general rule was for engines to be replaced with reconditioned engines.

Dick Hunt followed Bill to Rootes and brought his skills to bear in production planning. Graham Turner hints at the scale of this challenge when he writes of Rootes that 'in order to turn out its light car range it has to order correctly, schedule and marshal no less than 16,000 parts'.[14] Dick's experience of tank assembly would have been priceless.

The New Year's Honours list for 1947 contained the name of Harold Kenward, created Knight Batchelor for service to the British motor industry. This announcement delighted Bill and a great many of his new colleagues within the motor industry. In August, Kenward and his wife set out on the new *Queen Elizabeth* for New York. Tragically, only one day into the voyage, Harold was taken ill and died. He was such a well-respected name in the motor industry and so well liked, that it must have sent shock waves. I have already quoted from the appreciation in Bill's archive. I also found online that the Society of Motor Manufacturers and Traders presented a scholarship fund, in memory of Kenward, to St Catherine's College Cambridge of whose association Kenneth Johnson-Davies was then chairman.[15]

The completion of the Ladbroke Hall project coincided with Bill's and Betty's wedding in April 1948. Bill's best man was Gordon Richards, his great friend from the war years who had also remarried. My sister and I remember his new wife, Lynn, with great affection; she became my sister's godmother. Bill's and Betty's honeymoon was short, for the Rootes job continued to demand. Bill was asked to move to New York to head up the Rootes USA sales business. Both he and Betty had fallen in love with the States from their many trips. They had made good friends and it would have been exciting. However, Bill's mother, who lived with them, was getting old and Betty's parents weren't in the best of health. They also wanted to start a family and they thought that this was best done in England. William Rootes respected Bill's decision and sent his son Geoffrey in Bill's place. Geoffrey made a huge success of the appointment.

A party at the Dorchester in 1948 with an intriguing invitation entitled 'Darby's Detours' is the first mention of a relationship that would extend over generations. Bill Darby was an entrepreneur and among his interests was Lewis Berger, the paint company, and among his guests was the name W.A. Shapland, which would appear on the letterhead of a good number of companies in the years to come. Bill had been invited through his Rootes connection, but perhaps also because one of the major shareholders in Lewes Berger, Vera Lilley, was the widow of one of Bill's former fellow officers. Two years later, on 17 November 1950, Lewis Berger held a lunch party at the Dorchester for some thirty guests from a broad spread of industry from Thorne Lighting and Plessey to Cunard, Jack Olding and a number from the motor industry, including Bill from Rootes and Colonel Waite, a director of Austin. The lunch was hosted by Bill Darby and Cyril Fry as Finance Director. As a young auditor, I remember meeting Fry when he was chairman of one of our clients, Tremco, a specialist paint manufacturer. Looking further down the guest list there was, once more, W.A. Shapland but then as a partner in Allan Charlesworth & Co., the firm with which I trained as an accountant. Of the other names, Jack Olding is significant. His company had supplied the army with Caterpillar equipment, and, at their premises known as 'Tank Central', prepared many tanks for deployment; later thousands of tanks were decommissioned there. He was also the host at a shoot which Bill attended each year at King's Forrest, Culford.

The final entry for 1948 has an echo of Bill's and Betty's final trip to the USA, and is a letter from the actor, Ronald Coleman, saying how sad he and his wife, Benita, were not to have seen them on their recent trip to England.

Themes begin to emerge in the albums, a particularly strong one being city livery companies. In my study as I write this, the photograph I have of my father is of him with his Master's robes of his beloved Carmen which I have already mentioned in relation to wartime relationships. In the peace and, particularly, now in business, Bill set out, in 1949, on his path to Master's chair, when he was elected Junior Warden and so a member of the Court of the Carmen. There is a photograph of the Court in Session.

As a member of the Court, there were invitations from a number of other livery companies: the Farriers, the Paint-Stainers and the Basketmakers, the Fruiterers, the Dyers, the Glaziers and Painters of Glass, although these may equally have come through personal contacts: that old adage of his, 'it's not what you know, it's who you know'. Bill attended the first livery dinner for the Company of Farmers in 1953. A name from the past appeared, when Bob Lillico of Lucas invited Bill to a Skinners company dinner. Lucas, itself, featured in the albums with regular invitations to the Lucas Agents dinner.

Bill was installed as Senior Warden of the Carmen in November 1950 and in 1951 he was elected Master. I can't help seeing the small boy sitting at the kneehole chest in Trossachs Road all those years before. He took to the role, which lasted for one year, with characteristic energy and enthusiasm. There are, in Betty's album, letter after letter sent to the leaders of the day inviting them to key events. Some accepted, some declined, but always most graciously. One who did attend was the high commissioner of Rhodesia who, at a dinner, made a plea for union in Africa, as well as congratulating Bill as Master for the success of Sunbeam-Talbot in the Monte Carlo Rally: politics, business and sport hand in hand. There were also lunches including one at the Tallow Chandlers Hall with Humphrey Gale as guest. Gale had been Bill's host at dinner in North Africa in 1943.

The high point, and indeed final point, of Bill's year as Master was the livery dinner in the Egyptian Hall at the Mansion House with Minister of Transport Rt. Hon. A.T. Lennox-Boyd MP as principal speaker. Bill wrote a personal letter of thanks to the Lord Mayor, Sir Leslie Boyce, who gave permission for the dinner to be held in 'his' Mansion House. The Duke of Sutherland and Earl Alexander of Tunis were on the invitation list, but had prior engagements. MP Rupert De la Bère (Lord Mayor elect) wrote a letter of thanks to say how much he had enjoyed his conversation with the Rootes brothers about diesel transport in Africa; it was all about networking. The Duke of Sutherland was the young man Bill met on his way out to Africa. Earl Alexander was, of course, the celebrated soldier. That he and Bill knew each other is evidenced in a photograph, reproduced in the *Tatler*, of Earl and Countess Alexander warmly welcoming Bill and Betty to a ball raising money for the Trinidad Empire Games in 1954. Digging deeper, I found a copy of Bill's letter to Alexander inviting him to the livery dinner, and, in the letter, he reminded Alexander that he had served under him a number of times in his army career. In the file where I found the letter to Alexander, there was also a copy of the speech Bill made in reply to the Minister of Transport.

Bill spoke of the need for better roads, both to reduce the large number of road accidents but also to facilitate door-to-door delivery of goods. He told how he saw the Carmen as 'the arteries and veins of the country through which flow the goods to our ports and imported food and raw materials'. He added that,

> we number amongst our Livery not only a large number of representatives of the road haulage industry, but also members of shipping and air ... for example we are glad to include in our Livery Sir Miles Thomas, who has done so much to make BOAC one of the greatest air transport operators in the world ... last, but not least, we have some distinguished members of the very ancient craft, the wine merchants, who provide the oil which is such a help in so many difficult business negotiations.[16]

For Bill, this last point would prove prophetic.

With Ladbroke Hall up and running, Bill was asked to move to the exports department of Rootes to work alongside the export managing director, Joe Caldecott. This, Bill was happy to do; Caldecott spent most of his time travelling and Bill addressed the organizational issues at home. He also did possibly what he did best: he nurtured his extensive network of contacts. Outside the hallowed walls of the City of London, the Society of Motor Manufacturers and Traders was of particular note. The 1948 SMMT dinner was addressed by the Minister of Supply, G.R. Strauss. In the album, there is then a photograph of Bill with his opposite numbers at Morris Commercial. There is a suggestion that Rootes and Morris were considering a merger of their commercial vehicle businesses.[17] In 1952 Morris and Austin did indeed merge to become the British Motor Corporation. On 11 February 1948, Bill attended a dinner at Claridge's in honour of Henry Ford with the great and the good of the British motor industry. It was hosted by the chairman of Ford UK, Lord Airedale, and had speeches from Henry Ford, Sir Rowland Smith, Managing Director of Ford UK, and G.R. Strauss, the Minister of Supply. Bill was invited to the Automobile Association celebration of one million members. Bill and Betty received an invitation to the Road Haulage Association annual banquet and ball on 10 March 1952, and Bill one to the Roadfarers' Club Traders Road Transport Association later in the year. The chairman of the RAC invited Bill to the presentation of the Dewar Trophy to Sunbeam-Talbot for the outstanding performance of the three Sunbeam-Talbot cars in the international Alpine Rally, 1952, and the research and development that made this possible. Bill Duck of Firestone Tyre and Rubber invited Bill to a reception with Harvey Firestone on Monday, 8 June 1953.

There were also invitations from foreign governments: the Egyptian ambassador and the Belgian ambassador; the Egyptian invitation was followed up in 1949 by one to the Anglo-Egyptian Society. The involvement with groups from other countries is further evidenced by an invitation to a commemorative dinner of the New Zealand Society on 22 January 1952, to the Canada Club on 29 April 1952, to the Brazilian Chamber of Commerce and Economic Affairs, to the British and Latin Chamber of Commerce and to the high commissioner of India. There is a photograph of a motor industry meeting with potential customers from Nigeria in 1952. The Kuwait Oil Company features frequently, with invitations to dinners but also to a showing of the film *Desert Harvest* at the Curzon on 27 August 1952. It wasn't only Bill; there is an invitation to the 1953 Canada Lodge Ladies' Night with photographs of Bill and Betty with their hosts. Betty was also invited to the Anglo-Arab Association Coronation reception on 8 June. It was back to men only for the Royal Central Asian Society in July 1953, the Iraqi military attaché in October 1953 and the Sudan Agency in London on 6 October 1954. Bill, now in his sixties, was approaching his job with energy and enthusiasm. He loved it.

A third theme comes from the first mention in the albums of the Pilgrims, a society promoting Anglo-American dialogue; it was part of the 'special relationship'. There are many guest lists in Betty's albums, and the speakers were the most prominent men of the time. On 4 May 1949, Bill was elected as a member and attended a dinner at which the US Secretary of State, The Hon. George Marshall (of the Marshall plan) spoke; the Earl of Halifax was in the chair. In 1940, it had either been Halifax or Churchill who would succeed Chamberlain as prime minister. Dean Acheson, the US Secretary of State, spoke at the dinner in May 1950 and Dr James B. Conant, President of Harvard, on 18 March 1952. The June dinner had as its guest the Foreign Secretary, Anthony Eden. The speaker on 14 October 1952 was General Matthew B. Ridgway, Supreme Commander Allied Powers in Europe, and on 21 January 1953, Walter S. Gifford, the US ambassador. Perhaps more memorably, on 18 March 1954, Dag Hammarskjöld, Secretary-General of the United Nations, spoke, followed, on 21 June 1956, by Harry S. Truman, President of the USA 1945–53. Ominously, on 25 November 1958, Richard M. Nixon, Vice-President of the USA, was the speaker. At possibly Bill's last dinner, on 14 August 1962, General Dwight Eisenhower, President of the USA 1953–61, spoke. Of course, it wasn't just the speaker, it was the opportunity to mingle in such a group.

There were other not dissimilar groups: The Ends of the Earth Dinner on 1 June 1955 with speaker, Harold Macmillan, Foreign Secretary, and The Saints and Sinners Club, with Bill Darby. Then a lunch at the Dorchester for an unnamed group which had a guest list with names that for me rang a bell: Kenneth Horne (radio comedian, but also at one time managing director of Triplex Glass which supplied most of the motor industry and was part owned by Pilkington), Colonel John Pye (later Master of the Carmen), Douglas Gluckstein (present at Bill's and

Betty's wedding with his secretary, Susan Barry, who was my sister's other godmother) and the Earl of Courtown whose son, Patrick Stopford, is Conservative Chief Whip in the House of Lords. There is also an intriguing press cutting from *The Recorder* of 1 November 1952 listing the best-known London restaurants and which famous people ate where. Bill was amongst those listed and, apparently, ate at the Caprice!

The day job was, of course, the export of motor vehicles and, in evidence, there are three photographs of 'West African Chiefs' at the London Motor Show. This meeting was followed by a trip to the Brussels Motor Show and then the Geneva Motor Show from 17 to 27 March 1949; Bill was there showing off the new ranges. The *Rootes Gazette* of July 1949 is full of export news with a photograph of the Australian distributors conference, a visit to Ladbroke Hall by Mr Patel, the Defence Minister of India, and actor Richard Murdoch, of the BBC radio programme, *Much Binding,* taking delivery of his Super Snipe. On 7 October 1949, Bill was invited to the Sunbeam-Talbot Owners' Club, and he spoke at a car dealers' conference in Ireland on Rootes' progress in world markets. Nubar Gulbenkian was a well-known society millionaire and Betty had on file a letter of thanks from him to Bill about a Humber Hawk.

Just two months later, an event occurred which, I suspect, Bill had thought would never happen: at the age of 58, he became a father. Marian Nancy was born to Betty on 7 December 1949. I would follow just under two years later. The presence of children, alongside a job where a wife was expected to accompany her husband, meant that Betty needed a nanny, and Moira Broadbridge joined those resident at Long Grove House. Moira would become a very close friend of my sister.

With children taken care of, Bill and Betty travelled to the Paris Salon, the Copenhagen Motor Show and the Amsterdam Motor Show in 1952. In December 1954, Bill visited H.J. Wallin, the Rootes agent in Copenhagen which the *Rootes Gazette* reported extensively. It was a period of great success: a Humber Super Snipe won the Monte Carlo Rally.

It wasn't all selling. An invitation to the Institute of Packaging dinner was coupled with an article giving an account of what Bill had said in his speech, as he recalled the efforts he and his team had gone to in the war to ensure efficient use of shipping space and appropriate packing for the rough handling stores would receive.

It is clear, also, from the albums that Bill involved himself with Rootes employees. As I have already mentioned, one of his treasured possessions was a silver cigarette case given to him to commemorate a production of *Aladdin* performed in Gibraltar in 1925. On 26, 27 and 28 November 1949, there was a performance of the Ben Travers farce *Rookery Nook* with Bill named as president of the Rootes Players. *The Barton Mystery* by Walter Hacket followed on 23–24 January 1952 and, throughout his time with Rootes, such programmes appear regularly in Betty's albums. Was this a love of theatre or evidence of involvement with the workforce? There are, of course, photographs of annual staff dinner dances. That of 11 March 1949 had the most wonderful invitations with an image of Ladbroke Hall. I don't recall Bill having an interest in cricket, but the *Rootes Group Review* of January 1952 shows him presenting the end-of-season prizes at the Rootes Cricket Club.

Another possible sub-theme I think can be traced to Frank Rokison, the Rootes shipping manager. It emerges, in December 1948, with an invitation from Cunard to join them for a coastal trip on their new liner RMS *Caronia*. Betty records in her album that they met and talked to the Duke of Edinburgh. In the albums, there are guides to passengers on the *Queen Mary* and the *Queen Elizabeth*, from which I certainly infer a distinct interest, confirmed perhaps by another invitation to join the maiden voyage of a new ship, this time from the Orient Line, RMS *Orcades*. More shipping companies feature: the New Zealand Shipping company, Swedish Lloyd and the British India Steam Navigation Company and Orient Line with their SS *Uganda*. There is an invitation from Ellerman Lines for a coastal trip on the *City of Port Elizabeth*. Bill attended the Spithead Review 1953 on SS *Kenya*, with guests including the Sultan of Zanzibar. Bill and Betty sailed on Ellerman Lines *City of Durban* to Holland on 3 September 1954. The Royal Mail Lines Ltd. invited Bill to view their *Highland Princess* on 17 December 1957. Bill was invited to a lunch on the Ellerman Lines *Iberia* with a guest list including one Mac Escombe of shippers Escombe, McGrath. An invitation from P&O Far Eastern Freight Services to lunch on 26 April 1956 is in the album, with a handwritten note of that same name 'Escombe'. An invitation from Escombe to Bill to the Merchant Taylors Hall on 24 April 1958, perhaps demonstrates the path of a growing friendship/business relationship. This becomes even clearer with subsequent invitations to Merchant Taylors events. All the time, Bill is expanding his network of contacts.

On 30 September 1952, Mildred, Bill's mother, died. In the album, shortly after this announcement, there is an article on Cecil, Bill's brother, who was managing director of Stein & Atkinson Ltd., manufacturers of furnaces for steel and glass. It told how Cecil was a founder member of the Institute of Fuel and had been a member of the Society of Glass Technology since 1935 and of the Iron and Steel Institute since 1936. I can't help thinking that Mildred must have been proud of her sons. She was buried in Seer Green cemetery where she would be joined by Bill thirteen years later and by Betty well over half a century later, in 2009.

Bill loved the company of interesting people. His continuing wider involvement in business is evidenced by an invitation from Sir Patrick Ashley Cooper of the Hudson's Bay Company on 12 April 1949. Bill had first met Cooper when he was with Cunard in New York during the war. There is then an invitation to luncheon at the Dorchester from the Earl of Cottenham and Peter Merchant Ltd. entitled 'Feeding Industry'. Present were industry leaders including Bill, but also Maurice Laing (J.M. Laing of the builders John Laing & Son who would serve on the Middle East Mission with Bill, which I write about below). Bill and Betty attended the 1951 general election night at the Savoy with speeches from Churchill, Attlee and Clement Davies. The albums feature regular invitations from Illustrated Newspapers and the Albany Club, but also one from Vincent Jobson of Qualcast 'At Home' at the Dorchester. This is a name that resonates from my childhood. It is perhaps strange to remember names of businessmen, when other children may recall favourite bedtime stories or visits to football matches! Having said this, one of my fondest memories of my father was of trips to Woolworths in nearby Uxbridge where we would buy tools which we would then use in building my Marklin model railway which came in instalments every Christmas from 'Father Christmas' aka a friend of Bill's in Germany.

There is clear evidence of Bill's own sporting interest with invitations to both football and boxing. There are regular invitations to boxing matches at the Harringay Arena, and also to football matches at Charlton Athletic. One of the football matches was against Derby County which Betty had, as a girl, watched with her family. There was an invitation to the Henley Royal Regatta on 1 June 1949 and the Football Association 90th anniversary with England v Rest of the World at the Empire Stadium, Wembley.

In looking at Bill's export efforts, one name stands out, that of Emile Bustani, chairman of the Contracting and Trading Company of Beirut in the Lebanon. In Betty's album there is a newspaper cutting about him under the title 'Woodrow Wyatt's Commentary', dated 3 June 1956. Wyatt was a well-known journalist and politician and his piece on Bustani is headlined: 'Emile: Do-gooder of the Middle East'. It continues:

> When I was in Cairo before Christmas, he was almost the first person I saw. He was having lunch at my hotel. He arranged an interview with Col Nasser days before I could have got it any other way.
>
> In Baghdad a few weeks ago, I had just finished interviewing Nuri Pasha Prime Minister of Iraq. Walking across the lawn there he was again. His name is Emile Bustani and his influence reaches all over the Middle East.[18]

Wyatt goes on to explain that from humble origins, Bustani graduated from the American University in Beruit and that his first job was teaching mathematics at a Quaker school in Palestine. He then went to America and, with a degree in engineering, returned to work in Palestine. Soon he set up his own contracting company, with work across the Middle East. The company was a great success, and Bustani became Minister of Public Works in the Lebanese government, foregoing any salary. As Wyatt says, 'he does care about what happens to ordinary people. In many ways he is a natural "do-gooder".' In the Middle East where corruption was never far away, 'even his enemies say he is not a corrupt politician'.

There are a number of photographs with him and Bill indicating a warm relationship. There are then photographs of a business trip Bill made to see him in the Middle East and to meet colleagues and connections. He died in a flying accident whilst still in his prime and there is a website dedicated to his memory.[19]

The Coronation on 2 June 1953, I have placed in civvy street, since, whilst Bill attended in his capacity as Colonel Commandant of the RAOC, the best photographs were of the Rootes party in Devonshire House in Piccadilly with Emile Bustani and American chat show host, Jinx Falkenburgh, together with Bill and Billy Rootes.

This leads quite naturally into a high point in Bill's business career when he was invited to take part in the Middle East Mission. Betty records it by including the text of a reply to a question in Parliament on 10 November 1953, when Mr Heathcoat Amery said:

As the house is aware the oil producing regions of the Middle East are very important export markets and her Majesty's government have decided to send a trade mission of prominent businessmen to these countries and to Syria and Lebanon in the immediate future. The team has now been constituted under the leadership of Sir Edward Benthall, and I should like to take this opportunity of expressing the grateful thanks of her Majesty's government to these gentlemen for volunteering their services. The mission will leave in a few days' time and will visit over a period of about five weeks Baghdad, Kuwait, Damascus, Beirut and Jeddah as well as other important commercial centres in the countries in question.[20]

The letter of appointment added the list of members:

W.R. Beswick – Director Power Gas Corporation

D. Maxwell Buist – Export Director British Electrical and Allied Manufacturers Association

C.H. Colton – Director British Celanese

S.R. Halton – Director Balfour Williamson Merchant Shippers Ltd.

J.M. Laing – Director, John Laing & Son Ltd. (civil engineers)

T.A.L. Paton – Partner, Sir Alexander Gibbs & Partners (consulting engineers)

Major General Sir Leslie Williams – Rootes Motor Group

It added that:

The Mission hope to spend about twelve days in Iraq and a few days in each of Kuwait, Lebanon, Syria and Saudi Arabia. Their aim is to persuade the countries visited of our desire to help in the rapid development of their economies and our ability to provide them with the goods and services that they need. The Mission hopes to study export opportunities in the area for British industry and commerce and also any forms of hindrance there may be to the speedy expansion of our exports to these rich markets. It wishes on its return to make worthwhile suggestions which may help in such an expansion of exports and foreign earnings generally.[21]

The report produced by the Mission is in the National Archives and there is a copy in Bill's archive. Bill spoke of his trip in his speech to the Carmen, as Past Master, and it was indeed a rousing speech. Bill encouraged his audience, which included the Lord Mayor, saying 'encourage your sons to go out to the world to capture more export trade, which is the lifeblood of this country'. He continued,

> I have just returned from a visit to the Arab countries as a member of the British Government Trade Mission. These countries are the new Aladdin's cave. Oil wealth is pouring into the laps of the rulers, largely as a result of the vision and energy of our own countrymen and I hope that our young men from the City of London will go out and ensure that we get the lion's share of their trade.[22]

A number of related invitations followed: the National Union of Manufacturers, the Lebanese ambassador, the Iraqi ambassador, the high commissioner for India, the Kuwait Oil Company, and repeat invitations would follow in subsequent years. There is a letter of thanks to Bill from the Mutasarrif of Baghdad for 'the Honour the Queen had bestowed'. There is no note of what the honour was. There was reciprocation when Bill hosted a visit from the Sudan Military Mission to Rootes. On a more personal level, Bill and Betty received an invitation from Maurice Laing and his wife to a buffet lunch at their home on 20 November 1954 and they became good friends. Sir Edward Benthall wrote to Sir William Rootes on 27 January 1955 saying how he appreciated 'the sterling work of Bill Williams on the mission to the Middle East'. On 28 July 1954 Bill attended a dinner with politicians, businessmen and export targets: Barbara Castle MP, George Brown MP, Terry Clarke MP, Sir Rupert de la Bère (Lord Mayor), Emile Bustani, and companies such as Wimpey, Shell and Electrolux plus journalists from the *Evening Standard* and Arab News Agency.

The Rootes Group prizegiving for apprentices of 15 April 1954 was reported in the *Coventry Evening News* which told how Bill, presenting the prizes, spoke of his recent trip and how export markets needed to be regarded as 'oysters which will have to be opened'. The headline writer referred to the winning apprentices as the new 'oyster-openers'. Bill's interest in education was also evidenced when, on 18 June 1949, he was invited to unveil the war memorial at his old school, Alleyn's. He subsequently became deputy president, and then president of the Alleyn's Old Boys' Association in 1953. On 7 March 1955, Bill wrote to those former Rootes apprentices now undertaking national service:

> Last April I had the occasion to meet a number of you pupils and apprentices when I presented the prizes at your annual prize giving at Coventry.
>
> It provided me with the opportunity to give you a brief, and I hope, realistic, picture of National Service and to stress its value to you in developing your character, personality and powers of leadership. Those of you at the presentation who are now receiving this letter as one of our National Servicemen, have had an opportunity to sample service life – and I feel sure that you are finding it a most interesting experience.
>
> The final result largely depends, of course, on your personal reaction when you join up. My advice, which is the result of many years' service in most ranks of the Army, is to make your mind up in advance that you are going to like it and benefit from it. You are bound to get some humble and uninteresting jobs during your service, but if you make up your mind to do them better than the other man, you will almost certainly be picked out for promotion which will bring you training in leadership, one of the most valuable assets to a young man in any and every part of the Rootes Group.
>
> In the Export Division, in particular, we need men not only with sound technical qualifications but with personality and powers of leadership to develop our business in the markets of the world.[23]

Bill again gave the prizes in 1955.

1956 began with sadness, first with a memorial service for Sir George Kenning on 6 February 1956, and then for Bill's great friend, Gordon Richards, on 18 April 1956. There are handwritten letters from Gordon to Bill suggesting that Bill and Betty visit Gordon and Lynn in Tenerife where they had rented a villa. Betty had been seriously ill and it was hoped that a holiday in the sun would aid her recovery. Tragically, Gordon died before the visit could be arranged. As I told in the previous chapter, Bill and Betty took a short holiday in Algeciras. Bill retired from Rootes on 19 July 1956. Retirement offered a little more space for time with Betty, and in April 1957 they took the holiday in Tenerife; characteristically, Bill combined this with a visit to Hernandez Hermanos, the Rootes distributors in the Canary Islands. The Hernandez family would become good friends and further holidays would follow.

On leaving Rootes, Bill set up as an industrial consultant and in that capacity he worked for Lewis Berger and a number of motor-related companies. He also became a director of transport company, Howard Tenens. I had noticed a couple of events to which Bill had been invited in Newport, Monmouthshire, but had failed to make a connection. Further research revealed that this was where Howard Tenens and chairman, Norman Foster, were based. Bill had met them through Frank Rokison of the Rootes shipping department. The Rootes connection hadn't ceased as is evidenced by a copy of a report in Bill's archive. This was dated 1958 and concerned the Rootes internal procedures for processing orders for new cars. It is damning and highlights again Bill's attention to detail.[24]

A further continuation of motor industry interest is evidenced by an invitation by Ford to the launch of new models, but also the Motor Industry Research Association and Rover Company to celebrate the tenth birthday of the Land Rover. Betty includes an anecdote of Bill visiting Lewis Berger's factory at Shadwell Heath in East London, that Ford of Dagenham had sent a car to the station to take him to the factory. I can add my own memory of being told how he would arrive at Marylebone Station in the morning desperate for a pee (something I now know all too well), but Bill would stride into British Railways headquarters and use their gents. It happened so often that the doorman would salute.

There is then the first hint of one of the most enjoyable activities that would occupy Bill in his retirement, and this was a dinner for the City Fellowship of Wine held at the Tallow Chandlers Hall on 7 November 1957. The activity was his appointment as chairman of wine shippers, Grierson Oldham & Adams Ltd. Betty tells that this came about from Bill's habit of lunching at the Washington Hotel in Curzon Street. This hotel was owned by a then well-known hotelier, Max Joseph. It seems that Bill got to know Joseph, and the latter asked him if he would like to become involved with a business in which Joseph had an investment. That business was Grierson Oldham and it was merging with Adams Brothers. In Betty's album there are a few pieces from the company that suggest the appointment was fun.

> An invitation presenting Grierson's No. 1 Gin to the '67' Liquor Shop, 67 West 67th St, New York

> General Sir Leslie Williams – soldier of fame, gentleman of taste, advisor to industry and a world traveller of great experience, insists that only the finest distillations are used for his company's product ...[25]

And from *International Beverage News*:

> Two-day Hock and Moselle Tasting

> Major General Sir Leslie Williams, chairman of Grierson, Oldham & Adams Ltd., his boardroom colleagues, Derek Butler Adams and Peter Adams (joint managing directors) were At Home to around three hundred wine merchants at London's Park Lane Hotel on 28 and 29 May 1962.

> The two-day event, which was splendidly arranged was a Hock and Moselle wine tasting, mainly devolving on 1959 vintages.[26]

Bill had first become ill on 15 June 1959, but then suffered a second stroke. At the same time, Betty's father became ill and her pocket diaries show that she made frequent visits to Long Eaton. Francis George Perks died on 30 July 1960 and Betty's mother on 24 December 1963. In 1964, Bill was diagnosed with prostate cancer and spent some weeks in hospital for an operation. Betty's albums show that he kept his interests as long as physically possible: his beloved Carmen, RAOC reunion dinners and the Pilgrims. He also kept up with former colleagues.

Jack Omond had long since retired, and had remarried on the death of his first wife. His step-grandson contacted me and told how he remembered Grandpa Jack driving a Hillman Minx. I suspect that Bill found Rootes cars for many old friends. Cutters Cutforth had retired from the army in 1958, but continued as Colonel Commandant until 1965, serving also as Director-General of Inspection in the Ministry of Supply, and then as Assistant Master General of Ordnance. He then served as chairman of the London Transport Users' Consultative Committee from 1964 to 1972. He and his wife, Vera, were frequent visitors to Long Grove House. Wolffy was living in Malta and, to no one's surprise, had become a major cog in the life of the ex-pat community. He visited Bill in September 1963.

Bill Williams died on 7 August 1965 following a long and painful struggle with cancer. I remember that morning, and my mother sitting by the knee-hole chest telephoning those who needed to be informed. The RAOC was top of the list and, possibly, the next day, John Hildreth visited to discuss preparations for what would be a full military funeral. I have seen photographs of the coffin on a gun carriage and I remember columns of marching soldiers taking the same route that we as a family had taken many Sundays to the village church. The military party was from Bicester and Blackdown and a piper from the London Scottish played a lament from the church to the cemetery where Bill's mother, Mildred, was also buried. The funeral was taken by the Reverend Bob Crawley-Boevey who, unusually for the time, had welcomed Bill as a divorced man into his church.

Listed among those attending were the 'top brass', but also, I noted R.C. Hiam from Old Dalby and the D-Day advanced depots, and Harry Whitaker from Chilwell and the Middle East. A memorial service was held at St Martin's in the Fields on 30 September and, again, as well as 'top brass' including Cutters, John Hildreth, Lionel Hoare, Jim Denniston, Reddie Readman and Clifford Geake, there were listed Jack Omond, R.F. Johnson and C.H.E. Lowther. From the business world was Reggie Rootes and from the next generation, Geoffrey and Brian Rootes. Bob Lillico from Lucas came; Lillico had been one of those to whom Bill had written for help in 1938. Picky Pickthall and Harold Kenward had died in 1947, Geoffrey Palmer in 1952, Bill's best friend, Gordon Richards, in 1956, Ronald Weeks, Dicky Richards and Basil Hill in 1960, and Dick Hunt in 1961. Wolffy was living in Malta and Cyril Cansdale in Portugal, and both would live a further twenty years. Lionel Hoare would live well into his nineties.

These were soldiers who had armed an army, a task of such a magnitude that would never be repeated. It had consumed their lives through unremitting hours of work, year in and year out. We owe them, and those who served with them, a massive debt.

Notes

Author's Note

1. Max Hastings, *Overlord: D-Day and the Battle for Normandy, 1944* (London: Book Club Associates, 1984), p.201.

Chapter 1: The Photograph

1. Alfred Goldstein, *RAOC Gazette*, 1962, p.13.
2. NMP album, RLC Archive.
3. LHW private papers, RLC Archive.
4. Philip Hamlyn Williams, *War on Wheels* (Brimscombe: The History Press, 2016), p.53.

Chapter 2: Family and Childhood in Victorian London

1. NMP, Leslie's Story, Family Archive.
2. Philip Hamlyn Williams, *Charlotte Bronte's Devotee* (Lincoln: Independently Published, 2019), p.220.
3. Charles de Wolff, unpublished autobiography, Imperial War Museum Archive.
4. Arthur R. Chandler, *Alleyn's The Coeducational School* (Henley: Gresham Book, 1998), p.33.

Chapter 3: The World of Work in Edwardian London, East Africa and Malaya

1. T.C. Barker, *The Glassmakers Pilkington: The Rise of an International Company, 1826–1976* (London: Weidenfeld & Nicholson, 1977), p.236.
2. NMP, Leslie's Story, Family Archive.
3. NMP, Leslie's Story, Family Archive.

4. NMP, Leslie's Story, Family Archive.
5. Barbara Lamport-Stokes, *Blantyre Glimpses of the Early Days* (Blantyre: The Society of Malawi, 1989).
6. Consular Reports, 'Report of the Trade of Portuguese Possessions in East Africa, 1911' (London: HMSO 1912).
7. Eric Macfadyan, *Rubber Planting in Malaya* (Malay States Information Agency, 1924), p.54.
8. NMP Leslie's Story, Family Archive.
9. Private papers of J.S. Omond, RLC Archive.

Chapter 4: The Great War
1. Interview with Clifford Geake, Imperial War Museum.
2. Lecture on the Army Ordnance Department, its organization and duties at home and in the field delivered to Officers of Staff Courses, Clare College, Cambridge by Lt-Col T.B.A. Leahy, 30 September 1916, RLC Archive.
3. Lecture on the Army Ordnance Department, its organization and duties at home and in the field delivered to Officers of Staff Courses, Clare College, Cambridge by Lt-Col T.B.A. Leahy, 30 September 1916, RLC Archive.
4. Private papers of J.S. Omond, RLC Archive.
5. Private papers of J.S. Omond, RLC Archive.
6. Charles de Wolff, unpublished autobiography, Imperial War Museum Archive.
7. Interview with Clifford Geake, Imperial War Museum.
8. Philip Hamlyn Williams, *Ordnance* (Brimscombe: The History Press, 2018), p.89.
9. 'Obituary,' *The Times*, 20 August 1960, p.8., The Times Digital Archive, http://tinyurl.gale.com/tinyurl/Bzeiq4 accessed 23 October 2019.
10. Sir John Hildreth's obituary of Alfred Goldstein, *RAOC Gazette*, 1976, RLC Archive.
11. Private papers of J.S. Omond, RLC Archive.
12. Wilfred d'A Collings and Juliet Campbell, *One Small Island and Two World Wars: The Life and Times and Maj Gen Wilfred d'A Collings, CB, CBE* (Rimes House, Oxford, 2016), p.63.
13. Everard Wyrall, *The History of the 19th Division, 1914–1918* (London: Edward Arnold, 1932).

14. LHW private papers, RLC Archive.
15. Private papers of J.S. Omond, RLC Archive.
16. Philip Hamlyn Williams, *Ordnance* (Brimscombe: The History Press, 2018), p.175.
17. Everard Wyrall, *The History of the 19th Division, 1914–1918* (London: Edward Arnold, 1932), p.114.
18. LHW private papers, RLC Archive.
19. Philip Hamlyn Williams, *Ordnance* (Brimscombe: The History Press, 2018), p.209.
20. LHW private papers, RLC Archive.
21. Major F.P. Stoodley, *RAOC Gazette*, 1986, p.297.
22. Philip Hamlyn Williams, *Ordnance* (Brimscombe: The History Press, 2018), p.213.

Chapter 5: Interwar Years and Mobilization

1. www.historic-uk.com/HistoryUK/HistoryofBritain/The-Spanish-Flu-pandemic-of-1918/ accessed 16 February 2020.
2. *RAOC Gazette*, 1980, p.10.
3. Douglas C. Oldham, *A history of rolled heavy armour plate manufacture at the Sheffield works of Charles Cammell and Vickers (merged as part of the English Steel Corporation in 1929)* (Sheffield: South Yorkshire Industrial History Society, 2010), p.3.
4. www.gracesguide.co.uk/1953_Who's_Who_in_the_Motor_Industry:_Persons_S accessed 28 November 2019.
5. T.C. Barker, *Pilkington Brothers and the Glass Industry* (London: George Allen & Unwin, 1960), p.244.
6. T.C. Barker, *The Glassmakers Pilkington: The Rise of an International Company, 1826–1976* (London: Weidenfeld & Nicholson, 1977), p.331.
7. Ian Hay, *R.O.F.: The Story of the Royal Ordnance Factories, 1939–48* (London: His Majesty's Stationery Office, 1949), p.16.
8. Private papers of J.S. Omond, RLC Archive.
9. Obituary of Sir Basil Hill, *RAOC Gazette*, September 1960, Vol. 42. No. 4.
10. A.H. Fernyhough, *History of the Royal Army Ordnance Corps, 1920–1945* (Deepcut: RAOC 1963), p.44.
11. A.H. Fernyhough, *History of the Royal Army Ordnance Corps, 1920–1945* (Deepcut: RAOC 1963), p.45.

12. Frank Steer, *To the Warrior his Arms: The Story of the Royal Army Ordnance Corps, 1918–1993* (Barnsley: Pen and Sword, 2005), p.40.
13. Obituary of Major General W.W. Richards, *RAOC Gazette*, April 1961, Vol. 42, No.11.
14. *RAOC Gazette*, October 1929, p.353.
15. Captain G. Hodgson, *Now It Can Be Told*, TELA, The Journal of the London and War Office Branch of the Royal Army Ordnance Corps Association, May 1952.
16. Ian Hay, *R.O.F.: The Story of the Royal Ordnance Factories, 1939–48* (London: His Majesty's Stationery Office, 1949), p.39.
17. Philip Hamlyn Williams, *War on Wheels* (Brimscombe: The History Press, 2016), Chapter 3.
18. *RAOC Gazette*, 1986, p.470.
19. Philip Hamlyn Williams, *Ordnance* (Brimscombe: The History Press, 2018), p.98.
20. LHW private papers, RLC Archive.
21. Philip Porter and Phil Skilleter, *Sir William Lyons: The Official Biography* (Yeovil: Haynes Publishing, 2001, 2011), p.56.
22. Jack Omond appreciation of Sir Basil Hill, *RAOC Gazette*, 1960, p.128.
23. Lionel Hoare appreciation of Sir Basil Hill, *RAOC Gazette*, 1960, p.127.
24. LHW private papers, RLC Archive.
25. Major Harries, *RAOC Gazette*, 1959, p.9.
26. Charles de Wolff, unpublished autobiography, RLC Archive.
27. *RAOC Gazette*, 1979, p.208.
28. 'Obituary', *The Times*, 20 August 1960, p.8. The Times Digital Archive, http://tinyurl.gale.com/tinyurl/Bzeiq4 accessed 23 October 2019.
29. Report on BEF, RLC Archive.
30. Major Bullock, *RAOC Gazette*, 1978, p.371.
31. J.K. Stanford, *Tail of an Army*, (London: Phoenix House, 1966), p.28
32. Philip Hamlyn Williams, *Ordnance* (Brimscombe: The History Press, 2018), p.131.
33. Report on BEF by COS, the private papers of W.W. Richards, WW2, Imperial War Museum.
34. Frank Steer, *To the Warrior his Arms, The Story of the Royal Army Ordnance Corps, 1918–1993* (Barnsley: Pen and Sword, 2005), p.68.

35. *RAOC Gazette*, 1980, p.10.
36. www.britannica.com/event/Dunkirk-evacuation

Chapter 6: The Depots and the Motor Industry
1. D.S. Robinson, *RAOC Gazette*, 1965, p.176.
2. D.S. Robinson, *RAOC Gazette*, 1986, p.388.
3. Charles de Wolff, unpublished memoir, RLC Archive.
4. Sir John Hildreth, *RAOC Gazette*, 1965, p.131.
5. National Archives, Fitch Committee, WO 32/9720.
6. LHW private papers, RLC Archive.
7. Eric Bennett, *The Worshipful Company of Carmen of London: A Short History* (Simpkin Marshall, London, 1952), p.9.
8. LHW private papers, RLC Archive.
9. National Archives, DWS War Diaries, WO 167/110.
10. National Archives, Beveridge Report, CAB 66/21/24.
11. National Archives, PREM 4/55/3.
12. Philip Hamlyn Williams, *War on Wheels* (Brimscombe: The History Press, 2016), p.129.
13. LHW private papers, RLC Archive.
14. Cutting from *Modern Transport*, 3 February 1945, LHW private papers, RLC Archive.
15. Winston S. Churchill, *The Second World War* (London: Cassell, 1950), Vol. III, p.777.
16. Sir John Hildreth, *RAOC Gazette*, 1965, p.131.
17. Sir John Hildreth, *RAOC Gazette*, 1961, p.37.
18. NMP album, RLC Archive.
19. National Archives, Beveridge Report, CAB 66/21/24.
20. W.W. Richards private papers, Imperial War Museum.
21. NMP album, RLC Archive.

Chapter 7: The Middle East and Africa
1. W.W. Richards private papers, Imperial War Museum.
2. R.A.C Parker, *The Second World War: A Short History* (Oxford: OUP, 1989), p.98.
3. NMP album, RLC Archive.
4. Obituaries of W.W. Richards, *RAOC Gazette*, 1961, p.436

5. NMP album, RLC Archive.
6. Alan Fernyhough, *The History of the Royal Army Ordnance Corps, 1920–1945* (Deepcut: Royal Army Ordnance Corps, 1965), p.210.

Chapter 8: Bill, Betty and the USA
1. Report on visit to USA 1943, LHW private papers, RLC Archive.
2. Report by Sir William Rootes, LHW private papers, RLC Archive.
3. NMP album, RLC Archive.
4. NMP album, RLC Archive.
5. Album of USA visit 1943.
6. Private papers of Geoffrey Vale, Imperial War Museum.

Chapter 9: D-Day Before and After
1. Sir John Hildreth, *RAOC Gazette*, 1965, p.131.
2. A.H. Fernyhough, *History of the Royal Army Ordnance Corps, 1920–1945* (Deepcut: RAOC 1963), p.171.
3. Sir John Hildreth, *RAOC Gazette*, 1965, p.131.
4. NMP album, RLC Archive.
5. NMP album, RLC Archive.
6. Herbert Ells, *Autocar* magazine, 16 June 1944, p.416.
7. Philip Johnson, *The Star*, 12 June 1944.
8. Charles Graves, *The Sphere*, 3 June 1944, p.294.
9. NMP album, RLC Archive.
10. Charles de Wolff, unpublished memoir, p.74, RLC Archive.
11. NMP album, RLC Archive.
12. Philip Hamlyn Williams, *War on Wheels* (Brimscombe The History Press, 2016), p.119.
13. NMP album, RLC Archive.

Chapter 10: The Middle East and Africa to VE Day
1. NMP diary, RLC Archive.
2. Philip Hamlyn Williams, *War on Wheels* (Brimscombe: The History Press, 2016), p.123.
3. Ronald Weeks, *Organization and Equipment for War* (Cambridge: Cambridge University Press, 1950), p.62.

Chapter 11: India and South East Asia to V-J Day

1. Engine Power – A Talk by Major General L.H. Williams, Controller of Ordnance Services with a foreword by Major General E.B. Rowcroft, Director of Mechanical Services, LHW private papers, RLC Archive.
2. Ordnance Services – Supply and Maintenance of Ordnance Stores for South-East Asia Command and the Static Units and Formations in India Proper, LHW private papers, RLC Archive.
3. NMP album, RLC Archive.
4. Sir John Hildreth, *RAOC Gazette*, 1965, p.131.
5. *RAOC Gazette*, January 1955, p.233.
6. Comments and Advice by Controller of Ordnance Services War Office on Ordnance Problems in India and ALFSEA Commands, LHW private papers, RLC Archive.
7. LHW private papers, RLC Archive.

Chapter 12: The Post-war Army

1. National Archives WO 167/100.
2. National Archives WO 167/110.
3. George Fyfe, *Daily Telegraph*, 19 September 1945.
4. NMP album, RLC Archive.
5. NMP album, RLC Archive.
6. A.H. Fernyhough, *History of the Royal Army Ordnance Corps, 1920–1945* (Deepcut: RAOC 1963), p.470.
7. NMP album, RLC Archive.
8. NMP album, RLC Archive.
9. *RAOC Gazette*, 29 April 1946.
10. NMP album, RLC Archive.
11. Newsletter, Canbedoneans, NMP album, RLC Archive.
12. L.T.H. Phelps, *A History of the Royal Army Ordnance Corps, 1945–1982* (Deepcut: Royal Army Ordnance Corps, 1991), p.4.
13. NMP album, RLC Archive.
14. Lancelot Cutforth, *RAOC Gazette*, 1953, p.353.
15. *RAOC Gazette*, June 1951, p.350.
16. COD Donnington visit, 7 February 1957, RLC Archive.
17. NMP album, family collection.

18. Sir Edward Ford KCVO, Private Secretary to Her Majesty the Queen, copy of the original letter of 12 April 1958 presented to the RAOC officers' mess.
19. Letter to Bill Williams from R.F. Johnson, NMP album, family collection.

Chapter 13: Civvy Street

1. C.P. Hill, *British Economic and Social History, 1700–1982* (London: Edward Arnold, 1985, 5th edition), p.283.
2. C.P. Hill, *British Economic and Social History, 1700–1982* (London: Edward Arnold, 1985, 5th edition), p.285.
3. James McMillan, *The Dunlop Story* (London: Weidenfeld & Nicholson, 1989), p.97.
4. James McMillan, *The Dunlop Story* (London: Weidenfeld & Nicholson, 1989), p.131.
5. 'Obituary', *The Times*, 20 August 1960, p.8. The Times Digital Archive, http://tinyurl.gale.com/tinyurl/Bzeiq4. Accessed 23 Oct. 2019.
6. J.D. Scott, *Vickers: A History* (London: Weidenfeld & Nicholson, 1962), p.307.
7. J.D. Scott, *Vickers: A History* (London: Weidenfeld & Nicholson, 1962), p.335.
8. *Scope*, November 1944, p.86.
9. Graham Turner, *The Car Makers* (London: Eyre & Spottiswood, 1963, revised edition by Penguin 1965), p.30.
10. LHW family archive.
11. Geoff Carverhill, *Rootes Story: The Making of a Global Automotive Empire* (Marlborough: Crowood Press, 2018), p.131.
12. *Scope*, November 1944, p.82.
13. LHW private papers, Rootes Archive,
14. Graham Turner, *The Car Makers* (London: Eyre & Spottiswood, 1963, revised edition by Penguin 1965), Chapter 4.
15. www.society.caths.cam.ac.uk/Public_Magazines/1948r.pdf accessed 21 February 2020, *St Catherine's Gazette* online.
16. LHW private papers, Rootes Archive.
17. Geoff Carverhill, *Rootes Story: The Making of a Global Automotive Empire* (Marlborough: Crowood Press, 2018).

18. Woodrow Wyatt, 'Emile Do-gooder of the Middle East', *Reynolds News*, 3 June 1956.

19. http://www.emilebustani.org/about-emile.html accessed 22 February 2020.

20. https://api.parliament.uk/historic-hansard/written-answers/1953/nov/10/middle-east-mission

21. Middle East Mission, letter of appointment, NMW album, Rootes Archive.

22. NMW album, Rootes Archive.

23. NMW album, Rootes Archive.

24. Report for the Rootes Group, LHW private papers, Rootes Archive.

25. Grierson, Oldham & Adams Ltd. invitation, NMW family album.

26. *International Beverage News*, June, 1962, NMW family album.

Further Reading

Barker, T.C., *Pilkington Brothers and the Glass Industry* (London: George Allen & Unwin, 1960).

Barker, T.C. *The Glassmakers Pilkington: The Rise of an International Company, 1826–1976* (London: Weidenfeld Nicholson, 1977).

Bennett, Eric, *The Worshipful Company of Carmen of London, A Short History* (Simpkin Marshall, London, 1952).

Carverhill, Geoff, *Rootes Story: The Making of a Global Automotive Empire* (Marlborough: Crowood Press, 2018).

Chandler, Arthur R., *Alleyn's: The Coeducational School* (Henley: Gresham Book, 1998).

Churchill, Winston S., *The Second World War* (London: Cassell, 1950).

Collings, Wilfred d'A. and Juliet Campbell, *One Small Island and Two World Wars: The Life and Times of Maj Gen Wilfred d'A Collings, CB, CBE* (Rimes House, Oxford, 2016).

de Wolff, Charles, unpublished autobiography, Imperial War Museum Archive.

Fernyhough, A.H., *History of the Royal Army Ordnance Corps, 1920–1945* (Deepcut: RAOC 1963).

Forbes, Maj Gen A.F., *A History of The Army Ordnance Services* (London: The Medici Society, 1929).

Gilbert, Martin, *The Second World War* (London: Weidenfeld & Nicolson, 1989).

Hastings, Max, *Overlord: D-Day and the Battle for Normandy, 1944* (London: Book Club Associates, 1984).

Hay, Ian, *R.O.F.: The Story of the Royal Ordnance Factories, 1939-48* (London: His Majesty's Stationery Office, 1949).

Hill, C.P., *British Economic and Social History, 1700–1982* (London: Edward Arnold, 1985, 5th edition).

Lamport-Stokes, Barbara, *Blantyre Glimpses of the Early Days* (Blantyre: The Society of Malawi, 1989).

Lecture on the Army Ordnance Department, its organization and duties at home and in the field delivered to Officers of Staff Courses, Clare College, Cambridge by Lt-Col T.B.A. Leahy, 30 September 1916, RLC Archive.

LHW private papers, Rootes Archive.

LHW private papers, Royal Logistic Corps Archive.

Macfadyan, Eric, *Rubber Planting in Malaya*, (Malay States Information Agency, 1924).

McMillan, James, *The Dunlop Story*, (London: Weidenfeld & Nicholson, 1989).

NMP albums, Royal Logistic Corps Archive.

NMW albums, Rootes Archive.

Oldham, Douglas C., *A history of rolled heavy armour plate manufacture at the Sheffield works of Charles Cammell and Vickers (merged as part of the English Steel Corporation in 1929)* (Sheffield: South Yorkshire Industrial History Society, 2010).

Parker, R.A.C., *The Second World War: A Short History* (Oxford: Oxford University Press, 1989).

Phelps, L.T.H., *A History of the Royal Army Ordnance Corps, 1945–1982* (Deepcut: Royal Army Ordnance Corps, 1991).

Porter, Philip and Phil Skilleter, *Sir William Lyons: The Official Biography* (Yeovil: Haynes Publishing, 2001, 2011).

Private papers of J.S. Omond, Royal Logistics Corps Archive.

RAOC Gazette, Royal Logistic Corps Archive.

Scott, J.D., *Vickers: A History* (London: Weidenfeld & Nicholson, 1962).

Stanford, J.K. *Tail of an Army* (London: Phoenix House, 1966).

Steer, Frank, *To the Warrior his Arms: The Story of the Royal Army Ordnance Corps, 1918–1993*, (Barnsley: Pen & Sword, 2005).

Turner, Graham, *The Car Makers* (London: Eyre & Spottiswood, 1963, revised edition by Penguin 1965).

Weeks, Ronald, *Organization and Equipment for War* (Cambridge: Cambridge University Press, 1950).

Williams, Philip Hamlyn, *Charlotte Bronte's Devotee* (Lincoln: Independently Published, 2019).

Williams, Philip Hamlyn, *Ordnance* (Brimscombe: The History Press, 2018).

Williams, Philip Hamlyn, *War on Wheels* (Brimscombe: The History Press, 2016).

Wyrall, Everard, *The History of the 19th Division, 1914–1918* (London: Edward Arnold, 1932).

Index